5. 12. 2018

In Dankbarkeit

Women in the History of Philosophy and Sciences

Volume 2

Series editors

As the historical records prove, women have long been creating original contributions to philosophy. We have valuable writings from female philosophers from antiquity and the Middle Ages, and a continuous tradition from the Renaissance to today. The history of women philosophers thus stretches back as far as the history of philosophy itself. The presence as well as the absence of women philosophers throughout the course of history parallels the history of philosophy as a whole. Edith Stein, Hannah Arendt, and Simone de Beauvoir, the most famous representatives of this tradition in the twentieth century, did not appear from nowhere. They stand, so to speak, on the shoulders of the female titans who came before them.

The ever-growing market of scholars and students of women's contributions to philosophy and science is a strong indicator that the series Women in the History of Philosophy and Sciences will be successful as the series Women Philosophers and Scientists published by Springer VS, the 4-Volume series a History of Women Philosophers and several other works the editors have published with Springer. WHPS will be of interest not only to the international philosophy community, but also for scholars in history of science and mathematics, the history of ideas, and in women's studies.

More information about this series at http://www.springer.com/series/15896

Antonio Calcagno
Editor

Gerda Walther's Phenomenology of Sociality, Psychology, and Religion

Springer

Editor
Antonio Calcagno
Department of Philosophy
King's University College
London, ON, Canada

ISSN 2523-8760 ISSN 2523-8779 (electronic)
Women in the History of Philosophy and Sciences
ISBN 978-3-319-97591-7 ISBN 978-3-319-97592-4 (eBook)
https://doi.org/10.1007/978-3-319-97592-4

Library of Congress Control Number: 2018950778

This Springer imprint is published by the registered company Springer Nature Switzerland AG
The registered company address is: Gewerbestrasse 11, 6330 Cham, Switzerland

To Ruth Hagengruber

—In Dankbarkeit

Series Foreword

Women in the History of Philosophy and Sciences

The history of women's contributions to philosophy and the sciences dates back to the very beginnings of these disciplines. Theano, Hypatia, Du Châtelet, Agnesi, Germain, Lovelace, Stebbing, Curie, Stein are only a small selection of prominent women philosophers and scientists throughout history.

The Springer Series *Women in the History of Philosophy and Sciences* provides a platform for publishing cutting-edge scholarship on women's contributions to the sciences, to philosophy, and to interdisciplinary academic areas. We therefore include in our scope women's contributions to biology, physics, chemistry, and related sciences. The Series also encompasses the entire discipline of the history of philosophy since antiquity (including metaphysics, aesthetics, philosophy of religion). We welcome also work about women's contributions to mathematics and to interdisciplinary areas such as philosophy of biology, philosophy of medicine, sociology.

The research presented in this series serves to recover women's contributions and to revise our knowledge of the development of philosophical and scientific disciplines, so as to present the full scope of their theoretical and methodological traditions. Supported by an advisory board of internationally esteemed scholars, the volumes offer a comprehensive, up-to-date source of reference for this field of growing relevance. See the listing of planned volumes.

The Springer Series *Women in the History of Philosophy and Sciences* will publish monographs, handbooks, collections, anthologies, and dissertations.

Paderborn, Germany — Ruth Hagengruber
Cleveland, USA — Mary Ellen Waithe
Vercelli, Italy — Gianenrico Paganini
Series editors

Contents

Editor and Contributors

About the Editor

Antonio Calcagno is Professor of Philosophy at King's University College, London, Canada. He is the author of *Giordano Bruno and the Logic of Coincidence* (1998), *Badiou and Derrida: Politics, Events and Their Time* (2007), *The Philosophy of Edith Stein* (2007), *Lived Experience from the Inside Out: Social and Political Philosophy in Edith Stein* (2014).

Contributors

Angela Ales Bello Pontifical Lateran University, Rome, Italy

Kimberly Baltzer-Jaray King's University College (UWO), London, Ontario, Canada

Antonio Calcagno Department of Philosophy, King's University College, London, ON, Canada

Christina M. Gschwandtner Fordham University, New York, NY, USA

Manuela Massa Society and Culture in Motion, Halle (Saale), Germany

Julia Mühl Paderborn University, Paderborn, Germany

Rodney K. B. Parker Department of Philosophy, Center for the History of Women Philosophers and Scientists, Paderborn University, Paderborn, Germany

Marina Pia Pellegrino Italian Centre for Phenomenological Research, Rome, Italy

Anna Maria Pezzella Pontifical Lateran University, Rome, Italy

Alessandro Salice University College Cork, Cork, Ireland

Genki Uemura Okayama University, Okayama, Japan

Introduction

Gerda Walther (1897–1977) was a prominent member of the early phenomenological movement, which was founded by the philosophers Edmund Husserl, Alexander Pfänder, Moritz Geiger, and Max Scheler. A student of Pfänder, she travelled from Munich to Freiburg to study under Husserl to expand her understanding of phenomenology. There, she met the philosopher Edith Stein and began to develop her friendship with her fellow phenomenologist Hedwig Conrad-Martius. Having no one definitive, systematic method, phenomenology was guided by the insight that lived experience can make present the reality of "things themselves." Phenomenologists largely studied phenomena that were not absolutely reducible to empirical or psychological quantification (for example, the subject, the person, the inner experience of time, sense-making, the self, psyche, and community).

This book brings critical philosophical reflection to bear on an important but understudied thinker, whose original contributions lie in a novel understanding of social ontology, psychology, religion, mysticism, and paranormal or parapsychological phenomena. Walther's background in Marxist political thought and psychology deeply influenced her own engagement with phenomenology. Pfänder, Husserl, and Stein recognized her unique talent for philosophy, but the combination of history and sexism in the German university system during her early years of study and research prohibited her from obtaining a university professorship. The goal of this book is to introduce English-speaking readers to the important legacy of this early 20th-century thinker.

Each of the chapters in this book highlights a specific aspect or claim in Walther's philosophy, much of which still remains in manuscript form in the archives of the Munich Staatsbibliothek. The chapters are arranged chronologically and move from an introduction to Walther's life, work, and method to her writings on social ontology to her later engagement with a philosophy of mysticism and religion. We also consider various aspects of her phenomenological psychology. Our focus here is primarily philosophical, and we do not engage the large amount of psychological and parapsychological work that comes to occupy Walther's later life. The latter work is rooted in both quantitative and qualitative analysis of data based on experiments, events, or narrative accounts to establish the possibility or impossibility of certain psychological phenomena, including telekinesis and telepathy. The leading, international scholars we have gathered here all have an interest in Walther's philosophical work and they bring it into dialogue with their own philosophical interests, resulting in a rich tapestry of ideas and possibilities for thinking.

Rodney Parker's opening chapter "Gerda Walther (1897–1977): A Sketch of a Life" presents a brief biography of the philosopher, situating her in relation to members of the phenomenological movement while highlighting Walther's own unique philosophical achievements. Parker's sketch belongs to Part I of the book, which is dedicated to Walther's life and work method. The second chapter "Gerda Walther: Searching for the Sense of Things, Following the Traces of Lived Experiences" of Part I is written by Marina Pia Pellegrino. It chronicles how Walther's understanding of the phenomenological method evolved throughout her life. Pellegrino maintains that what is fundamental for Walther's philosophy is the centrality of sense-making and the obtaining of an essence, and she shows how these two methodological components come to structure Walther's early analyses of social phenomena and her later writings on mysticism.

Part II of the book focuses on Walther's analyses of social ontology and the self. Phenomenologically speaking, Walther's discussion of community is ground-breaking, as she develops a view that is related but distinct from her contemporaries Edmund Husserl, Max Scheler, Edith Stein, and Dietrich von Hildebrand. One finds in Walther's early writings deep traces of her earlier Marxist commitments as well as an astute understanding of the passive mental structures that condition the possibility of community, including the unconscious and habit. Alessandro Salice's and Genki Uemura's chapter "Social Acts and Communities: Walther Between Husserl and Reinach" explores an important aspect of all social ontology (namely, social acts). The authors show how Walther reformulates Reinach's famous understanding of social acts though her engagement with Husserl's ideas. Social acts, in Walther's understanding, are not merely I–you acts of address; rather, they are also communal acts in which an individual acts in the name of or on behalf of the community, thereby extending the scope and influence of social acts from a phenomenological perspective. Anna Maria Pezzella's chapter "On Community: Edith Stein and Gerda Walther" discusses the views of Stein and Walther on the highest, most intense form of sociality (namely, community). Although Walther and Stein share many convictions about the nature of community, the dialogue that emerges between them brings to the fore an important difference between the two thinkers. Whereas Stein ascribes a prominent and distinct role to the ego in the formation of community, Walther makes the I less prominent, giving it both a background role as well as claiming that identification between different Is is possible in the lived experience of community. Stein's egology is much more pronounced and defined: the I can never become absorbed by a super-individual, collective being like a community or a we. Community is a shared sense of togetherness between individual persons, and the I remains the foundation of community.

Antonio Calcagno's chapter, "Gerda Walther and the Possibility of a Non-intentional We of Community", explores an original aspect of Walther's social ontology (namely, the possibility of non-intentional communities; that is, a consciousness of community that has no traditional object, understood in the phenomenological sense). For example, families, lovers, and friends can come to constitute a sense or meaning of a very intense lived experience of community, but the ability to understand such relations as communal does not require that they present some kind of objectivity—say, a purpose or a recognizable social form: the reflexive relationship itself is the community and does not express itself in some other objective form. Calcagno demonstrates that although no object may be fully present or manifest to consciousness, at the passive level, however, we find evidence in Walther's writings that these unique relationships present some kind of pre-reflective or pre-conscious object-like formations that leave behind traces of content that allow them to be understood as unique forms of social relationships, especially at the level of remembered habits of being. Julia Mühl's chapter "Human Beings as Social Beings—Gerda Walther's Anthropological Approach" mines Walther's unique position that all community formations presuppose some kind of deep anthropological foundation in which a common humanity is shared among individual members of communities. Walther's claim that a universal human community exists is radical. Mühl shows how this encompassing and shared sense of a human community manifests itself in consciousness and how it functions in all particular forms of community.

The next chapter of Part II is Christina Gschwandtner's "*Körper, Leib, Gemüt, Seele, Geist*: Conceptions of the Self in Early Phenomenology". Edith Stein and Hedwig Conrad-Martius, two of Walther's contemporaries, had a marked influence on Walther's thinking, especially in terms of her analyses of religion and psychology. Gschwandtner shows how the three women phenomenologists share and diverge conceptually on notions of the body, lived body, soul, *Gemüt*, and spirit. The author shows how these rich philosophical and psychological concepts frame our experience of selfhood, especially when they are experienced as working together as a unity that forms an identity. The chapter concludes by bringing the early phenomenologists into dialogue with arguments in recent French philosophy that distance phenomenology from the traditional phenomenological concepts employed by Walther, Stein, and Conrad-Martius, ultimately resisting the possibility of a defined subjectivity. Gschwandtner shows how women phenomenologists challenge recent developments about selfhood in contemporary French phenomenology. The final chapter of Part II is Manuela Massa's "What is the Condition for the Members of Social Communities to Be 'Real' People According to Gerda Walther?". The author demonstrates that Walther understands community as having both internal (for example, relationality, social bonds, or sociality between individual members) and external aspects (for example, concrete social formations like political parties). Phenomenology usually but not exclusively privileges the inner structure of reality that conditions its external appearing and functioning in the world. In this chapter, Massa shows how both inner and outer aspects work together to structure a fuller experience of community. Empathy is identified as the key intersubjective act that demonstrates how the inner and outer aspects work together to shape the lived experience of community

The value of Part II, taken as a whole, consists in showing how unique aspects of Walther's social ontology (including a broader understanding of social acts, resituating I experience in deep, unconscious layers of an I-center, non-intentional communities, human community, empathy, and a robust psychology constituent of selfhood) distinguish her social ontology from her contemporaries. Furthermore, Walther's original views can certainly come to challenge contemporary views and claims in social ontology. We hope that scholars, once they become familiar with Walther's philosophy, will bring her valuable insights into dialogue with contemporary positions, thereby expanding our philosophical understanding of sociality, the self, and the social world.

Part III of the book investigates Walther's philosophical writings on religion and mysticism. It opens with the chapter "*Phenomenology of Mysticism*, Introduction and Chapter One"—Rodney Parker's translation of Gerda Walther's work. These texts display a unique phenomenological approach to the question of mysticism while commenting on the various structures that make possible mystical experience itself. For example, Walther's discussion of the I echoes Husserl's analysis, but she decenters the I in that the I-center also has a background from which flow all kinds of unconscious and less conscious realities. One also gleans from the brief extract a sense of how Walther envisioned the phenomenological method. Angela Ales Bello's chapter, "The Sense of Mystical Experience According to Gerda Walther", explains Walther's concept of mystical experience, highlighting not only its methodological reliance on Husserl's thought but also its hyletic and noetic aspects. Walther's ideas are brought into conversation with Stein's views of mystical experience (as found in her discussion of Saint Teresa of Avila). Ales Bello demonstrates the novelty of Walther's ideas and how they may be of use today in investigations of the nature of religious and mystical experience.

Kimberly Baltzer-Jaray's chapter "Phenomenological Approaches to the Uncanny and the Divine: Adolf Reinach and Gerda Walther on Mystical Experience" fittingly closes the book as we explore Walther's discussion of paranormal psychological phenomena. The author extends Walther's thought by bringing it into conversation with the work of Adolf Reinach on foreseeing and the uncanny. Both philosophers try to account for forms of knowing that lie outside traditional epistemological and phenomenological frameworks. Baltzer-Jaray makes the case that what Walther and Reinach both extraordinarily experience in their own lives comes to be investigated under the rubric of mystical and religious experience. The chapter also includes translations of Reinach's notes on God and religious experience. The dialogue that emerges in the chapter manifests a conception of God that cannot be confined to rational categories of the mind. God is an Absolute and an Other, with whom we can relate but whom we cannot completely define. The phenomenological account of mystical experience that both Reinach and Walther deliver creates a space of encounter between the human and the divine. The chapter concludes with a bibliography of Walther's work, which is impressive and which spans numerous decades. The bibliography also shows how Walther's interests changed from politics and psychology to philosophy to religion and mysticism to parapsychology.

Gerda Walther was an original thinker, whose involvement in the phenomenological movement gave birth to novel ideas about selfhood, sociality, and religion. The volume serves as a critical introduction and assessment of some of her important ideas. It is our hope that the chapters in this book will spawn further dialogue and scholarly research. As Walther's work is made more accessible through translation and critical editions, we know that her contributions to philosophy and phenomenology will inspire future scholars and philosophers to delve into the vital human questions that Gerda Walther helped raise and answer.

Antonio Calcagno

Part I
The Life and Work of Gerda Walther

Gerda Walther (1897–1977): A Sketch of a Life

Rodney K. B. Parker

Abstract Gerda Walther, a student of Alexander Pfänder and Edmund Husserl, penned numerous interesting contributions to phenomenology and phenomenological psychology during the 1920s, including her dissertation on social ontology and her studies on religious and mystical experience. This chapter gives a brief overview of Walther's life and her relationship to both Marxism and the phenomenological movement, drawing attention to some of the interesting unpublished materials contained in her *Nachlass*. While Walther's legacy has been widely neglected in the years since her death, there is renewed interest in her work on communities and we-experience. However, this only represents a small subset of her writings. Other aspects of her thought are relevant to contemporary philosophical debates in the phenomenology of religion and abnormal psychology.

Keywords Historical materialism · Social ontology · Mysticism · George-Kreis

Gerda Walther was born on March 18, 1897 in Nordrach, a small village near Offenburg, Germany. She was the daughter of Otto Walther, a medical doctor, and Ragnhild Bajer, his second wife and former patient at the Nordrach Clinic for the Treatment of Tuberculosis. Prior to being married to Ragnhild, Otto had been married to Hope Bridges Adams, with whom he had founded the Nordrach Clinic. They divorced in 1895. From this first marriage Gerda Walther inherited two half-siblings: a brother, Heinz, and a sister, Mara. The three siblings spent holidays together with their father.

For a more detailed account of Walther's life see her autobiography, *Zum anderen Ufer: Vom Marxismus und Atheismus zum Christentum* (Walther 1960), as well as "Gerda Walther and the Phenomenological Community" (Parker 2017). I would like to thank Marcela Venebra, editorial director of *Acta Mexicana de Fenomenología*, for permitting me to reproduce parts of my 2017 article herein. A comprehensive list of Walther's publications, compiled by Eberhard Avé-Lallemant, can be found in (Resch 1983: 50–78). The contents of signature A. I. 1–6 - *Veröffentlichungen* of Gerda Walther's Nachlass correspond directly and are numbered according to that list.

R. K. B. Parker (✉)
Center for the History of Women Philosophers and Scientists/Department of Philosophy, Paderborn University, Paderborn, Germany
e-mail: rodney.k.b.parker@gmail.com

A. Calcagno (ed.), *Gerda Walther's Phenomenology of Sociality, Psychology, and Religion*, Women in the History of Philosophy and Sciences 2,
https://doi.org/10.1007/978-3-319-97592-4_1

Ragnhild died on July 4, 1903 and a year later Otto married her sister, Sigrun. Walther described her relationship with her aunt as a relentless struggle with and against this interloper that lasted from 1904 until after Otto's death.[1] In 1908 the clinic in Nordrach was sold to the city of Offenburg, and the family moved to Lake Starnberger, 25 km southwest of Munich.

From a young age Walther was immersed in Marxism and socialism. Her father was a well-known social democrat, and his comrades, such as August Bebel and Adolf Geck (whom Walther knew as "Onkel August" and "Onkel Geck"), frequented the Walther household. Her "formal" education in Marxism began in 1913 at the hands of Karl Kautsky and Gustav Eckstein. With them she studied not only Marxist economics, but also the works of Hegel and Feuerbach.[2] As her father had wished, when Walther entered the Ludwig-Maximilians-Universität München in winter semester (WS) 1915/16 her intent was to study sociology, economics, and politics in the hopes of becoming a political agitator. However, her interest shifted to philosophy and psychology.

When Walther arrived at university she enrolled in courses with Edgar Jaffé,[3] a student of Max Weber, and Walther Lotz, a student of Lujo Brentano.[4] However, she was disappointed by their lack of engagement with Marx and their limited knowledge of historical materialism. She chalked this up to the fact that she was attending a bourgeois university whose aim was to train future bankers and businessmen, rather than free thinkers and socialist activists.[5] Disillusioned by her university experience up to that point, Walther decided to attend an introductory lecture on psychology being given by a little-known professor from the faculty of philosophy, Alexander Pfänder.[6] Walther was immediately drawn to Pfänder. The following semester she enrolled in his lectures on *Logik und Erkenntnislehre*[7] and the corresponding *Übungen im Philosophischen Seminar über D. Hume's Erkenntnislehre*, and in WS 1916/17 his course *Sachliche und historische Einleitung in die Philosophie*.[8] These lectures were a decisive influence on Walther. In them Pfänder introduced her to phenomenology and discussed the writings of Edmund Husserl, prompting Walther

---

[1] Walther (1960: 52–53).

[2] For a detailed account of Walther's time studying with Kautsky and Eckstein see Walther (1960: 133–168).

[3] See Walther's seminar presentation (*Refarat*) for Jaffés seminar, Ana 317 A.III.1.1—*Karl Marx System* (19.I.1916). References to Walther's *Nachlass* throughout refer to the holdings of the Bavarian State Library in Munich, which she bequeathed to the library in 1966 (Avé-Lallemant 1975: 257).

[4] Walther also attended a course with L. Brentano himself. See her notes from his *Wirtschaftsgeschichte* (WS 1916/17) in Ana 317 B.V.4.

[5] Walther (1960: 183).

[6] Walther (1960: 185). The "Einführung in die Psychologie" that Walther refers to here was Pfänder's *Grundzüge der Psychologie des Menschen,* WS 1915/16, though she was not enrolled in this course. See her notes for this course, Ana 317 B.V.1.1.

[7] Ana 317 B.V.1.2.

[8] Ana 317 B.V.1.3.

to read both the *Logical Investigations* and *Ideas I*.[9] In 1917 Walther transferred to Albert-Ludwigs-Universität Freiburg to study with Husserl.

Beginning in the summer of 1917, Walther spent six semesters in Freiburg, taking courses with Husserl,[10] Martin Heidegger,[11] and Jonas Cohn.[12] According to Walther, Husserl was initially hesitant to accept her as a student. He felt that the Munich phenomenologists had gotten "bogged down" in metaphysics, and wondered if Walther had followed his transcendental turn.[13] As a result, Husserl sent her to participate in Edith Stein's "philosophical kindergarten" for beginners in phenomenology. In WS 1918/19 Walther gave the opening lecture for the inaugural meeting of the Freiburger phänomenologischen Gesellschaft.[14] The paper was well received, and Walther even considered submitting an expanded version of this paper to the *Jahrbuch für Philosophie und phänomenologische Forschung*.[15] Unfortunately, the manuscript for Walther's lecture, *Zur Problematik von Husserls reinem Ich*, is not extant. According to Walther, she lent her only copy to Robert Steiger while in Heidelberg in 1923, who had inadvertently taken it with him to Vienna and lost it.[16] During her time in Freiburg, Walther also compiled an extensive subject index for *Ideas I*, which was included as an appendix to the second edition and published as a standalone pamphlet in 1923.[17] It was later replaced by a shorter index attributed to Ludwig Landgrebe, much to Walther's chagrin.[18]

Walther returned to Munich in time for WS 1919/20 to write her dissertation under the supervision of Pfänder.[19] During this time, she also enrolled in courses

[9] Walther (1960: 193–194).

[10] Contained in Ana 317 B.V.2 are Walther's notes from *Phänomenologie und Kants Transzendentalphilosophie* (SS 1917), *Logik und Wissenschaftslehre* (WS 1917/18), *Einführung in die Philosophie* (SS 1918), *Fichte's Bestimmung des Menschen* (SS 1918), and *Seminar über Kant* (SS 1919). Also in this container is Walther's seminar presentation on Fichte's *The Way Towards the Blessed Life*, presumably written for Husserl's SS 1918 course.

[11] Contained in Ana 317 B.V.3 are Walther's notes from *Idee einer Philosophie und Weltanschauungsproblem* (KNS 1919), *Universitätstudiums* (SS 1919), and *Wertphilosophie und Phänomenologie* (SS 1919).

[12] In Ana 317 B.V.4 one can find Walther's notes from Cohn's course *Weltanschauungen des deutschen Idealismus* (WS 1917/18). Her seminar presentation for Cohn's course on Hegel in SS 1918 is located at Ana 317 A.III.1.9—*Hegels Staatsbegriff*. A complete list of the courses in which Walther was officially enrolled can be found in Parker (2017: 63–66).

[13] Walther (1960: 202).

[14] Walther (1960: 213–214); Husserl (1994: 160).

[15] See Pfänder's letter to Husserl from 17.I.1920 (Husserl 1994: 160).

[16] Ana 317 C.II Gerda Walther an Erich Przywara, 04.I.1958.

[17] Walther (1923a).

[18] See Walther's letter to the publisher, Max Niemeyer, dated 18.IV.1932, which is included as a footnote in Husserl (1994: 266).

[19] Walther took numerous courses with Pfänder during this time. See Ana 317 B.V.1.5—*Einführung in die Philosophie (WS 1919/20—Aus der Nachschrift von Ph. Schwarz)*, B.V.1.6—*Person und Lebewesen (Seminar/Diskussion)*, and B.V.1.7—*Person und Lebewesen (Vortrag in der Münchener philos. Gesellschaft, 1920)*.

with Moritz Geiger[20] and attended the final lectures of Max Weber before his death in June 1920.[21] The original intention for her doctoral thesis was to explore issues of social determinism and individual free will—issues that hark back to her early interests in Hegel's historical materialism and Marxist sociology. However, Walther had started to drift away from Marxism and, after studying with Husserl and Pfänder, she decided instead to write on social communities from both an ontological and phenomenological perspective. Walther defended her dissertation, "Ein Beitrag zur Ontologie der sozialen Gemeinschaften (mit einem Anhang zur Phänomenologie der sozialen Gemeinschaften)" on March 10, 1921.[22] She was awarded her doctorate *summa cum laude*, and the text was published with a slightly altered title in Husserl's *Jahrbuch* in 1923.[23]

It was also during this period that Walther turned toward mysticism. In November of 1918, while on a train to Freiburg after visiting her dying father, she underwent an intense spiritual encounter. Walther claimed that she was touched by a presence that enveloped her in a sense of warmth and goodness, which she took to be an experience of the Divine. This event prompted her to pen "Ein Beitrag zur (bewusstseinsmäßigen) inneren Konstitution des eigenen Grundwesens als Kernpunkt der Persönlichkeit (und Gottes)"[24] in early 1920. A version of this text was presented to Pfänder in honour of his 50th birthday, and served as the basis for her *Phänomenologie der Mystik* (1923).[25] Shortly after her experience on the train, Walther stumbled upon a copy of Stefan George's *Der siebente Ring* while visiting Karl Löwith's apartment.[26] She found the writings of the members of the George-Kreis compelling, and after returning to Munich she became romantically involved with Percy Gothein, a close associate of George.[27]

Upon completing her dissertation, Walther took steps to obtain her Habilitation at the Ruprecht-Karls-Universität Heidelberg with Karl Jaspers. She moved to Heidelberg for WS 1922/23, and in addition to Jaspers[28] she took courses with Heinrich

---

[20]There are a few pages of notes in Ana 317 B.V.6 that appear to be from Geiger's WS 1919/20 course, *Übungen zur Geschichtsphilosophie*.

[21]Walther's notes from Weber's *Wirtschaftsgeschichte* (WS 1919/20) are contained in Ana 317 B.V.4.

[22]Walther (1922).

[23]Walther (1923b).

[24]Ana 317 A.III.2.1.

[25]This work should not be confused with her essay titled "The Phenomenology of Telepathy" which was (reportedly) rejected from inclusion in the *Pfänder-Festschrift* in 1933. (See Linda McAllister Lopez, p. 203; Michael Gubser, *The Far Reaches: Phenomenology, Ethics, and Social Renewal in Central Europe*, p. 257.)

[26]Walther (1960: 291).

[27]Walther (1960: 298–303); Baumann (1995: 69–71). Cf. Ana 317 A.III.5.3—*Zum Problem des Bindens, Anhaftens*.

[28]Walther's essay from Jasper's seminar on Hegel's *Logic* (WS 1922/23) can be found at Ana 317 A.III.2.4—*Hegel's dialektische Methode* (14.XI.1922).

Rickert,[29] Friedrich Gundolf (a member of the George-Kreis),[30] and Hans Gruhle.[31] However, due to both financial problems and the lack of prospects for women to obtain academic positions, Walther was forced to leave Heidelberg at the end of 1923. In the spring of 1924 Walther moved to Berlin and took a series of short-term jobs, first in a job as a nurse's assistant,[32] and then as a ghostwriter for Katharina von Oheimb.[33] In February of 1925 she moved to live with relatives in Leipzig and began working for a book dealer, and then as a translator. During her time in Leipzig, Walther published her essay "Zur Psychologie der sogenannten" ("moral insanity"),[34] and attended lectures by Hans Dreisch.[35] With the help of Alfred Schwenninger, she obtained a position working as a secretary for Willy Hellpach, and then at a state mental hospital in Emmendingen.[36] While working in Emmendingen, Walther became interested in the lived experience of schizophrenia. She presented an essay on this topic, "Zur innen psychischen Struktur der Schizophrenie,"[37] at the 1926 meeting of the Southwest German Psychiatric Association. At the conference Walther met Hans Prinzhorn and was hired as his research assistant. In 1928 Walther became the last scientific secretary to the psychiatrist and parapsychologist Albert von Schrenck-Notzing.[38] She assisted Schrenck-Notzing with his investigation of the mediums Willi and Rudi Schneider, his work on telekinesis and materialization, and edited a number of his

---

[29]From Rickert's course *Übungen über den Begriff der Intuition* (SS 1923) we have outlines for two presentations Walther gave on the concept of intuition: *Der Begriff der Intuition der Husserl'schen Phänomenologie* and *Die Rolle der Intuition in der Schriften des Georgekreises* (which she presented with Herrn Jakobs) (both at Ana 317 A.III.2.5). Cf. Walther (1960: 333–334). Unfortunately, we only have a single page of her notes on Husserl's concept of intuition.

[30]See her notes on Gundolf's *George* (Berlin 1920), Ana 317 A.III.2.6—*Einige Fragen und Bemerkungen zu dem Georgebuch von Prof. F. Gundolf* (ca. 1923).

[31]See her presentation from Gruhle's *Psychologie der Sprache* (WS 1923/24), Ana 317 A.III.2.7—*Was heißt: Sprachgedächtnis. Referat in dem sprachpsychologischen Seminar von Prof. Gruhle, 17.XII.23*. It is clear that my list in the 2017 publication (Parker 2017: 66) is not completely accurate, since it omits courses from WS 1923/24.

[32]While in Berlin, Walther attended a lecture by Romano Guardini. See Ana 317 B.V.5—*Der religiöse Vorgang der Gottfindens im Neuen Testament (Berlin, 1924)*. Cf. Walther (1960: 361).

[33]Ana 317 A.III.3.1—*Die moderne Deutsche Frau/La femme allemande modern. Katharina von Oheimb*; Ana 317 B.II.3. Cf. Walther (1960: 375).

[34]Walther (1925).

[35]Walther (1960: 376).

[36]Walther (1960: 382–383). Walther may have also briefly worked for Schwenninger himself. In a footnote to Husserl's correspondence with Walther, Karl Schuhmann notes: "Walther war von 1925 bis zum 1. April 1927 als Schwen(n)ingers Sekretärin tätig gewesen und übernahm nun eine ähnliche Stellung in Frankfurt" (Husserl 1994: 265). Walther and Schwenninger were certainly close during this period. There is a picture of her with Schwenninger and his family in Ana 317 B.III.4 dated ca. 1926, and in the Schwenninger Nachlass we have her handwritten notes on an article by Ludwig Binswanger (Ana 545 C.I.1) as well as what appears to be a typescript made by Walther of Karl Löwith's notes from Heidegger's lecture *Die Zeit*, delivered on 25.VII.24 (Ana 545 C.I.2).

[37]Walther (1927).

[38]Walther (1960: 406).

posthumously published writings. After Schrenck-Notzing's death in February 1929, Walther's work focused almost exclusively on parapsychology.

Excluding the later editions of her *Phänomenologie der Mystik* and her article "Die Bedeutung der phänomenologischen Methode Edmund Husserls für die Parapsychologie,"[39] Walther's last truly phenomenological writings were published in 1928 and 1929. These works are important in that they quite clearly lay out the concepts from Husserl and Pfänder that Walther attempted to criticize and develop in not only her dissertation, but in her lost lecture on Husserl's concept of the pure ego, and in her own work on the phenomenology of mysticism. These include her articles "Ludwig Klages und sein Kampf gegen den 'Geist',"[40] and "Sören Kierkegaards Psychologie der Verzweiflung,"[41] along with a short newspaper article dealing with Pfänder titled "Ein Münchner Philosoph" ("A philosopher from Munich").[42] The article was written following a lecture on "Phänomenologie und Erkenntnistheorie" ("Phenomenology and epistemology") that Pfänder had delivered at the Charles University in Prague in April of 1929.[43] In it Walther mentions the influence of Neo-Kantian idealism, particularly Paul Natorp, on Husserl's phenomenology, whereas Pfänder's phenomenology grew out of a sympathy for critical realism, noting the importance of Pfänder's collaboration with Nikolai Hartmann. But, more importantly, she gives important clues in this piece about the influence of Pfänder on her *Phenomenology of Mysticism*.

At the outbreak of WWII, Walther was forced into national service and assigned to work in the Foreign Postal Censorship office. In June of 1941, she was arrested by the Gestapo and jailed for several weeks. She was interrogated concerning her acquaintance with Kurt Eisner, a leader in the Socialist Revolution in Munich 1918, though she later deduced that her imprisonment was in part due to her work on the paranormal. Her home was ransacked and many of her writings were confiscated or destroyed. Alhough Walther had veered away from phenomenology in her published writings, she maintained contact with numerous phenomenologists, including Roman Ingarden and Hedwig Conrad-Martius, after the war. Throughout her life, Walther worked on an autobiography (with the working title *Wandlungen (Metanoia)*),[44] which was finally published in 1960 as *Zum anderen Ufer: Vom Marxismus und Atheismus zum Christentum*. Walther died on January 6, 1977.

---

[39] Walther (1955).

[40] Walther (1928a).

[41] Walther (928b).

[42] Walther (1929).

[43] Walther had written a similar, though much longer, piece following Husserl's London Lectures in June of 1922, but this does not appear to have been published. See Ana 317 A.III.2.3—*Die phänomenologische Richtung in der neueren deutschen Philosophie, 1922.*

[44] Ana 317 A.II.1.

References

Avé-Lallemant, E. (1975). *Die Nachlässe der Münchener Phänomenologen in der Bayerischen Staatsbibliothek*. Wiesbaden: Otto Harrassowitz.

Baumann, G. (1995). *Dichtung als Lebensform. Wolfgang Frommel zwischen George-Kreis und Castrum Peregrini*. Würzburg: Königshausen & Neumann.

Husserl, E. (1994). *Briefwechsel Bd. 2. Die Münchener Phänomenologie* (Husserliana Dokumente, III). Dordrecht: Kluwer.

Parker, R. (2017). Gerda Walther and the phenomenological community. In *Acta Mexicana de Fenomenología* (Vol. 2, pp. 45–66).

Resch, A. (1983). *Gerda Walther*. Innsbruck: Resch.

Walther, G. (1922). *Ein Beitrag zur Ontologie der sozialen Gemeinschaften (mit einem Anhang zur Phänomenologie der sozialen Gemeinschaften)*. Max Halle: Niemeyer.

Walther, G. (1923a). *Ausführliches Sachregister zu Edmund Husserls "Ideen zu einer reinen Phänomenologie und phänomenologischen Philosophie Bd. 1"*. Halle: Max Niemeyer.

Walther, G. (1923b). Zur Ontologie der sozialen Gemeinschaften (mit einem Anhang zur Phänomenologie der sozialen Gemeinschaften). In *Jahrbuch für Philosophie und phänomenologische Forschung* (Vol. 6, pp. 1–158).

Walther, G. (1925). Zur Psychologie der sogenannten "moral insanity". In *Japanisch-deutsche Zeitschrift für Wissenschaft und Technik* (Vol. 3, pp. 174–184).

Walther, G. (1927). Zur innenpsychischen Struktur der Schizophrenie. In *Zeitschrift für die gesamte Neurologie und Psychiatrie* (Vol. 108, pp. 56–85).

Walther, G. (1928a). Ludwig Klages und sein Kampf gegen den 'Geist'. In *Philosophischer Anzeiger* (Vol. 3(1), pp. 48–90).

Walther, G. (1928b). Sören Kierkegaards Psychologie der Verzweiflung. In *Zeitschrift für Menschenkunde, Blätter für Charakterologie und angewandte Psychologie* (Vol. 4(4&6), pp. 208–219, 336).

Walther, G. (1929). Ein Münchner Philosoph. In *München-Augsburger Abendzeitung* (Vol. 124, p. 7).

Walther, G. (1955). Die Bedeutung der phänomenologischen Methode Edmund Husserls für die Parapsychologie. *Psychophysikalische Zeitschrift, 1*(22–29), 37–40.

Walther, G. (1960). *Zum anderen Ufer. Vom Marxismus und Atheismus zum Christentum*. Remagen: Otto Reichl.

Rodney K. B. Parker is a postdoc and lead researcher on Women in Early Phenomenology at the Center for the History of Women Philosophers and Scientists at Paderborn University. After receiving his PhD in 2013, he worked at Western University and its affiliated Colleges at the rank of Assistant Professor (Adjunct) before moving to Germany in 2017. He publishes widely on the history of the phenomenological movement and Husserl's idealism.

Gerda Walther: Searching for the Sense of Things, Following the Traces of Lived Experiences

Marina Pia Pellegrino

Abstract Gerda Walther's life and thought can be grasped through her various interests, including human community, the paranormal, and mysticism. These seemingly divergent topics are held together through her use of Edmund Husserl's phenomenological method. Tracing the flow of lived experience back to its point of origin, Walther distinguishes different "spheres" constitutive of the fundamental human essence (namely, the vital-bodily, the feelings of the psyche, and the sphere of the spirit, which is marked by a spiritual, personal core). Her analysis makes evident a background or embedment that lies behind the I, from which lived experiences arise. This "background" life of the I is essential not only to describe experiences like telepathy but also to grasp communal and mystical phenomena. The I-center is always necessary for lived experience to be actualized

Keywords Fundamental human essence · I-center · Telepathy · Embedment Community · Mysticism

Orienting Oneself in Multiple Experiences

One finds the question of the sense or meaning of things addressed in Gerda Walther's early works. In the preface to the second edition of her *Phenomenology of Mysticism*, she claims that life would have appeared meaningless or even not worthy of being lived, had the reality of the divine not existed. She notes that the idea of a divine reality, especially in specific contexts she knew well, including Marxist and atheistic ones, was presented as the "trick of priests," as the "self-delusion of human beings fleeing the world," a "sign of decadence of those belonging to certain social classes

Translated by Antonio Calcagno.

M. P. Pellegrino (✉)
Italian Centre for Phenomenological Research, Rome, Italy
e-mail: marinapiapellegrino@gmail.com

A. Calcagno (ed.), *Gerda Walther's Phenomenology of Sociality, Psychology, and Religion*, Women in the History of Philosophy and Sciences 2,
https://doi.org/10.1007/978-3-319-97592-4_2

whose historical task had come to its end."[1] Through diverse lived experiences, Walther claims to have discovered the world of spirit, which was strictly understood as having a divine foundation. She began to become aware of the dominant prejudices of her education and began to seek other more convincing approaches to the question of the divine (for example, a study of the writings of mystics, to obtain a clearer understanding of the interior universe that was slowly unfolding in her).

A unique characteristic of Walther's existential and speculative itinerary was her ability to hold together multiple interests and areas of research, including her writings on society and human community, parapsychology, theosophy, anthroposophy, Yoga, and mysticism, which she saw as a phenomenon common to all religions.[2] She holds all of the foregoing interests together thanks to the philosophical method deployed by phenomenology. By being faithful to the things themselves, following Husserl's dictum, it becomes evident that all that appears (phenomenon) is a complex reality (that is, every appearing has multiple aspects and its own proper essential characteristics that both distinguish it from and connects it to other phenomena). Following the phenomenological philosophical line, Walther is able to examine, without prejudice, that which presents itself as "exceptional" or lying outside the normal state of affairs (for example, paranormal experiences), for we are able to "bracket" the judgments and preconceptions that are tacitly given in the natural and spontaneous living of our daily lives. I would like to underscore here Walther's courage as a thinker, for she seeks to understand the meaning of her own and others' experiences, mindful of the need to evaluate them in a rational manner. Phenomenology, especially Husserlian phenomenology, convinces Walther of its philosophical validity because it deploys the epoché as an essential step to be taken in order to begin a rigorous philosophical investigation without prejudice and by investigating everything.[3]

The Phenomenological Method

As a young student, Walther first encountered phenomenology while following the lectures of Alexander Pfänder at the University of Munich. He introduced Walther to questions about knowledge of the psyche. The thought of her first teacher of philosophy would come to inform much of Walther's early analysis, and her learning was also amplified by following Husserl's courses at the University of Freiburg. Although Pfänder had devoted himself to understanding the life of the human psyche or soul to develop a comprehensive psychology that could combat the soulless psychology of positivism, he could not follow Husserl's transcendental turn. Edith Stein, whom

[1] Gerda Walther, *Phänomenologie der Mystik* (Olten: Walter Verlag, 1955), 16.

[2] Walther, *Phänomenologie der Mystik*, 18.

[3] Alexander Pfänder makes use of the epoché, but as Michael Konrad asserts, "It is not a permanent attitude, as it is for Husserl; rather, it is a provisory measure of precaution taken against hasty conclusions." See Michael Konrad, "Alexander Pfänder. L'anima umana e i suoi moti", in *Le fonti fenomenologiche della psicologia*, ed. by A. Ales Bello and A. De Luca (Pisa: Edizioni ETS, 2005), 136.

Walther knew while frequenting Stein's introductory courses on phenomenology that she gave for Husserl, also took seriously Pfänder's work, but Stein felt that Pfänder did not fully address the relations between body and the soul, and between the soul and spirit. He did not undertake a comprehensive investigation of the soul as such and as an individual soul.[4]

The study of the soul would remain foundational for both women phenomenologists. They both followed a personal theoretical–existential itinerary to know human being in itself and in its multiple relations. In Stein's work, her intent to clarify the three aspects of the human (namely, the corporeal, psychic, and spiritual aspects) can already be found at the end of her doctoral dissertation on empathy. She asks whether it is possible to access the spiritual lives of other individuals without the mediation of the body, and whether one can think of relations between persons as purely spiritual.[5] We know that Stein's continued research on spirit led her to an analysis of the essential possibility that there exist pure, created spirits (for example, angels). This is a possibility that throws new light on our understanding of the spirit or the spiritual human soul. Also revealing is the fact that Walther wanted to enter, through reflection, into the inside of certain lived experiences, including those of telepathy, to comprehend how the presence of the other invades interiority, but from "behind," from the background of consciousness. In such experiences the other is not present before me in flesh and blood. In certain cases, however, this invasion by the other happens without the I simply representing the outside other, whose "atmosphere saturates" [*durchtränkt*] the interiority of psyche.

For both Stein and Walther the complexity of being an embodied, psycho-spiritual person is analysed through the various layers or aspects constituent of the human being, from the periphery to the deep-seated core, from that which comes to light to that which remains hidden. Following Husserl's classes at Freiburg, Walther developed a profound understanding of his thought, as developed in his book *Ideas Pertaining to a Pure Phenomenology and a Phenomenological Philosophy*. She even prepared an index for the work.[6] In this work, Husserl makes two important foundational moves. First, with eidetic intuition the subject captures the essence or sense (*eidos*) of the object, be it external or internal, to which the subject is intentionally directed. Sensible perceptions as well as intellectual ones of an essence become legitimate sources of knowledge. To "see," to intuit "what the thing is," one needs to "bracket" the thesis inherent in the spontaneous natural attitude, which posits naively the existence of the world in its factuality. "Bracketing" or the epoché does not possess a sceptical sense of negation or radical doubt; rather, what remains bracketed is not negated: it is only temporarily "put out of circulation" [*Ausschaltung*]. The second move is the *transcendental reduction*, which assumes that an object of

[4]See Edith Stein, *Die Seelenburg* in *Endliches und Ewiges Sein. Versuch eines Aufstiegs zum Sinn des Seins*, introduced and ed. by A.U. Müller, ESGA 11/12 (Freiburg: Herder, 2006), 522.

[5]Edith Stein, *On the Problem of Empathy*, trans. by Waltraut Stein (Washington, DC: ICS Publications), 117–118.

[6]Gerda Walther, *Ausführliches Sachregister zu Edmund Husserls* (Ideen zu einer reinen Phänomenologie und phänomenologischen Philosophie, Vol. 1) (Halle: Max Niemeyer, 1923).

consciousness is correlated to a lived experience [*Erlebnis*] of *pure consciousness*. Pure consciousness was the domain that Husserl marked off as a field of phenomenological investigation. He was interested in the pure flow of lived experiences, which emerge and pass away much like the waves of the sea and which have the conscious I as their starting point.

In the introductory chapter of her long essay on social communities, Walther considers at length the difference between eidetic and transcendental reductions.[7] The former is connected to ontology (understood in the sense of Husserl's regional ontologies) and seeks to grasp the essentiality of objects. The latter is phenomenological in the sense that it investigates the modes of manifestation of the objects within the conscious flow of lived experiences (that is, within pure consciousness). Walther demonstrates how these two reductions intersect: the object, which stands opposite the I and, therefore, which transcends the I and which ontology defines as an essence, is also perceived, remembered, etc.; the object as a lived experience is lived "immanently" and is investigated in its essence by phenomenology. For example, in her essay on community, Walther asks what community is and what are its essential traits, but she also asks about the essence of the communal lived experience and how members consciously constitute themselves as members of a community. In addition, in her work on mysticism she wishes to show the essential characteristics of the lived experience of the mystical, understood as a correlate of a particular region that is the reality of the divine.

The Fundamental Human Essence: The I-Center and Embeddedness

Walther seeks in her work to understand the fundamental essence [*Grundwesen*] of the human being, which, metaphysically, could be understood as a kind of "entelechy." By referring to entelechy, a concept taken up by Aristotle, Stein, and Hedwig Conrad-Martius, Walther wishes to delineate a real, metaphysical essence or an originary type (*Urtypos*), the *eidos* that incarnates and actualizes itself in real, living beings. The force (their real founding source, *Quellgrund*) that one finds in this essence is found in living beings.[8] One finds in plants, therefore, a fundamental essence of a living body, and in animals one finds a psycho-corporeal one. In human beings one finds a corporeal-psycho-spiritual essence. Examining the flow of lived experiences, Walther uncovers the human essence as a personal spiritual core, which Edith Stein also develops in her own phenomenological anthropology that draws inspiration from her encounter with medieval philosophy.

Walther traces the content of certain, particularly exceptional ("Es gibt ... besonders ausgezeichnete Erlebnisse") lived experiences that form the very foundations

[7] Gerda Walther, "Zur Ontologie der sozialen Gemeinschaften", in *Jahrbuch für Philosophie und phänomenologische Forschung*, Vol. VI (Halle: Max Niemeyer, 1923), 1–17.

[8] Walther, *Phänomenologie der Mystik*, 45–46.

of our being. These particular lived experiences flow in a certain direction and erupt into a "new creation" [*Neuschöpfung*] that the I is able to grasp in a pure intuition, as an originary phenomenon with its own essence.[9] But how can one go behind lived experiences, especially if they unceasingly flow? Husserl, in *Ideas I*, affirms that "the phenomenological method completely moves within acts of reflection."[10] The fact that every I lives its own lived experiences does not mean that they are completely visible; rather, they can come to appear through reflection. Reflection on lived experiences "retained" by pure consciousness, in themselves and in their structure, is like an "interior light," following an image of Edith Stein, that illumines the flow of lived experiences. Even in the flowing out and passing away of lived experiences, reflection can clarify what appears, even though the I may not appear as present.[11] Originary consciousness, which has collected and conserved within the unity of a lived experience (for example, joy) the past moments of the lived experience, is able to grasp the lived experience as an object of reflection, as an originary object whose constituent aspects are able to be observed. Walther remarks:

> We grasp our life and our psycho-spiritual experience as fully living when we observe it from within, above all, when the I reflexively turns its interior gaze backward to a lived experience that it is living without entering into a new experience that observes another experience without suffocating or disturbing it. The I must interiorly focus itself such that it can be led by the lived experience, silently observing and accompanying it [instead of, for example, unfavorably analyzing and judging it]. The essence of the lived experience must not be changed within its "normal" flow. Since the essence of the metaphysical and real core of personality is psycho-spiritual, it must also undoubtedly be able to be brought to interior givenness in "reflective" contemplation such that it becomes immediately intelligible in a living manner and not through the long path of a series of deductions.[12]

There also exist moments that do not appear on account of the gaze of the I: there are stirrings [*Regungen*] that come out of a background [*Hintergrund*] that lies behind (*a tergo*) the I that Walther describes as "being embedded" [*Einbettung*]. Here, the I is not a pure subject of consciousness, but is an I embedded within the background of psyche. If we do not carry out the phenomenological reduction on the pure I, Walther notes, we speak of the I and its background within the framework of a concrete psychological attitude. Again, the I is given, but it is given as a real "point" (not in the spatial sense) in a subject: it is an I-center [*Ichzentrum*], following the terminology of Pfänder, or it is a moment endowed with the consciousness of a real psychic subject and with power over the self that clearly expresses itself in acts of will.[13] We see this power of the will in lived experience (for example, I can choose, not to cede to the emergence in me of a certain possible embedment, for

[9]Walther, *Zur Ontologie der sozialen Gemeinschaften*, 16.

[10]Edmund Husserl, *Ideen zu einer reinen Phänomenologie und einer phänomenologische Philosophie* III/I, ed. by K. Schumann (The Hague: Martinus Nijhoff, 1976), 144.

[11]Edith Stein, *Einführung in die Philosophie*, Hinführung, ed. and introduced by Claudia Mariéle Wulf (Edith Stein Gesamtausgabe No. 8) (Freiburg: Herder, 2004), 106. AU: should "Hinführung," be removed?

[12]Walther, *Phänomenologie der Mystik*, 48–49.

[13]Walther, *Zur Ontologie der sozialen Gemeinschaften*, 13.

I can choose to repress, remove, or even quash it). Hence, the I is free in relation to such risings in me (we shall see how important the will is for telepathy). The I, however, cannot cause the risings to occur, but it can place itself in another position vis-à-vis these moments of emergence in me insofar as the I can allow the emerging moments to appear or it can likewise negate them. The I, then, can remain in contact with the sources from which the spirituality of the person emerges. This contact can also serve as the basis for the formation of enduring or habitual attitude necessary for the communal union between human and/or divine persons. Actual lived experience can become habitual.

Walther sketches a description of the I that is different from the usual one in which the I is conceived as simply tending to something. The I is capable of lifting itself out of its own lived experiences in an act of reflection ("sich über seine Erlebnisse zu erheben").[14] Simply being "conscious of" does not in itself guarantee the freedom of the I. Although the I may know its lived experiences, it can also freely choose to abandon itself to living the very flow of the experiences. This moment of the force of the will, which implies self-consciousness but is not reducible to it, is a sign of freedom proper to human beings alone. Here, we also can establish the difference between the purely psychic and spiritual aspects of human beings.

In embedment or sedimentation, one finds, for example, buried lived experiences that were once actual and which can become objects of memory. One also finds psychic dispositions in which are inscribed the risings of habitual or potential lived experiences. In telepathy, embedded movements or risings of another individual appear within the psychic experiences of a subject. It is important to recall the importance that Husserl ascribes to this obscure base, even though he does not treat parapsychic or mystical experiences. In *Ideas II*, which Edith Stein edited and pieced together from the "Master's" notes, one finds in the chapter dedicated to motivation as the fundamental law of the spirit a section titled "The Spiritual I and its Base": "This specifically spiritual I, the subject of spiritual acts, the personality, depends on an obscure base of characterological inclinations, originary, hidden dispositions, and nature."[15]

The difficulty of the description lies in the aspect of the I embedded in an obscure "where" that coincides with a pure I. This background [*Hintergrund*], embedment [*Einbettung*], self [*Selbst*], or subconsciousness [*Unterbewusstsein*] (even though Walther prefers the term embedment because it is less contaminated by various other senses, she also uses the other aforementioned terms) is a background lived experience [*Erlebnis-hintergrund*], a lived backdrop that manifests itself to the gaze of the I in phenomenological reflection. Evidently, there is a need here for a universal structure with its own essential characteristics in order for the concrete living to be grasped. Because consciousness accompanies the lived experience and because living is structurally present in all lived experiences, knowledge, reflection, and the description of all individual lived experiences become possible, including those that emerge from the profound depths.

[14] Walther, *Phänomenologie der Mystik*, 43.

[15] Edmund Husserl, *Ideen II*, 276.

By deploying concrete experiences, Walther retrospectively reflects on the directions that the lived experiences follow. She asks: How do lived experiences flow from the I? For example, while we may find ourselves in a determined lived experience, we could suddenly be grasped by another one. While looking from the window, for example, we become conscious of a problem, as if this problem emerged from the obscure background of the I, as if it had been dragged out from what the I had been observing; the problem is led back to my interiority to reflect on it.[16] When the I moves from one lived experience to another, we experience how the lived experience emerges from one direction in the psychic interior background, in its embedment, and how only later it drags the I into itself such that its point of departure and the conscious I itself begin to fuse with one another.

One can distinguish different "spheres" in an embedment, according to the direction taken by the lived experience as it emerges from its own embeddedness. In these spheres the I can grasp its own spiritual person, its fundamental metaphysically real essence, as an ultimate form of givenness. The spiritual sphere, understood as a source of lived experiences (perceptions and ultimate, scientific, artistic, ethical, etc. intuitions) is placed in a layer of embedment "above" the I. Walther observes:

> Perhaps the I finds itself in a difficult moral crisis that affects its entire life and, deprived of any form of help, the I finds itself facing its own impulses that resist the situation. Suddenly, the crisis is no longer; the lifting of the crisis feels like an interior tremor: one finds oneself shaken free from his or her confines in that interior circle of light, which discloses itself above the I and which seems to exist "above" and "behind" the I's habitual embedment. Now the I suddenly sees what it clearly and distinctly must do. It now stands in a pure and clear interior light, raised "above" the confusion of its instincts.[17]

The sphere of light from which certain rays emanate shines beyond the human being and its psychic, interior confines, even though, simultaneously, the rays seem to spring from the very same direction of its own embedment. The rays flow from a central source of spiritual light, a source that is connected to the human being. This source prefigures the divine Spirit from whom the "spark" in human beings stems. The individual experiences herself or himself here as a spiritual being, as a member of the spiritual realm; she/he can distinguish very clearly her/his own spiritual qualities from those of others. For example, only certain spiritual rays emanating from the same species are able to awaken interior rays.

One can also experience a realm of feelings of the soul arising in one's interiority, feelings that surge from the "depths" of the heart, that flow from the "bottom" to the "top" (for example, psycho-spiritual love for a person or an ideal, etc.). The flow of feelings of the heart, or those that flow from the depths of the soul, becomes more manifest when the I is abandoned to its object, a person, or a value that elicits the feeling itself. But the moment the I turns away from the object to return to itself and its feelings, as if in a "self-mirroring," the I has already distanced itself from its source. It is only from a higher level, for example, when one contemplates oneself from a "God's-eye" view as God's creation that one does not run the risk of collapsing into

---

[16]Walther, *Phänomenologie der Mystik*, 37–38.

[17]Walther, *Phänomenologie der Mystik*, 120.

narcissistic self-contemplation. It is only from this view that one can meaningfully understand the commandment: "Love your neighbour as yourself." The interior gaze that grasps the source of feelings and its particularity, although it has been absorbed by the feelings, can only perdure for a moment, much like a flash. In this flash the I seizes its own basic essence as soul, as the warm flame of sentiment [*Gefühlsflamme*] "colored" by individual characteristics.[18] With other forms of embedment there arise the self-lived experiences that refer to the vital, corporeal sphere.

If the I-center grasps the lived experiences that stem from the spiritual sphere or from the realm of deep feelings, even without actually living in one single act of or in the other spheres, although the I radiates within these spheres, the I-center continues to rest in its fundamental essence. If the lived experience of the I-center becomes habitual, then the body will be animated and transfigured by the forces of the soul and spirit. Like Edith Stein, who deploys the image of the interior castle of Saint Teresa of Avila, the decisive importance of one's ultimate end arises for the existence of the person by virtue of the "place" in which the I comes to permanently stand.

Telepathic Union

We have already discussed the various movements that arise from embeddedness and that saturate the other's psyche. Here, one finds lived experiences that, in their origin, refer back to the interiority of the subject in question (A) and the other subject (B). These lived experiences immediately, telepathically penetrate the embeddedness of A through its I-center. Gerda Walther devotes much attention to the question of telepathy, and she even discusses her own experience of it, which she closely studied. She asserts that even those who do not believe in telepathy must account for the fact that there exists much discussion about it, especially at the conceptual level. What does telepathy mean and what are the essential traits of such a lived experience? Although telepathy manifests a deep inherence of one individual in another, it does not mean that subjects identify with one another, for the I that is entered into by the other is conscious that the other does not belong to it.

Telepathy is distinguished from empathy, which Edith Stein eminently described in her doctoral dissertation.[19] Walther knew Stein's text and cites it. In the lived experience of empathy, I seize through the expressions of others (gestures, words, etc.) the mind of the other: I hear what the other tells me, and through his sad face I can grasp his pain or though his radiant eyes I can grasp his joy. All that stands before me is transmitted through consciousness. All that empathy facilitates, the totality of the other, from her corporeity to her personality, comes to light before my gaze. The characteristic of telepathy, however, is that this very same experience described above actualizes itself unbeknown to me, from "behind" (*a tergo*). The thoughts and

---

[18] Walther, *Phänomenologie der Mystik*, 115–117.

[19] Edith Stein, *On the Problem of Empathy*, trans. by Waltraut Stein (Washington, DC: ICS Publications, 1989).

feelings of the other subject penetrate my very embeddedness, thereby affirming my I-center. From her various studies of telepathy, Walther offers a rich discussion of the particularities of telepathy. She maintains that telepathy is unique because the living of the experience is carried out from the viewpoint of the other, at the very same time that the other lives it, as if one were present in the same place with the other, as if we were remembering it:

> Simultaneously, in a clear representation, for example, in a dream, we see the interior of something. I see what L, in this exact moment, experiences. I "see" L in his room [noticed by me] lying on his couch, and I see him as he sees himself: I experience him lying on the sofa, not as one observing him lying on the sofa, but as L lying on the sofa … I also see that he has a book in his hand that has slid down onto the sofa, a book that he no longer reads. Furthermore, I also grasp that he is smoking; I "smell" and "savor" in my interior the scent of his cigarette and I am stimulated to smoke. The sense of everything, the things around which the thoughts of L circulate, consists in the fact that he is reflecting on whether he should write me …"[20]

Walther concludes that it was her intention to dismiss her experience as "nonsense" (she had argued with this friend L and she did not expect him to write to her), but surprisingly she did receive a letter from him because mutual friends asked him to write to Walther.

Important here is the particular, interior psychic coloring of the lived experience, the transmitted "aura," which sometimes does not necessarily require the representation of the other person. From the beginning, the experience of telepathy is *saturated* by this aura that stems from the transmitter. Walther returns to the image of the ancient lamp, the image to which she compared the human person. The I-center is similar to a wick that burns and floats upon a combustible liquid [*Flüssigkeit*], which in ancient times was oil and which can be said to be like an embedment or the subconscious. All is surrounded by a container (namely, the lamp), strictly understood, to which the body is compared.[21] By drawing upon reported experiences of telepathy, Walther observes that we are each a different lamp with our own wicks that burn our own flames (our I-centers). However, the oil in the lamps seems to be able to flow from lamp to lamp, which means that each wick can be fed simultaneously by the oil of another person. The two lamps remain distinct. Often, the oils may not mix, and even in cases where the oils do mix, an individual wick may decide to withdraw from the oil of the other and burn one's own oil. Walther affirms, based on her studies, that one is able to preserve one's own freedom within the lived experience of telepathy insofar as that one is able to shake oneself off or even take one's own position vis-à-vis the lived experience of the other. Telepathic union, then, is achieved only in embedment and not in the I-center.[22]

---

[20] Gerda Walther, *Phänomenologie der Mystik*, 65–66.

[21] Walther, *Phänomenologie der Mystik*, 47.

[22] Walther, *Phänomenologie der Mystik*, 75.

Communal Union

Telepathic union is to be distinguished from the union between members of a community. In her work on the ontology of community, Walther differentiates a community from a societal relation. She warns, from the start, that the descriptor "social" refers to an exclusively human community, though it is not the most intense form of community, which is achieved when members have a "feeling of mutual belonging" [*Gefühl der Zusammengehörigkeit*].[23] Walther draws on the unpublished works of her teacher Alexander Pfänder (namely, *Psychologie der Gesinnungen* and *Psychologie der Menschen*), to develop her discussion of community. *Gesinnung* may be described as the disposition to react in a certain way (love, benevolence, malevolence, unfriendliness) to determined objects. Elicited by whatever object, it can produce in a subject the feeling of union though which an individual tends to unite with an object. For example, a warm, affirming psychic wave, emerging from the depths of consciousness, penetrates a waking consciousness. It is as if the wave returned the whole subject and its I, which is psychically pervaded by the wave, to its object (the term object may be understood in a wide sense, and may include also persons among its senses). The profiles of union are diverse: the subject may feel himself or herself as equal to or superordinated or subordinated to the objects, and this may happen until the object rests in the subject. This union is actual, and it proceeds from the I-center, which tends intentionally to its object.

Walther also maintains the possibility of simply "growing together" [*Zusammenwachsen*], which is achieved without the I having to take a stance within one's subconscious or depths. How does this happen? One becomes aware of the union in question at the very moment one begins to experience it. It is not something, however, that is characterized as only achievable now in the instant; rather, the union manifests itself as the reinforcement or confirmation of a union that is already present but unconscious. It is only in a now that growing together can be constituted for the experiencing subject.[24] This kind of union is to be distinguished from an actual union that has become habitual. When the actual union ceases the I no longer intends its object; rather, other new moving, lived experiences enter and the I moves toward their objects. The lived experience, so long as it perdures, is intentionally filled by its object, but in the case of growing together the lived experience cannot stand alone without a relation to the object. Hence, the "fabric" of the union is not ripped apart and the earlier lived experience continues to vibrate within the flow of consciousness, even though it may have retreated into the background behind the I-center. The lived experience of union is awakened by some external occasion and it re-emerges in waking consciousness, and not as the faint image of a memory. In habitual unions, even though they may lie deep within the depths of an individual, within the embedment of the I, the feeling of union is not spent. It continues to have a vital force that

[23]Gerda Walther, *Ein Beitrag zur Ontologie der sozialen Gemeinschaften*, 33–34.

[24]Walther, *Ein Beitrag zur Ontologie der sozialen Gemeinschaften*, 36–37.

flows out of its own inexhaustible source.[25] The transformation of an actual union into a habitual one is fundamental for the life of a community.

The subject may feel itself united to other human beings "that also … feel and value the same thing."[26] This "also" constitutes, according to Walther, a category fundamental for understanding community. The "also" does not only refer to external ends, but also encompassing attitudes regarding existence. The notion of human beings, who are "also" present in the embedment of the I wherever community exists, does not simply arise from a single individual; rather, it surges from the unity of others in the notion of human being, from a we. The we is not to be understood properly as a subject, an I-center community. Even the lived experiences of community have to come to fullness in the I-center of every individual. They flow from my embedment to my I-center, from which they ultimately are actualized. In the lived experience of union, one also seizes others within oneself, in one's own embedment.

Walther adds that for the constitution of an authentic community the union must be intentional on both sides; there must always be an exchange between individuals. The tendency to union, which rises from the depths of the subject, finds adequation or fulfillment in the depths of the other, in his or her spiritual essence. In communal union, as opposed to telepathic union, the I has intentionally seized in itself others, and the I feels one with them. Edith Stein, in her "Individual and Community,"[27] also carried out a phenomenological analysis of community from the perspective of the individual who is a member of a community. The accounts of both philosophers may be read in parallel to one another. Stein's text was published in 1922 in Husserl's *Jahrbuch*, while Walther's essay on social communities appeared in 1923 in the same journal. Walther admits in a footnote[28] that she was not able to consider Stein's work, but she remarks in opposition to Stein that community may also be viewed from the "outside." Yet, even if viewed from an external point of view, community arises from the deepest "layer" of the subjects who are its members.

Mystical Union

The Phenomenology of Mysticism may be considered Gerda Walther's main work. In this text, one finds a consolidation of all her fields of interest. She affirms that she wishes to follow as closely as possible the lived experience of mystics, ultimately distilling the essential aspects of their experience, which she denotes as a living experience of "the real [*leibhaftig*] presence" of God. Although she privileges Christian mystical experience, she sets the object of her study within a broad framework by distinguishing the union with God from a spiritual force or a force of love. She also

[25] Walther, *Ein Beitrag zur Ontologie der sozialen Gemeinschaften*, 39–40.

[26] Walther, *Ein Beitrag zur Ontologie der sozialen Gemeinschaften*, 69–70.

[27] Edith Stein, *Philosophy of Psychology and the Humanities*, trans. by Mary Catharine Baseheart and Marianne Sawicki (Washington, DC: ICS Publications, 2000).

[28] Gerda Walther, *Ein Beitrag zur Ontologie der sozialen Gemeinschaften*, 17.

distinguishes between communion with God, God as infinite spiritual person, or the God of interpersonal relations.

The reference to the lived body and all that is given as embodied allows one to enter into a dimension in which all is living. This dimension allows Walther to assert that the Eucharistic union, understood as the living presence of Christ, may be connected with mystical lived experiences. The discussion of mysticism in her book is preceded by a philosophical anthropology that seeks to uncover and describe the lived experiences that arise from the foundation or essence of the human person, especially those stemming from the individual's personal core.

Walther claims that there are two descriptors that grasp the essence of the individual (namely, abandonment and desolation—*Verlassenheit*). In these two states the I can be said to be enclosing itself in its own constitutive emptiness, ultimately comporting itself as the personification of a vicious circle,[29] thereby either falling prey to nonsense or tending to something else. The I can be seen to be entering the dimension constitutive of the relation between human and divine persons. The I opens itself up to the divine. Sometimes, this mystical experience is referred to as a kind of madness or folly; it is not described as a psychic state, yet it is also described as the metaphysical possibility of losing oneself. The latter occurs when one remains wrapped up in one's being-alone-with-one's I, without any relation to the fullness of being of the divine essence. Walther views this being trapped in the immanence of the I as diabolical or Satanic.[30]

Walther will often describe her own personal mystical experiences, drawing out what is of universal value in them. The state of abandonment is described as *wakeful*. Here, the I lives with the highest concentration. Echoing her past investigations, Walther affirms that the I-center is free to remain in contact with the deep sources of lived experience, but she can also distance herself from them. The I-center is like the "eye" (that is, the actualizing point of consciousness not only for embedment—as in telepathic experiences—but also for the basic body–psyche–spirit human essence, without which the I would be "blind").

The I, perhaps because of a crisis that afflicts a person's existence (Walther tells of such a crisis while returning on the train to Freiburg after visiting her gravely ill father), seems to unconsciously lapse onto itself in its inability to grasp any content, be it of the external world or from within. The I experiences itself as being completely "empty," as being nothing but an I. The I knows, but all it knows is itself and its inconsolable state; it is as if the I has been "blocked" from the external world and its values, as well as the I's own psycho-spiritual world and its own self and embedment. A dark abyss appears before the I, an abyss into which it may fall. The I here has neither world nor soul nor embedment nor a foundational essence. The I has no life, objects, and goals from which certain possibilities and forces may arise. The I has contracted into itself with the greatest tension and intensity.[31] This solitary life is

[29]"Der wie ein personifizierter circulus vitiosus sich verhält …" Gerda Walther, *Phänomenologie der Mystik*, 140.

[30]Walther, *Phänomenologie der Mystik*, 140–141.

[31]Walther, *Phänomenologie der Mystik*.

not bearable for the human being: either the individual lapses into the emptiness or she/he desperately tends toward something of the highest value that cannot be degraded:

> The I only knows one thing: Its something else [*Es*] must be totally different than what it has up until now known and experienced. This is what the I feels … It does not know where its something else is and whether it is true. With imperturbability, calmness, and cold and clear certainty, it knows in a completely determined way one thing: The I will lapse into ruin and wants to do so, if it does not find something else. This is the case because otherwise nothing from within or outside the I could lead it to want to continue to exist.[32]

In this description, Walther does not include a specific religious context. The something else toward which the I tends, at this point in her work, has neither name nor identity. Its coming to be is free and is understood to be a *grace*. Here, the source moments of religious consciousness emerge: the desire for a fullness that cannot be obtained by oneself, the waiting for a freely given event that blocks one from lapsing into the void.

In an immeasurable interior distance and beyond all that from which the I is blocked, something appears, as a sea of light and color that envelops the I and whose radiance fills the heart, soul, spirit, and the self. It is only in this sea that I rests peacefully, full of gratitude because that something or *Es* has arrived. The I finds itself now abandoned over to trust; the abandonment is different than desolation. If, previously, all had contracted into an unextended I-point, now there is an opening, a dilation that opens up onto the infinity of everything. Here, the I "sees" its fundamental essence and it enters again into it; it sees and feels itself with the "eye" and "heart" of God. The I becomes open to the possibility of seeing all creatures in this light. Yet, the I is not annihilated within this sea of light and color. Only insofar as it was born or in that it was never in the union described above, although it has received the foundational essence of body–psyche–spirit and a self while being placed in the world, thereby having for itself a lived history, can the I be aware of all that it has in the living experience of the divine. Therefore, in mystical union, in the pure abandonment of love, even though the subject may be only a contemplating I, the I is never identical with its object (namely, God).

The mystical experience cannot be confused with the telepathic one. One need only think here of the incommensurable distance of that something (*Es*) and the tension of the I as it awaits it, not knowing whether it will die or become mad if this something does not come.[33] In the last chapters of the *Phenomenology of Mysticism* the divine essence is described as God, Infinite Spiritual Person, and as a being in communion with It. Salvation comes, then, from the Person of God, who can bring the I home, ultimately reinserting it into the totality of the I's own aspects. The Person of God can truly heal the human being from what is diabolical, from the complete estrangement from one's own self.

The two results of Walther's analysis of desolation recall, on the one hand, the metaphysical dependence of the individual on the foundation of his or her essence

---

[32] Walther, *Phänomenologie der Mystik*, 144.

[33] Walther, *Phänomenologie der Mystik*, 145.

and, on the other hand, the constitutive freedom of the I, understood as a center of willing and choice. It seems to me that Walther wishes here to condense in a powerful way (because she does not avoid the possibility of a tragic result) the sense of things, even the abysmal sense, as they unfold in the flow of lived experience. In this flow, she uncovers our being as unique and responsible persons capable of actualizing our own ends in a united, communal way, with others and with the Other.

Marina Pia Pellegrino holds a *laurea* in Philosophy and has taught philosophy and pedagogy in secondary schools. She has also taught courses on Edith Stein's philosophy for Catholic teachers and the Diocese of Turin. She collaborates with the Italian Center for Phenomenological Research and sits on the Executive Committee of the International Research Area Dedicated to Edith Stein and Contemporary Philosophy. She has published various papers on philosophy and Gerda Walther, including *L'essere umano e la sua vita interiore. Linee di fenomenologia della mistica in Gerda Walther* [*The Human Being and Its Interior Life: Outline for a Phenomenology of Mysticism in Gerda Walther*] (Naples: Edizioni Scientifiche Italiane, 2007). Along with Angela Ales Bello, she is the co-editor of the book *Edith Stein–Gerda Walther. Incontri possibili. Empatia, telepatia, comunità, mistica* [*Edith Stein and Gerda Walther: Possible Encounters—Empathy, Community, Mysticism*] (Rome: Castelvecchi, 2007).

Part II
Social Ontology and the Self

Social Acts and Communities: Walther Between Husserl and Reinach

Alessandro Salice and Genki Uemura

Abstract The chapter contextualizes and reconstructs Walther's theory of social acts. In her view a given act qualifies as social if it is performed in the name of or on behalf of a community. Interestingly, Walther's understanding of that notion is patently at odds with the idea of a social act originally propounded by Reinach. According to Reinach, an act is social if it "addresses" other persons and if it, for its success, requires them to grasp it. We claim that to explain Walther's reconfiguration of this concept, one has to look into the use that Husserl makes of it. Husserl adopts this idea from Reinach to tackle a problem that is not discussed by the latter. This is the problem of how communities, by means of social acts, are "constituted" in consciousness. Walther shares with Husserl the concern about the constitution of communities and her radical revision of Reinach's idea is presented as an attempt to offer an alternative solution to Husserl's problem.

Keywords Social act · Walther · Reinach · Husserl · Constitution

Introduction

It is almost a truism to claim that the mind is one of the core topics—if not *the* core topic—of research in phenomenology. Moreover, exploring the mind from a phenomenological perspective is to a great extent an investigation into the structures of experiences lived through by a singular subject. Among other results, the phenomenological approach to the mind has produced detailed descriptions of different

The authors equally contributed to this chapter. Uemura's research was supported by the Japan Society for the Promotion of Science (KAKENHI, Project No. 26770014).

A. Salice (✉)
University College Cork, Cork, Ireland
e-mail: alessandro.salice@ucc.ie

G. Uemura
Okayama University, Okayama, Japan
e-mail: uemurag@okayama-u.ac.jp

A. Calcagno (ed.), *Gerda Walther's Phenomenology of Sociality, Psychology, and Religion*, Women in the History of Philosophy and Sciences 2,
https://doi.org/10.1007/978-3-319-97592-4_3

kinds of experiences. One particularly important description concerns the distinction between what we suggest labeling "infra-personal" and "social" experiences.

Many of a subject's experiences can be qualified as infra-personal. Among others, perceptions, beliefs, acts of imaginations, and (at least, some kinds of) emotions are infra-personal in the sense that they *may* involve, but *do not necessarily* require, the existence of other subjects. By contrast, and as a first approximation of a characterization, experiences of the social kind *necessarily* require the existence of other subjects in one way or the other (that is, they require the subject to interact with others in a social environment). For instance, issuing an order always involves issuing an order *to* somebody. And declaring war always involves declaring war *on behalf of* a nation. The main question of this chapter concerns the essential structure of social experiences: How to understand, precisely, the claim that these experiences require the subject to interact with others in a social environment?

This chapter reconstructs and scrutinizes the discussion about social experiences in early phenomenology. To be more precise, the chapter is concerned with a *specific* class of social experiences (namely, *social acts*), and with two arguably irreconcilable positions thereof, which were developed by two early phenomenologists. The first position, advocated by Adolf Reinach, holds that what characterizes an act as social is the peculiar way in which this act is addressed to another person or other persons (and hence has "addressee(s)"). The second position, defended by Gerda Walther, maintains that, for an act to qualify as social, this act must stand in the right relation with a community: The act must be performed *in the name of* or *on behalf of* a community. Walther, who presents her view in an article of 1923, was certainly aware of Reinach's theory, which leads to the question as to why she reconfigures Reinach's notion in such a radical way. We claim that her revision of Reinach's position depends on (and is mediated by) Husserl's understanding of (Reinach's notion of) social acts.

The chapter is organized as follows. In section "Reinach's Conception of Social Acts (and Walther's Departure from It)" we introduce Reinach's theory of social acts by drawing a parallel with what have been called "speech acts" in Ordinary Language Philosophy. After this, we briefly show how Walther's view of social acts conflicts with Reinach's. In section "Husserl on the Constitutive Function of Social Acts" we investigate how Reinach's ideas have been adopted by Husserl to address a problem that was not originally discussed by Reinach. This is the problem of how communities are given or "constituted" in consciousness. In section "Walther on Social Acts" we turn to Walther to highlight that she shares with Husserl the concern about the constitution of communities and that her original and radical revision of Reinach's notion of a social act is an attempt to offer a different and alternative solution to Husserl's problem.

Reinach's Conception of Social Acts (and Walther's Departure from It)

Reinach developed his theory of social acts between 1911 and 1913, and he formulated it succinctly in his monograph titled *A priori Foundations of the Civil Law*. This theory shows many significant analogies with the notion of a speech act developed by Austin in the 1950s (and later refined by Searle and others). Notoriously, these analogies have motivated several commentators to suggest that Reinach should be credited with discovering the notion of a speech act (see Mulligan 1987; Smith 1990).

This chapter's primary interest does not lie in comparing Reinach's and Austin's views (which is a task that has been taken on by others; see Crosby 1990; Mulligan 1987), yet we think that such a comparison may be relevant for the topic at stake as it may enable us to uncover an important aspect of Reinach's theory that is core to the phenomenological understanding of social acts, but which is not appreciated in the Oxonian approach to speech acts. The main difference between these two theories, roughly, is this: Whereas Austin (and those working in his tradition) considers speech acts to be a class of ritual, ceremonial, or conventional actions, Reinach describes social acts as *intentional experiences* of a particular kind.

One way to identify the similarities between these two theories is by pointing to the idea that Reinach and Austin concur in claiming that successfully performed social/speech acts fulfill at least three conditions. We call these conditions the "preparatory," the "sincerity," and the "essential" conditions (to paraphrase John Searle's classical terminology introduced in 1969; see also Salice 2015).

The first condition is qualified as "preparatory," for the entire act is miscarried if that condition is not aptly fulfilled. To be successfully performed, all social acts must "secure uptake" in their addresses (Austin 2011: 117) or, in Reinach's terms, they must "be heard" (*vernommen*) by the addresses. All and only those acts that necessarily are in need of being heard (that exemplify the property of being in need of being heard—*Vernehmungsbedürftigkeit*) qualify as social (Reinach 2012: 18ff.). A social act performed between two or more human beings is "heard," according to Reinach, when three things occur: First, the linguistic utterance is acoustically or visually perceived by the act's addressee; second, the addressee understands the content of the utterance; and, finally, the addressee understands the type of the act—this is its "quality," in Husserl's terminology of the *Logical Investigations*, or its "mode"; see Crane (2001) (that is, she understands whether a given utterance is a promise, an order, etc.). Puzzlingly, however, Reinach believes that this last condition does not apply to the social act of informing somebody about something (Reinach 2012: 21).

Although Reinach argues that social acts can also be performed in non-linguistic communication (for example, in mien and gestures; Reinach 2012: 20), it is the linguistic dimension that most clearly characterizes social acts. Indeed, all these acts have what could be called a *locutionary* component (in Austin's sense, see 2011: 94ff.): in performing a social act the subject by necessity also performs a so-called "act of meaning something" (*Meinen*, *Meinensakt*). Reinach describes this act as consisting in the use of syntactically organized strings of words that belong to the vocabulary of a language, refer to entities, and predicate something of these entities (Reinach 1989a: 102ff., 127ff.). In social acts (but only in social acts), the act of meaning something is always verbalized or uttered, which makes *Meinen* the visible "body" of the act (Reinach 2012: 20).

In addition to a body, social acts also have a "soul." Indeed, every social act presupposes or is founded (*fundiert*) upon a further mental state that represents the "sincerity condition" of that very act. This further state, Reinach argues, is an *inner* or non-social intentional experience: Insofar as it is not social, this experience is not in need of being heard and, insofar as it is intentional, it has an intentional correlate, which is said to coincide with the correlate of the act of meaning something mentioned above (Reinach 2012: 20). For example, if Jim informs Joel that p, then Jim's act of informing is constituted by an act of meaning that p and by a conviction that p. Analogously, the promise to φ is constituted by the act of willing or intending to φ and, again, by the act of meaning φ. If the social act merely *pretends* to be founded by an inner act of a given type, while in reality it is not, it experiences a "modification" (that is, the act is insincere). For instance, if Jim merely pretends to be convinced that p is the case, then Jim is not *informing* Joel about p, he is belying him; analogously, a promise that lacks the will to act is not a promise, but the deceptive modification of a promise (Reinach 2012: 22). While describing several other ways in which social acts can be modified, he identifies the present modification as the origin of social hypocrisy (Reinach 2012: 22; see Austin's notion of insincerity, 2011: 39ff).

The last condition that both Reinach and Austin delineate for a social act to be successful concerns the consequences of these acts. In fact, social acts have a point, which is to generate effects of a peculiar sort. These are what Austin calls the illocutionary consequences or "effects" of a speech act (2011: 114ff). What are these effects or consequences? They can be illustrated most clearly by looking at the social act *par excellence* (namely, the promise). *If*, say, Jim's promise to Joel is successful in the sense that it meets the preparatory and the sincerity conditions, *then* the promise has brought about Jim's commitment to realize the content of his promise and Joel's claim that Jim does so. But then, what are claims and commitments? They are certainly not material objects like tables and trees, but they are not mental objects like beliefs or desires either, as they exist even if their bearers sleep or are unconscious. Furthermore, they are not abstract objects like numbers or propositions, since such objects are atemporal, whereas the effects of a social act, as they are brought to existence by this very act, start to exist at a given time t and (potentially) disappear at a given time t' (Reinach 2012: 14ff.). Claims and commitments, hence, belong to a *sui generis* ontological category, they are social (or perhaps, more precisely, institutional) objects (see Salice 2013).

If the reconstruction offered so far is on the right track, then there are good reasons for thinking that Reinach and Austin are trying to conceptually model the very same phenomena. But this is not to say that there are no important differences between these accounts, and one of them is particularly relevant for our purposes. Austin is adamant in describing speech acts as "conventional, ceremonial or ritual actions." To put this differently, speech acts belong to a specific class of actions whose existence is premised on an accepted convention. We will soon come back to this point, but it is important to highlight one consequence of this understanding already now: In the case in which either there is no convention or the agent does not respect the convention, then the action (that is, the speech act) has literally not taken place: "lots of things have been done [...] but we shall not have done the purported act [...]" (Austin 2011: 17). For example, if Jim says to Joel, "I promise to...," but Joel does not understand Jim, then, literally, no promise has occurred. In other words, to promise is to commit oneself to do something for somebody else. If Jim were to be asked whether he has promised something to Joel, he would reply that no promise has been made. In a sense, he has tried to promise, but the action was not performed.

Reinach's understanding of a social act is completely different: A social act is an experience (*Erlebnis*), that instantiates an essence. We have already pointed to some essential properties of social acts: First and foremost, social acts are in need of being heard. Moreover, it is because they are in need of being heard that they must be announced, for the addressee must be put in a position to understand the act (in the many senses of the term "understanding" described above). This is why they consist of a locutionary component (*Meinen*), which is accompanied by an inner experience. But there are other essential features: What distinguishes social acts from other classes of intentional experiences (like beliefs or emotions) is their spontaneity (*Spontaneität*). The subject of a social act deliberately performs her act (that is, she determines times and forms of her act), whereas this is not the case for beliefs or emotions. If my eyes move upon an artwork, my belief that I face an artwork or my emotions of enjoyment toward the artwork are not spontaneous in any comparable sense.

But now let us go back to our previous example: Jim utters a certain sentence, "I promise that…," but Joel does not understand him. In Reinach's view an experience has occurred. This is an experience that is intentional, spontaneous, and in need of being heard, which presupposes an intention and an act of meaning something. Hence, given that all essential properties of a promise are exemplified by the experience, Jim's experience *does* qualify as a promise, contrary to what Austin claims. In fact, Reinach writes: "If we put ourselves in the position of the promisor, we see that a genuine promise can be performed and expressed, yet without reaching the subject to whom it is directed" (2012: 28). So, were Jim to be asked whether he has promised something to Joel, then he—again, in Reinach's view—would not have to reply that he *tried* to promise, but rather that he indeed promised something, although his promise was not successful.

To elaborate, one could argue that, in Reinach's view, what makes a given experience a *social* act, is not primarily the fact that this act is premised on a social convention, but that it is the peculiar way in which the other is addressed by the subject. To further expand on this idea, Reinach seems to develop what could be characterized as an "internalistic" account of social acts: In principle, a brain in a vat, to use Putnam's notorious example, would be able to perform all sorts of social acts as long as the brain is able to adopt the peculiar mental stance toward the other that characterizes social acts.

But, then, is not Reinach's understanding of an experience's sociality simply too minimal? How can a solipsistic mind be in a position to have social experiences? Within phenomenology, Reinach is not alone in embracing this form of internalism about social acts (for example, Scheler, too, seems to propound a similar view; Scheler 1954: 511). Now, pointing to this difficulty is not to mean that there are no conceptual resources in those accounts that may be able to dissolve this tension (as a matter of fact, we think such resources do exist). Yet, we suggest that one way to understand Walther's characterization of social acts can be seen as a reaction against that problem and as an attempt to fix what makes a given act a *social* act without falling prey to Reinach's internalism.

As we will see in sections "Husserl on the Constitutive Function of Social Acts and Walther on Social Acts", drawing on unpublished lectures and manuscripts of Alexander Pfänder, her teacher in Munich, Walther claims that social acts are characterized in terms of their being oriented toward [*sich richten auf*] the social community and that these acts are originated in the individual's "social self" [*soziales Selbst*] (see Walther 1923: 103). In her opinion, what deserves the name of "social acts" in the authentic (or, in her own words, "pregnant") sense are experiences that are performed "in the name of" or "on behalf [*Sinn*] of" the community (see Walther 1923: 104).

Reinach would strongly disagree with Walther's proposal. From his standpoint, her conception of social acts is partly too narrow, but partly also too broad. On the one hand, Walther's conception is too narrow because it captures only a certain subclass of social acts. Reinach would admit that an act of, say, promising can be performed in the name of or on behalf of a community, but he would take it only as a *modified* form of social acts (Reinach 2012: 25),[1] which are distinguished from experiences of non-social types precisely by the necessity of being heard (*Vernehmungsbedürftigkeit*). On the other hand, Walther's conception of social acts appears too broad because it encompasses experiences that are not social by Reinach's definition: On Walther's account, an experience may be social even if it lacks the necessity of being heard (for example, an emotion of fear felt "in the name of" a community would qualify as social, in Walther's view, although fear certainly does not require to be heard).

But, then, what are Walther's reasons for conceiving of social acts in such a way? Unfortunately, she does not elaborate on her reasons for departing from Reinach's positions. Moreover, if one is to understand how she arrives at her notion of social acts, these need to be reconstructed from the textual evidence available. The starting point of our reconstruction is the fact that she does not refer only to Reinach, but also to Husserl when she articulates her conception of social acts (see Walther 1923: 91, 103). Thus, section "Husserl on the Constitutive Function of Social Acts" is devoted to Husserl's understanding of social acts and in section "Walther on Social Acts" we explore how Walther adopts and transforms that notion. To put it negatively, we will see that Walther's conception of social acts is *distorted* by the conception of those acts advocated by Husserl. In more positive terms, we will highlight that Walther produces an original account of social acts based on, but also substantially transforming, Reinach's and Husserl's theories.

[1] To the best of our knowledge, Reinach only mentions the possibility of social acts performed in the name of other individuals, but not of groups. Yet, this possibility is essential for Edith Stein to develop a theory of state (on the basis of Reinach's theory see Gombocz and Salice 2006): "The state requires one person or a group of persons, to make itself audible [*um sich vernehmlich zu machen*], and a domain of persons to be heard and to come to existence. The state can perform acts only if persons who represent [*vertreten*] it perform those acts *on its behalf* [*für ihn*]" (Stein 1922: 313, our translation).

Husserl on the Constitutive Function of Social Acts

In her 1923 piece on social community Walther reports that Husserl discussed social acts in his *Nature and Spirit* [Natur und Geist] lectures, which she attended in 1919 (see Walther 1923: 91).[2] These lectures, which are now available in the Husserliana Materialien Series, help us to appreciate the important role played by Husserl in Walther's own reception of Reinach's idea of social acts. Husserl's description of social acts in those lectures belongs to his phenomenological analysis of community, and our interest in Husserl's analysis is limited to those parts of his theory that are relevant to Walther.[3]

According to Husserl, social communities, understood as bonds of subjects (*Subjektverbänden*), are different from mere aggregates of individuals because of the specific interrelation among the members of those communities. In his own words:

> The "relation" [*Verbindung*] is a "spiritual" one, this is an achievement [*Leistung*], which constitutes itself through the mutual relation [*Wechselbeziehung*] of subjects in subjective acts [*Subjektakten*] and which preserves and, possibly, reproduces itself in the exchange among deliberating and evaluating subjects (Husserl 2002: 133, our translation).

Social acts, in Husserl's understanding, are the subjective acts mentioned in the quotation. In fact, he continues by stating:

> Regarding the acts, which here function as originally meaning-grounding and *which therefore are originally constitutive for all sociality*, one can indicate already here that they belong to a peculiar group of I-acts [*Ichakten*], which are called "*social I-acts*." These are acts, which so to say have an addressee, in which an I refers to one or several other I-subjects, possibly including oneself, and from which the variations of the personal pronouns (you, he, we, they, etc.) gain their sense (Husserl 2002: 134, our translation and emphasis).

It seems clear that, here, Husserl is appropriating Reinach's conception of social acts as experiences in need of being heard.[4] However, it is crucial to note that Husserl is introducing this notion to deal with a problem that is not discussed by Reinach. According to Husserl, social acts are *constitutive* for all sociality and in particular for communities. This suggests that the discussion of social acts is part and parcel of his project of a constitutive phenomenology of sociality, which he already outlined in the first volume of *Ideen* (1913):

> These communities, although essentially founded in mental realities that are themselves founded in physical realities, prove to be new kinds of objects of a higher order. It is generally apparent that there are various kinds of objects that defy any psychologistic and naturalistic re-interpretation. Examples of these include every kind of object of value and practical

[2]These lectures were followed by Saturday discussions, which Walther also attended. See Schuhmann 1977: 234–235.

[3]For more on Husserl's discussions of *Nature and Spirit* in his 1919 lectures and elsewhere see Melle 1996.

[4]Husserl holds the same idea in his *Cartesianische Meditationen* (Husserl 1950: 159–160) and *Ideen II* (Husserl 1952/1969: 194), in both of which he claims that sociality is constituted in social acts (see below). For further reading on Husserl's notion of social acts and their role in his phenomenology of sociality see also Perreau 2013: 100–107.

> object, as well as all the concrete creations of culture that determine our current life as hard actualities, such as, for example, state, law, custom, church, and so forth. All these sorts of objectiveness must be described, just as they are given, in terms of their basic kinds and in their successive orders, and *the problems of constitution for them must be posed and solved* (Husserl 1913a, b: 318–319, our italics).

But, then, a question emerges: What does it mean that the bond among the members of a community is *constituted* in social acts? Moreover, and more generally, what is the meaning of the term "constitution" as it is used by Husserl in the foregoing quotation? Despite the legitimacy of this last question, two main reasons motivate us not to address it in the present chapter. First, the notion of constitution is a contentious issue in Husserl scholarship. Second, and more importantly for us, what is needed in the present context is not to reconstruct Husserl's constitutive phenomenology as such, but rather to reconstruct how Walther employs it in her work on social communities. For this purpose, it may suffice to give a minimal characterization of Husserl's notion of constitution, which we expect will not generate any exegetical controversy and which, crucially for our purposes, Walther agrees with and adopts in her work.

In the *Logical Investigations*, Husserl uses the phrase "to be constituted" [*sich konstituiren*] to capture the idea that "the objects of which we are 'conscious' are not simply *in* consciousness as in a box, so that they can merely be found in it and grasped in it" (Husserl 1913b: 165 [tr. vol. 2, 275], translation modified). According to him, "[objects] are first *constituted* as being what they are for us, and as what they count as for us, in various forms of objective consciousness" (Husserl 1913b: 166 [tr. vol. 2, 275], translation modified). His contention is that for any object there are various "forms" in accordance with which the object is given to consciousness. Here, for an object *to be constituted* is nothing over and above for this object *to be given in consciousness in certain ways*. In *Ideas I* Husserl takes on this idea with some important additions:

> Each objective region is constituted in accordance with consciousness. Insofar as it is actual, an object determined by the regional genus has, as such, *its way of being perceivable, clearly or dimly presentable, thinkable, demonstrable in general—all prefigured* a priori (Husserl 1913a: 309, translation modified, our italics).

Any object has its own ways of givenness and—this is the crucial point—those ways are determined a priori by the ontological region to which the object belongs. Since, phenomenologically, the a priori can be defined in terms of necessity and possibility that hold in virtue of the essence of something (see Husserl 1913b: 236), it is possible to rephrase his idea as follows: The ways in which the object is given in various forms or manners are determined by its essence. For instance, physical objects (or "things" [*Dinge*]) cannot be given in perceptual experience in a totally arbitrary manner because of some constraint that holds necessarily in virtue of the essence of those objects; since they are by their essence spatial, they are perceived only through adumbrations [*Abschattungen*].

This minimal notion of constitution should suffice to understand the primary objective of Husserl's constitutive analysis: Constitutive analysis aims at a phenomenological description of the most general manners in which objects of a various sort are given in consciousness by virtue of their essences. To apply all this to our topic: Communities are constituted in social acts in the sense that they are given to their members in social acts. To put this differently, subjects gain access to the communities they belong to by means of the social acts they perform. For instance, when Sam promises to φ to Pam, the I–thou community formed by Sam and Pam is given to Sam.

Against this background, it becomes possible to appreciate that Husserl's discussion of social acts and their relation to communities is closely associated with his idea of constitution. This makes a sharp contrast between him and Reinach, who never engaged in constitutive analysis of communities.[5] As a consequence, one may claim that Husserl somehow distorts Reinach's notion of social acts and, as we will see in section "Walther on Social Acts", the same distortion can also be found behind Walther's taking issue with Reinach. Indeed, her reception of the notion of social acts is mediated by Husserl. This does not mean, however, that she accepts everything Husserl maintains about social acts and their constitutive function; rather, her own conception of social acts aims at overcoming an important limitation in Husserl's discussion of these issues. In our opinion the limitation Walther faces is this: In the *Natur und Geist* lectures, Husserl deals only with the givenness of a community to an *insider* or to a group member of that community. To put it differently, he leaves untouched the following questions: How can the community be given to an *outsider* of the community? (How) is it possible for a community to be given to a subject regardless of whether she is an insider or outsider of the community? It is in attempting to answer these questions that Walther adopts her conception of social acts, as we argue in what follows.

Walther on Social Acts

As mentioned above, Walther adopts Husserl's notion of constitution in her "Zur Ontologie der sozialen Gemeinschaften." In the opening part of this paper she draws a distinction between ontology and phenomenology (see Walther 1923: 1). While ontology investigates the essence of objects of any sort, phenomenology investigates the way in which those objects are given, appearing, and apprehended [*erkannt*] in (pure) consciousness *in accordance with the essence of those objects*. To put it differently, the aim of phenomenology is to discover the way of givenness [*Gegebenheitsweise*] of an object, which is *predetermined* or "prescribed" [*vorschreiben*] by the essence of that object:

---

[5]In a posthumously published manuscript of his from 1911, Reinach writes that "social relations are constituted by social acts" (Reinach 1989b: 360). However, as the phrase "are constituted *by* [*durch*]" shows, he is obviously *not* operating with the Husserlian concept of constitution. His contention here is rather that social relations (such as promissory claims and commitments) are *produced* or *brought into existence* by social acts. In other words, the term "constitution" here should be understood as meaning what Walther calls *ontological* constitution (see section "Conclusion"). This interpretation is further corroborated by the fact that in his lectures in 1913 Reinach talks about the constitution of an object [*Gegenstandskonstitution*] when he deals with ontology or theory of objects [*Gegenstandstheorie*] as opposed to the investigation into the givenness of objects (see Reinach 1989c: 394).

> For all fundamental kinds and regions of objectivities, constitutive phenomenology has to investigate the construction [*Aufbau*] of the object (as this is prescribed to consciousness by the sense and essence of the object) in continuous series of experiences (relations of motivations), which are related to each other by means of the same intentional sense, i.e., [it has to investigate] *the "constitution" of the object in consciousness as prescribed by its essence (and this is to be confounded neither with the ontological constitution of an object* respectively of its essence in its essential traits, nor with the real constitution of a real individual in its real properties) (Walther 1923: 10, our translation and emphasis).

Accordingly, "constitution of an object" points to a specific process or, in her own words, to a "motivational connection" [*Zusammenhang der Motivation*] which is prescribed by the essence of the object and by means of which the object is given in consciousness. In this way Walther follows Husserl's conception of constitution in its *minimal* sense, as formulated above. However, what is remarkable about this quotation is that she also explicitly distinguishes constitution in this minimally Husserlian sense from what she labels "ontological constitution." Interestingly, this latter notion of constitution has nothing to do with how objects are given to us; rather, it concerns the structure of these objects *as such* (Walther 1923: 146). Consequently, in Walther's view, investigating communities boils down to pursuing a twofold task: It is the investigation of how communities are *phenomenologically* constituted, but also it is to investigate how they are *ontologically* constituted. It is to these two different tasks that we now turn our attention.

The Ontological Constitution of Communities

Let us start with Walther's *ontology* of communities. Here, the question is: What is the ontological constitution of communities? Or, what is the essential structural feature that makes communities different from mere aggregates of more than one (human) person? According to her, neither external features shared by members of a community (such as having the same tattoos) nor physical features shared by the members (such as being taller than 170 cm) can be the decisive factor (Walther 1923: 19–20). Rather, she contends that the key to the community lies in the mental and spiritual life of each individual. More precisely, a community emerges when several individuals undergo an *affective* experience called "inner unification" [*innere Einigung*]. Consider the following example:

> [...] just take a number of randomly picked workers from Slovakia, Poland, Italy, etc., who are all employed on a construction site. They do not understand one another's language, they do not know each other, they have never had anything to do with each other before—they just want to earn their living and have accidentally been hired by the same construction company. Now, for instance, they build a wall, some of them take the bricks, others pass them on to someone else and give them to the brick layers, who apply the mortar and place the bricks one on top of the other. [...] We have here a number of persons, who are aware of each other and who, in their behavior, are mutually [*in Wechselwirkung*] directed to each other [...]. Furthermore, at one level of their mental life, they are directed to the same intentional object in one unity of sense [*in einer Sinneinheit*]: [...] the entire construction. A partially

homogeneous mental–spiritual life, pervaded by one unity of sense and governed by the same intentional object (the construction and the earning of each his own living by working on that construction), results from this. [...] Do we have here a community? (Walther 1923: 31, our translation).

Walther responds negatively to this question (Walther 1923: 31–33): It is true that in her example each worker has an intention of the same kind. It is also true that the workers, to a certain extent, know each other and further that they interact together. But still, they *do not* form a community. Following Fernand Tönnies and Franklin Henry Giddings, she claims that the essence of communities as opposed to societies [*Gesellschaften*] lies in "inner bond" [*innere Verbundenheit*], "feeling of togetherness" [*Gefühl der Zusammengehörigkeit*], or "inner unification" (see Walther 1923: 33).

By using these expressions, Walther means to draw our attention to something that subjects *experience* as bond, togetherness, or unification. That is why she qualifies the bond and unification at stake here as *inner*. In what follows, to denote that experience, we conform to her terminology by using only "inner unification" or simply "unification" (except when we quote her own words).

But what is unification? We learn from Walther that this is not a cognitive act (like a state of knowledge or a judgment), but rather ought to be described as a sort of feeling or emotion [*Gefühl*]. In fact, one can feel the emotional experience of unification even in the absence of cognitive experiences (one can feel unified with a community without judging or knowing that one is a member of a community; see Walther 1923: 34). She further characterizes unification as a positive emotion in which the "contour" [*Kontur*] of its subject and object is "altered" [*verändert*] (see Walther 1923: 34–35). Walther adopts the idea of the altered contour from Pfänder, who illustrates it by means of the following example:

The motherly I, while preserving its own contours, absorbs [*aufsaugen*] the filial I more or less completely in itself; [the motherly I] coalesces [*einschmelzen*] it into its more extensive [*umfänglicheres*] self by destroying the contours and the existence [*Eigendasein*] [of the filial I]. The child is now no longer gently, internally, lovingly embraced [*umfangen*], but mentally engulfed [*veschlungen*] more or less entirely by the mother (Pfänder 1913: 380–381, our translation).

This example is about an extreme or even pathological case of unification,[6] but it serves to highlight the following point: Unification transforms its subject (the mother in the example) by enabling her to have another subject (her child) *in herself*, but the subject in this case does not cease to be an individual subject. Furthermore, subjects who undergo that particular transformation acquire a "social self." Walther, who operates with the notion of social self in her own investigations, reports that Pfänder discusses the idea of social self in unpublished lectures and manuscripts (however,

---

[6]Not all unifications are pathological, though. See "[The human soul] is absolutely not an isolated creature [*Wesen*], it is no monad, but from its beginning it is essentially a group member [*Gliedwesen*] (that is, it lies in essence to stay in intentional contact of unification with other creatures)" (Pfänder 1933: 225, our translation). For Pfänder's discussion of unification and Walther's adaptation of it see also Caminada 2014 (though note that *Einigung* is translated as "joining" in Caminada's paper).

we do not have access to that material and thus we cannot ascertain how Pfänder develops this idea).

Walther's idea of social self is closely related to the phenomenon of *habitual* unification. Unlike occurrent [*aktuell*] unification, habitual unification remains unexperienced unless it is actualized in some way or other (see Walther 1923: 38–44). According to Walther, "habitual unifications of all kinds are almost more important for the foundation of communities and for the communal life than the episodic [*einmalig*] occurrent [*unifications*], which immediately again disappears" (Walther 1923: 48, our translation). Habitual unification captures one important aspect of the relationship between a community and its members: Communities, for their existence, do depend on their members internally unifying, but it would be too demanding to impose on this form of unification the condition to be necessarily of an occurrent kind. For instance, a family persists even when all family members fall into dreamless sleep and thus do not have any occurrent experience in the first place. Introducing habitual unification as the foundation of communities may hence explain the existence of these social groups, even in absence of occurrent feelings of unification.[7]

But then, "how do we have to understand this foundation by means of habitual unification?" (Walther 1923: 69, our translation). To answer this question Walther resorts to the aforementioned transformative function of unification and thus to the notion of social self:

> Here, even if only in a vague awareness in the background [*in einem dunklen Innesein im Hintergrund*] and absolutely not in attentive knowledge or presentation, other humans—"humans who also…" —are *always* "given," in a more or less clear and noticed "co-presence" [*Mitgehabtheit*] (Walther 1923: 69, our translation and italics).

The notion of "humans who also…" [*Menschen, die auch…*] could best be understood as ranging over the subject's *fellows*. For, according to Walther, the gap expressed by the suspension points "…" is filled by psychological predicates which, depending on the kind of unification at work in each case, point to such things as aims, volitions, feelings, thoughts, etc. (see Walther 1923: 69). There is a sense in which others who share any of these experiences with me are *my fellows*. Now, once a subject has, one way or the other, involved fellows in one's mental life by virtue of habitual unification the subject makes up "a we" [*ein Wir*] with those fellows (see Walther 1923: 70). "Experiencing is here characterized for the experiencing subject *not only* as 'I experience that,' but as 'we experience so'…" (Walther 1923: 70, our translation and emphasis).

Notice the phrase "not only" [*nicht nur*] in Walther's expression: For her the experience in question, which in a sense is shared by *us* and thus characterized

[7] According to Walther, unification may be habitual from the beginning, without being occurrent [*aktuell*] (see Walther 1923: 44, 69; see also Zahavi and Salice 2016: 521). She does not give any example of such habitual unification, but the following would probably serve as one. A child who has grown up in a family may have habitual unification with the family without having any occurrent feeling of unification with it. Let us note that it may be difficult to convincingly argue for such a claim from a phenomenological point of view. We do not go into this issue any further, for the main line of our discussion would remain the same, even if this part of Walther's theory turns out to be untenable.

as a "communal experience" [*Gemeinschaftserlebnis*], nevertheless takes place in *me* (that is, in the subject as an individual). It is qualified as ours insofar as it is originated in [*entspringen aus*] the background of her consciousness or her "self" [*Selbst*] which lies behind her "ego-center" [*Ichzentrum*][8] (namely, in "the others in me"; see Walther 1923: 71).[9]

For example, let us suppose that, based on my habitual unification with another person, I share the same aim to write a paper with him and that I then deliberately decide to write a section of the paper to achieve that goal. In this case Walther would claim that my experience of making the decision is partly originated in the *other* in me. For, in the process of deliberation, my decision, by accommodating the preference of the other, may even have overridden my *personal* preference to do something else. Therefore, there is a sense in which my decision has as its source the *other* with whom I can be said to share the aim. At the same time, since I am the one who is making the decision, there is also a sense in which the other in question is in *me*; after all, I have not been forced or coerced into the activity. Accordingly, "other(s) in me" would be a suitable expression to describe—somewhat metaphorically—situations like the one portrayed in our example. In Walther's view, to sum up, a subject's having habitual unification with others is nothing over and above this subject having the others in the background of her consciousness in a certain way.[10]

Let us go back to Walther's claim that communities are primarily founded on the social self of their members. For Walther a community is a *sui generis* object that is founded upon, but is not identical with, the relevant social selves.[11] To put this differently, the community ontologically emerges out of the social selves on which it is founded. But there is more to it than this. Walther claims that an individual subject can have (actual and habitual) unification not only with other individuals, but also *with this community* "as such" [*als solche*] (see Walther 1923: 99–100).

It is with this idea in mind that, we suggest, one should interpret her claim that social acts in the authentic sense are experiences that are oriented toward the social community. When a subject of experience has established unification *with a community as such*, he can have communal experiences "which emerge in him from the background of his consciousness [*Bewußtseinshintergrund*], from his self, [and]

[8]The metaphorical expressions like "ego-center", "self", and so on are without any doubt inherited from Pfänder (see, for example, Pfänder 1911; for further references see Marbach 1974: 245–246).

[9]Thus, she explicitly rejects the conception of the we as a super-individual subject of experience (see Walther 1923: 70).

[10]This view is clearly echoed in Searle's idea of a background sense of the other as collaborative partner: "Collective intentionality presupposes a background sense of the other as a candidate for cooperative agency; that is, it presupposes a sense of others as more than mere conscious agents, indeed as actual or potential members of a cooperative activity" (Searle 2002: 104).

[11]This claim follows from the following two points Walther makes in her 1923 piece. First, Walther holds that a community itself [*Gemeinschaft selbst*] is different from the sum of items that founded it (namely, subjects and their relationship, see Walther 1923: 97; for a discussion of communities as objects of higher order within phenomenology, see also Salice 2016). Second, she qualifies that a community is founded primarily on the social self of its members (see Walther 1923: 147).

from the 'spirit of the community' [*Geist der Gemeinschaft*]" (Walther 1923: 104, our translation).

What is characteristic about such a communal experience is that it is had by the subject merely *in the name of* or *on behalf of* the community and that its subject thereby acts as a "representative" [*Vertreter*] of the community. This is exactly what she conceives as a social act in the authentic sense: In this case the individual subject of the experience needs not embrace and "jointly posit" [*mitmachen*] the purpose of the community; rather, she has the experience as a *social* person rather than as a *private* person (see Walther 1923: 105). To put this differently, the individual subject may have an intentional attitude, the motivation of which is grounded entirely in the group she belongs to and for which she, as an individual, may have no personal or individual motive. In other words, the social self in which the communal experience in question is originated is *entirely social*, as it were, insofar as it has nothing to do with the individual's personal aims, volition, thoughts, and so on. In this way experiences like this are distinctively social in a specific sense of the term *social.*[12]

The Phenomenological Constitution of Communities

Let us take stock. We have said that individuals have the ability to unify with other individuals and that this ability is a necessary precondition for the ontological constitution of communities. We have also highlighted that, on Walther's account, individuals also have the ability to unify with communities. When this happens the individual is in a position to perform a social act that is motivated entirely in accordance with the communal perspective. Such acts, in which the individual functions as a representative of the community, are what Walther calls "social acts."

Bearing all this in mind, we are now confident in arguing that Walther's discussion of social acts is relevant primarily for her *phenomenology*, rather than ontology, of social communities. In fact, she claims:

> Now we could call the genuine [*echten*] experiences and ways of behavior "on the purpose" and "in the name" of the community "communal experiences of third order" or "communal experiences in the most pregnant sense." They are especially typical for those members, who are the "organs" of the community, whether superordinate or subordinate organs. This kind of experience is one in which the community *phenomenologically constitutes* itself toward its own members as well as toward foreigners: they grasp the community through these [experiences]. They are "social acts" in the most pregnant sense (Walther 1923: 111, our translation and emphasis).

[12]Walther's ideas are in line with recent work in the theory of group agency. See "If we reach an alignment between what the group requires of us and our individual attitudes through adopting the group's viewpoint, [...] then we, the members, each have attitudes in whose propositional expression the group figures as we. Each of us acts on beliefs and desires that call for expression in first-person plural terms. They are desires that we do so and so, or beliefs that we can do such and such, that link up with our responses without the mediation of any belief about our membership in the group" (List and Pettit 2011: 192).

In this passage she talks about social acts "in the most authentic sense" on the basis of the constitutive function (in the minimally Husserlian sense), which she ascribes to those acts—meaning that she introduces the notion of social act to provide an answer on how communities are given to an individual subject. On the one hand, Walther does follow Husserl in that communities are *phenomenologically* (not *ontologically*) constituted in social acts. On the other hand, she proposes a conception of a social act that is totally different from, and in conflict with, Husserl's and Reinach's.

So, how are communities (phenomenologically) constituted, that is, how are they given in consciousness? To answer this question, we need to take into consideration her distinction between what she calls "genuine" [*echt*] and "non-genuine" [*unecht*] experiences (or actions). She proposes that an experience is evaluated as genuine or non-genuine, depending on its conformity to the personality of its subject (see Walther 1923: 108–109). To put it crudely, an experience is genuine if the personality that is typically revealed in the experience conforms to the personality of the experiencing subject; it is non-genuine if there is a discrepancy between the two personalities. To use Walther's own example (Walther 1923: 108–109), if a child has an attitude that conforms only to an adult, in the sense that the motivation for having that attitude only derives from the adult, then the child's attitude is non-genuine in this sense.

In this way, Walther first operates with an *individualist* conception of (non-) genuineness of experience; what is at stake here is the conformity of an experience with the personality of its subject. But this idea can be generalized and applied to the (non-)genuineness of a communal experience in accordance with the relevant community (see Walther 1923: 109–110).[13] Even if an experience in the name of or on behalf of the community is non-genuine (or genuine) from its subject's point of view, it may be genuine (or non-genuine) from the point of view of the community. No matter what the individual personality of the subject may be, the experience qualifies as a genuine communal experience as long as it conforms to the communal perspective.[14]

Now we can see what Walther has in mind when she talks about the constitutive function of social acts in the most authentic sense (that is, *genuine* experiences in the name of or on behalf of the community). Her contention is that a community is given in a communal experience *only if* that experience conforms with the community in some way or other.

So far, we have discussed how communities are given to their members—this being the *inner* (phenomenological) constitution of communities. For the *members*

---

[13] A similar idea is also found in Stein's *Beiträge*, but her discussion is conducted in slightly different terminology. According to her the key to the communality of an experience is the *Richtigkeit*, rather than *Echtheit*, of that experience in accordance with the relevant community (see Stein 1922: 125–126).

[14] To be precise, her claim is that a communal experience is genuine if it conforms either to the empirical viz factual characteristics and behaviors (at a given time) or to the essence viz idea of the community. According to her, this parallels the genuineness of experience from an individual point of view. In the present chapter, however, we do not go into details of this and related issues such as her discussion of the alleged personality of communities (see Walther 1923: 112–118).

the community is given in communal experiences or we-experience (namely, experiences that presuppose (habitual) unification with the community and that conform to the perspective of the community; see Walther 1923: 154). However, it is also the case that a community can be given in the consciousness of individuals who do *not* belong to that community. This observation motivates Walther in identifying an "outer" constitution of communities in addition to the "inner constitution" (Walther 1923: 17).

Compared with the inner constitution, the *outer* constitution of communities is more complex:

> From now on, in order to really bring social communities to givenness, it is required that the external observer adopts a social attitude [*sich sozial einstellt*] in empathy (as well as in the intuition) (that is, that he is intentionally directed to the grasping of the communal life and of the community every time a possibility for the fulfillment of this intention appears to be present) (Walther 1923: 155–156, our translation)

It seems, hence, that the main difference between these two modes or ways the phenomenological constitution of communities can be formulated is as follows. It is at least in principle possible for any insider of the community to grasp their social self by themselves alone, as long as they have some communal experience. For, at least in principle, I do not need a fellow member's presence when I am to qualify an experience of mine as *ours*.

By contrast, except for special cases we will discuss soon, the presence of some members of the community is indispensable for an *outsider* to have a community given in her experience. In fact, as the quotation suggests, an external individual must be able to *empathically adopt* the perspective of the community for this community to be given to her. Otherwise, her thought about the community would remain empty.

If we accept Walther's distinction between the outer and inner constitution of communities, which is missing in the relevant discussion of Husserl, we find some reason for her alternative proposal on how to think of social experiences. In talking about social experiences in the most authentic sense in the above-quoted passage, she writes, "This kind of experience is the one in which the community *phenomenologically constitutes* itself *toward its own members as well as toward foreigners*: they grasp the community through these [experiences]. They are 'social acts' in the most pregnant sense" (Walther 1923: 111, our translation and italics). Her idea is that experiences in the name of and on behalf of the community may also be performed by outsiders (namely, those who do *not* belong to the community). For instance, as a lawyer hired by a family, I can sign a contract for the family to which I do not belong; in this case I am living through an experience of promising that is performed in the name of and on behalf of the family. Given the constitutive function of social acts in Walther's sense, the family is given to me in my experience.

What is particularly noteworthy in this scenario is that the community is not given to me from the outside, as when a member or a set of members of the community is made the target of empathic acts. Rather, I experience the community in a participatory sense: I act on behalf of the community. When this happens, it is also possible to undergo the social experience even in the absence of group members. For instance,

I can sign a contract for the family in the absence of all the family members. Just as group members can live through social acts in absence of their fellows, so can outsiders perform acts on behalf of the community (and hence phenomenologically "access" the community), even in the absence of group members who have experiences of the same sort. In this way experiences in the name of and on behalf of the community serve for both outer and inner constitution of the community as long as they are genuine. Since Walther defines social acts in terms of their function to phenomenologically (not ontologically) constitute communities, there is a sense in which genuine experience in the name of and on behalf of the community are *the* social acts *par excellence*.

In this way, Walther reaches toward a view that overcomes the limitation which we have found in Husserl's constitutive analysis of communities (see section "Husserl on the Constitutive Function of Social Acts"). When Husserl ascribes the constitutive function to social acts in Reinach's sense he has in mind only the givenness of a community to an *insider* of the community. From Walther's perspective Husserl's theory falls too short because it leaves unexplained how the community is given to *outsiders*. Even more importantly, Husserl does not deal with (and possibly is not even aware of) a problem which Walther tackles by focusing on experiences in the name of and on behalf of a community: (how) is it possible for the community to be given to a subject regardless of whether this subject is an insider or outsider of the community?

Now we are able to reconstruct a reason for Walther adopting her conception of social acts. *If* one is to follow Husserl in defining social acts as experiences in which a community is constituted, and *if* one is, *beyond* Husserl, to analyze phenomenologically how the community is given to a subject whether or not she is a group member, it would be reasonable to claim that the role of social acts is best played by experiences in the name of and on behalf of the community.

It may be disputable whether the two presuppositions we have ascribed to Walther are well grounded. Reinach might disagree with the first one. Husserl's silence on the second might suggest that he is skeptical about whether the givenness of a community is phenomenologically analyzable from a standpoint that is sharable both for its insiders and outsiders. Be that as it may, however, the above conditional claim *as a whole* would explain very well Walther's departure from Reinach by drawing only on materials which she certainly was familiar with.

Conclusion

Let us summarize the three different conceptions of social acts which we have found in Reinach, Husserl, and Walther, respectively. For Reinach the essential property of social acts is being in need of being heard [*Vernehmungsbedürftigkeit*]; because of this property, what qualifies a certain act as a social act is the peculiar way in which this act is addressed to the other. Husserl accommodates this point, but he ascribes to social acts an additional function: Social acts are experiences in which communities are constituted. In other words, in addressing the other by means of social acts a community is given to the subject. Walther distinguishes two senses of constitution: Ontological and phenomenological. Ontologically, communities are founded upon, among other things, (habitual) feelings of unification. But how are communities given to subjects? In her view communities are phenomenologically constituted in social acts. Although she follows Husserl in this respect, her notion of a social act is completely transformed: A social act, according to Walther, is an act that is performed in the name of and/or on behalf of the community.

Although this is a matter of speculation, given that Walther never touches upon this issue, we believe that one additional reason that could have led her to develop this theory of social acts may be related to the attempt at blocking internalistic consequences (highlighted in section "Reinach's Conception of Social Acts (and Walther's Departure from It)") that seem compatible and consistent with Reinach's theory of social acts. In fact, the kind of act that Walther calls "social" cannot be had by a brain in a vat, given that this act necessarily presupposes the existence of a community with its own perspective. Only if one act accords with that perspective does the act qualify as "social" in the (most) authentic sense. All this obviously leaves open the question of whether or not Reinach's framework offers conceptual resources to resist that form of internalism. As we hinted in section "Introduction", we believe it is possible to find those resources, but pursuing this line of thought will be the topic for another paper.

References

Austin, J. L. (2011). How to do things with words. In J. O. Urmson & M. Sbisá (Eds.), *The William James lecture delivered at Harvard in 1955*. Oxford: Oxford University Press.

Caminada, E. (2014). Joining the background: Habitual sentiments behind we-intentionality. In: A. Konzelmann Ziv & H. B. Schmid (Eds.), *Institutions, emotions, and group agents* (pp. 195–212). Dordrecht: Springer.

Crane, Tim. (2001). *Elements of mind: An introduction to the philosophy of mind*. Oxford: Oxford University Press.

Crosby, J. (1990). Speech act theory and phenomenology. In: A. Burkhardt (Ed.), *Speech acts, meanings and intentions. Critical Approaches to the Philosophy of John R. Searle* (pp. 62–88). Berlin: de Gruyter.

Gombocz, W., & Salice, A. (2006). Edith Steins soziale Ontologie auf Grund ihrer Staatsschrift, Aufgang. In: *Jahrbuch für Denken, Dichten, Musik* (*Würzburg*) (Vol. 3, pp. 436–456).

Husserl, E. (1913a). *Ideen zu einer reinen Phänomenologie und phänomoenologischen Philosophie*, Vol. I. Halle: Niemeyer. (English translation: *Ideas for a Pure Phenomenology and Phenomenological Philosophy*, translated by D. O. Dahlstrom. Indianapolis: Hackett, 2013, page numbers of the original 1913 edition are indicated in the margin).

Husserl, E. (1913b). *Logische Untersuchungen* (2nd ed., Vol. 2). Halle: Max Niemeyer. (English translation: *Logical investigation*, 2 vols., translated by J.N. Findlay and edited by D. Moran. Routledge, 2001).

Husserl, E. (1950). *Cartesianische Meditationen*. In: S. Strasser (Ed.), (Husserliana vol. I). The Hague: Martinus Nijhoff.

Husserl, E. (1952/1969). *Ideen zu einer reinen Phänomenologie und Phänomenologischen Philosophie* (Vol. II). In: M. Biemel (Ed.), (Husserliana vol. IV). The Hague: Martinus Nijhoff.

Husserl, E. (2002). *Natur und Geist. Vorlesugen Sommersemester 1919*. In: M. Weiler (Ed.), (Husserliana Materialien vol. IV). Dordrecht: Kluwer.

Marbach, E. (1974). *Das Problem des Ich in der Phänomenologie Husserls*. The Hague: Martinus Nijhoff.
Melle, U. (1996). Nature and spirit. In T. Nenon & L. Embree (Eds.), *Issues in Husserl's Ideas II* (pp. 15–35) Dordrecht: Kluwer.
Mulligan, K. (1987). Promisings and other social acts: Their constituents and structure. In: K. Mulligan (Ed.), *Speech act and Sachverhalt. Reinach and the Foundations of Realist Phenomenology* (pp. 29–90). Dordrecht: Kluwer.
Perreau, L. (2013). *Le monde social selon Husserl*. Dordrecht: Springer.
Pfänder, A. (1911). Motive und Motivation. In: J. A. Barth (Ed.), *Münchner philosophische Abhandlungen* (pp. 163–195). Munich.
Pfänder, A. (1933). *Die Seele des Menschen Versuch einer verstehenden Psychologie*. Niemeyer: Halle.
Reinach, A. (1989a). Zur Theorie des Negativen Urteils (1911). In: K. Schuhmann, & B. Smith (Eds.), *Adolf Reinach. Sämtliche Werke* (Textkritische Ausgabe in 2 Bänden) (pp. 95–140). Munich: Philosophia.
Reinach, A. (1989b). Nichtsoziale und soziale Akte (1911). In: K. Schuhmann, & B. Smith (Eds.), *Adolf Reinach. Sämtliche Werke* (Textkritische Ausgabe in 2 Bänden) (pp. 355–360). Munich: Philosophia.
Reinach, A. (1989c). Einleitung in die Philosophie (1913). In: K. Schuhmann, & B. Smith (Eds.), *Adolf Reinach. Sämtliche Werke* (Textkritische Ausgabe in 2 Bänden) (pp. 369–513). Munich: Philosophia.
Reinach, A (2012). *The Apriori Foundations of the Civil Law (1913)* (pp. 2–142), translated by J. Crosby (with a foreword by A. MacIntyre). Frankfurt: Ontos.
Salice, A. (2013). Social ontology as embedded in the tradition of phenomenological realism. In: H. B. Schmid, M. Schmitz, & B. Sasha-Kobow (Eds.), *The background of institutional reality. Proceedings of the Inaugural Meeting of the European Network on Social Ontology* (pp. 217–232). Dordrecht: Springer.
Salice, A. (2015). Love and other social stances in early phenomenology. In D. Moran & T. Szanto (Eds.), *The phenomenology of sociality: Discovering the we* (pp. 234–247). London: Routledge.
Salice, A. (2016). Communities and values: Dietrich von Hildebrand's social ontology. In: A. Salice, & H. B. Schmid (Eds.), *The phenomenological approach to social reality. History, concepts, problems* (pp. 237–258). Dordrecht: Springer.
Scheler, M. (1954). Der Formalismus in der Ethik und die materiale Wertethik. Neuer Versuch der Grundlegung eines ethischen Personalismus. In: M. Scheler (Ed.), *Gesammelte Werke* (Vol. II). Berne: Francke.
Schuhmann, K. (1977). *Husserl Chronik*. The Hague: Martinus Nijhoff.
Searle, J. (2002). Collective intentions and actions (1990). *Consciousness and language* (pp. 90–105). Cambridge: Cambridge University Press.
Searle, J. (1969). *Speech acts: An essay in the philosophy of language*. Cambridge: Cambridge University Press.
Smith, B. (1990). Towards a history of speech act theory. In: A. Burkhardt (ed.), *Speech acts, meanings and intentions. Critical Approaches to the Philosophy of John R. Searle* (pp. 29–61). Berlin: de Gruyter.
Stein, E. (1922). Beiträge zur philosophischen Begründung der Psychologie und der Geisteswissenschaften. In: *Jahrbuch für Philosophie und phänomenologische Forschung* (Vol. 5, pp. 1–283). Halle: Max Niemeyer. (Reprinted as *Edith Stein Gesamtausgabe*, Vol. VI, edited by B. Beckmann-Zöller. Freiburg: Herder, 2010, page numbers of the original edition are indicated in the margin).
Walther, G. (1923). Zur Ontologie der sozialen Gemeinschaften. In: *Jahrbuch für Philosophie und phänomenologische Forschung* (Vol. 6, pp. 1–158).
Zahavi, D., & Salice, A. (2016). Phenomenology of the we. Stein, Walther, Gurwitsch. In: J. Kiverstein (Ed.), *The Routledge handbook of philosophy of the social mind*. London: Routledge.

Alessandro Salice is Lecturer at the Department of Philosophy of University College Cork. Previously, he held postdoctoral positions at the University of Graz, University of Basel, University of Vienna, and the Center for Subjectivity Research in Copenhagen. His expertise stretches from classical accounts of collective intentionality and joint action to phenomenology, philosophy of mind, and moral psychology. He has published widely on each of these topics. Recently, he edited *The Phenomenological Approach to Social Reality: History, Concepts, Problems* (2016) together with Hans Bernhard Schmid. He is responsible for the entry on the "Phenomenology of the Munich and Göttingen Circles" in the *Stanford Encyclopedia of Philosophy*. He is also a co-editor of the *Journal of Social Ontology*.

Genki Uemura is Associate Professor at the Graduate School of Humanities and Social Sciences of Okayama University. His research field topics are: Husserl's phenomenology, early phenomenology, metaphysics and philosophy of mind/action from a phenomenological perspective. His recent and forthcoming publications include: "Husserl's Conception of Cognition as an Action"; "Demystifying Roman Ingarden's Purely Intentional Objects of Perception"; and "Motives in Experience: Pfänder, Geiger, and Stein" (together with Alessandro Salice).

On Community: Edith Stein and Gerda Walther

Anna Maria Pezzella

Abstract Edith Stein and Gerda Walther place great value on community, for both thinkers view it as the fundamental, common, and necessary terrain in which one can grow and be formed as human beings. Although they share a phenomenological framework, they describe community in different ways. Stein starts from I-experience to reach her understanding community, which is analyzed deeply and in all its constitutive elements, whereas Walther moves from the social self and, hence, from the background of psychic interiority in which the communal we moves and lives. However, through different ways, both thinkers arrive at the same conclusion: they converge on the role played by the I-center in the actualization of the lived experience of community.

Keywords Ego · Community · Society · Humans, that also

Introduction

One finds constant reflection on intersubjective relations in phenomenology. Edmund Husserl, for example, tackles theoretically complex questions like the constitution[1] of alterity, and he explores in diverse texts[2] various forms of sociality, including community, society, and the state. He claims that others are fundamental because the person does not only see, listen, and experience with one's own senses but also with

[1] By constitution, Husserl means the mode in which objective unities (like the other) become manifest and known in consciousness.

[2] See Husserl's *Zur Phänomenologie der Intersubjektivität*, *Cartesianische Meditationen*, and *Pariser Vorträge*.

Translated by Antonio Calcagno.

A. M. Pezzella (✉)
Pontifical Lateran University, Rome, Italy
e-mail: annamaria.pezzella@virgilio.it

A. Calcagno (ed.), *Gerda Walther's Phenomenology of Sociality, Psychology, and Religion*, Women in the History of Philosophy and Sciences 2,
https://doi.org/10.1007/978-3-319-97592-4_4

the other's and vice versa.[3] One cannot think of the human being outside a human environment and context. One can choose to live as a hermit, but only after learning all the behavior typically associated with being human.

Because our relationships to others are fundamental for our growth and formation, we investigate deeply these very relationships. In addition to Husserl's own treatments of this topic, we also find other phenomenologists interested in it, including Adolf Reinach, Dietrich von Hildebrand, Max Scheler, Alexander Pfänder, Edith Stein, and Gerda Walther.

The two phenomenologists we explore here in this chapter were both students of Husserl. Edith Stein trained under Husserl at both Göttingen and Freiburg. She completed her thesis, *Zum Problem der Einfühlung* [*On the problem of empathy*] under his direction. Gerda Walther was a student of Pfänder in Munich—a philosopher whom Husserl held in high esteem. Husserl so valued him that "before making the transcendental turn and before knowing Heidegger, he thought [Pfänder] as the most suitable successor to his chair at Freiburg."[4] After his transcendental turn, Husserl, as Walther recounts in her autobiography *Zum anderen Ufer*, did not believe that the phenomenology being carried out at Munich was the same as his own insofar as the Munich phenomenologists remained fixed on the analysis of essence.[5] Walther completed her doctorate, "Zur Ontologie der sozialen Gemeinschaften," under Pfänder. It was published in 1923 in Husserl's *Jahrbuch*. One year earlier, in the same *Jahrbuch*, Stein published her *Beiträge zur philosophischen Begrundung der Psychologie und der Geisteswissenschaften*.

The two women phenomenologists knew one another. They met at Freiburg in what Edith Stein called her philosophical kindergarten. In a letter dated August 7, 1917 addressed to Roman Ingarden, Stein writes, "I believe you asked me again about the results of my teaching. Some of the students seem very promising, especially Mr. Clauss … and Miss Walther, who hails from Munich and who intends to work with Pfänder on the phenomenology of society."[6] In another letter to Ingarden dated June 24, 1918, Stein writes, "Clauss and Miss Walther (who participate in our discussions) will certainly become very capable phenomenologists …"[7] The active participation of Walther in phenomenology is also confirmed by another letter sent by Husserl to Ingarden on November 16, 1918. Husserl writes, "Miss Walther worked on the index [for my *Ideas I*] during the summer break and Mr. Clauss also wanted to help her."[8] Only two years later, however, Walther returned to Munich from Freiburg. Ingarden

---

[3] See Edmund Husserl, *Zur Phänomenologie der Intersubjektivität*, ed. by E. Marbach (Husserliana Materialien Series No. 14) (The Hague: Springer, 1973), 197.

[4] Michele Lenoci, "Logica, ontologia e fenomenologia in A. Pfänder," in *Il realismo fenomenologico. Sulla filosofia dei circoli di Monaco e Gottinga* (Macerata: Quodlibet, 2000), 673.

[5] See Angela Ales Bello, *Fenomenologia dell'essere umano. Lineamenti di una filosofia al femminile* (Rome: Città Nuova Editrice, 1992), 67. Angela Ales Bello was the first person in Italy to introduce Gerda Walther's philosophical work to the public.

[6] Edith Stein, *Lettere a Roman Ingarden 1917–1938*, Italian trans. by E. Costantini and Erika Schulze, revised by Anna Maria Pezzella (Vatican City: Libreria Editrice Vaticana, 2001), 69.

[7] Edith Stein, *Lettere a Roman Ingarden 1917–1938*, 103.

[8] Edmund Husserl, *Briefe an R. Ingarden* (The Hague: Martinus Nijhoff, 1968), 12.

asked Stein for Walther's address, but Stein replied that she no longer had contact with her[9] and that he should write to Pfänder for the information. Pfänder exerted a huge influence on Walther and she expressly notes in her autobiography that she was deeply touched by her encounter with him.[10]

The filiation of the two women philosophers also signals a difference in the way they understood and practiced phenomenology and responded to philosophical questions. Obviously, the differences between them can also be attributed to their different personalities, temperaments, theoretical and human experiences, but one must not underestimate the influence of their respective teachers. Although Husserl and Pfänder share a common field of phenomenological inquiry, they nonetheless have different perspectives and approaches to the same questions.

The Relation Between the I and the Community

The I-community relation is pivotal for understanding the different emphasis the two women phenomenologists place on the I within their own respective philosophical frameworks. We explore the difference by exploring two texts that appeared in Husserl's *Jahrbuch*. Edith Stein's "Philosophy of Psychology and the Humanities" [Beiträge der Psychologie und der Geisteswissenschaften], dedicated to Husserl for his 60th birthday, consists of two parts: "Psychic Causality" and "Individual and Community." Stein treats psychic causality for two reasons. First, she views her text as a contribution to then-contemporary debates, which Husserl also criticizes, on the status of empirical, positivist psychology, which grounded itself on the "fantasy of a natural scientific method that followed the model used by chemistry and physics."[11] Like Husserl, Stein refuses the idea of such a mathematization of the soul that renders it both determined and quantifiable. Both philosophers were convinced that the human being could not be investigated with the same criteria used by the natural sciences because the human being is a spiritual, free subject and, hence, it is impossible to quantify or determine human action with mathematical precision.

In her investigation of psyche, Stein does not negate the relation of causality that may exist between certain lived experiences, but she demonstrates that psychic causality is different than the model of causality followed by the natural sciences and the positivists. Stein claims that psyche is also conditioned by feelings of life and the life-force, and these remain unquantifiable. She also argues that cause and effect relations present within psyche are not always reiterable or exactly repeatable. For example, excessive tiredness (cause) may not permit me to go out (effect), but if I know that my presence will be of great benefit to a sick friend, I overcome my

[9] Stein, *Lettere a Roman Ingarden 1917–1938*, 69 and 103.

[10] Gerda Walter, *Zum anderen Ufer—Vom Marxismus und Atheismus zum Christentum* (Remagen: Otto Reichel Verlag, 1960), 185.

[11] Edmund Husserl, *La filosofia come scienza rigorosa*, trans. Filippo Costa (Pisa: ETS Editrice, 1990), 65.

tiredness and go visit her. In the human life, which is also a spiritual life, one finds the lawfulness of motivation that permits me to act despite unfavorable physical or psychic conditions. Motivation "... is the connection that acts get into with one another: not a mere blending like that of simultaneously or sequentially ebbing phases of experience, or the associative tying together of experience, but an *emerging* of the one *out of* the other, a self-fulfilling or being fulfilled of the one *on the basis of* the other *for the sake of* the other."[12]

Stein is aware that an analysis that only considers an individual being, without any relation to other human beings, remains abstract, for she maintains that the mechanism of psyche is not closed in on itself; rather, it draws strength from the external world and other human beings. There are constant references by psyche that go beyond the single individual and that open onto a social and spiritual world. In *Der Aufbau der menschlichen Person* [*The Structure of the Human Person*], she writes, "The observation of a single, isolated individual is abstract. The individual's being is a being in the world, and its life is life in community."[13] Stein begins her own philosophical explorations from the perspective of the solitary I because she wants to demonstrate the structure of lived experience and its interrelation with causality and motivation, ultimately leading to the investigation of how individual lived experiences can become interwoven with communal ones. The I has its own undeniable solitude, but it is also capable of dwelling in community. Stein moves from an analysis of the I to community because she wishes to understand "how this ego, notwithstanding its solitariness and inalienable aloneness, can enter into a *community of life* with other subject, how the individual subject becomes a member of a super-individual subject, and also how a super-individual current of experience is constituted in the active living of such a community-subject or community's subject."[14]

Stein's starting point is the I, which, for her, is essential, and remains so even when she distances herself from Husserl. His analysis of the I perhaps may be viewed as his most important teaching for Stein, despite all the differences between them and despite her criticisms of her old teacher. We see her fidelity to Husserl in *Kreuzeswissenschaft*, in which she maintains that God does not transgress a person's own freedom and that the soul can affect itself because it has the *conformation of the I*. Moreover, thanks to the I the person possesses itself and all that moves and lives in its own spatial sphere.[15]

Gerda Walther, in her text "Zur Ontologie der sozialen Gemeinschaften," proceeds differently than Stein: she explores the interior connection between subjects to arrive, in a second moment, at the reality of the I without first deeply analyzing the relation between the I and community. This notion of the I, Walther maintains, arises because

---

[12] Edith Stein, *Philosophy of Psychology and the Humanities*, trans. by Mary Catharine Baseheart and Marianne Sawicki (Washington, D.C.: ICS Publications, 2000), 41.

[13] Edith Stein, *Der Aufbau der menschlichen Person* (Vorlesung zur philosophischen Anthropologie) (Freiburg: Herder, 2004), 134.

[14] Edith Stein, *Philosophy of Psychology and the Humanities*, 133.

[15] Edith Stein, *Kreuzeswissenschaft:Studie über Johannes vom Kreuz* (Edith Stein Gesamtausgabe No. 18) (Freiburg: Herder, 2015).

"... the unity of the community is something that literally remains in the background or behind the I-center."[16] Others, in part, remain in the background of the subject, though subject and others exist together, with one another, forming a we that is not always immediately and clearly aware of itself. Further, it should be noted that Walther came to phenomenology from a Marxist background, hence it is reasonable to assume that she would give to the social a major place in her writing[17]:

> For this reason, from the period of my early university studies, I was inclined to doubt traditional theories that advocated a cause–effect model of a succession of level or grades of society and that grounded community in an aggregate of individuals that came into contact with one another based simply on the shared experience of their common, surrounding physical–spatial world.[18]

Hence, despite her time at Freiburg, she accepts neither Husserl's nor Stein's analyses of the primordiality of the I. This is one of the reasons that Walther may be viewed as preferring to return to the Munich School of Phenomenology led by Pfänder. She may be seen as not wanting to examine, as Husserl would have required, the modality in which the community externally constitutes itself in consciousness, a modality in which she later becomes interested, as witnessed in her later reflections. There, she posits a social self from and exclusively upon which a comprehension of the relation between the individual and the community becomes possible. Walther considers this approach to be a true and proper Copernican Revolution. Starting from this core insight, she develops an ontology of social communities that defines their essence and structure. She does not refute a priori the transcendental analysis, but she does not believe that it is the right starting point for an analysis of community. She remarks:

> Ontology investigates the ultimate sense of every objectivity, understood in its broadest possible sense, for phenomenology researches this objectivity through its necessary, manifest ways of givenness, appearance, and knowing in consciousness. Ontology begins from this *pure consciousness* and *its pure I,* from this most originary standpoint ...[19]

---

[16]Antonio Calcagno, "Gerda Walter. Sulla possibilità di un senso passivo della comunità e della coscienza interna del tempo," in *Edith Stein, Hedwig Conrad-Martius, Gerda Walter. Fenomenologia della persona, della vita e della comunità*, ed. by Angela Ales Bello, Francesco Alfieri, Mobeen Shahid (Bari: Edizioni Giuseppe Laterza, 2011), 774.

[17]Gerda Walther, *Zum anderen Ufer*, 270.

[18]Alice Togni, "Reciprocità e responsabilità: l'analisi delle comunità sociali in Gerda Walter," in *Per la filosofia*, vol. 100–101, May–December, 2017, 62.

[19]Gerda Walther, "Zur Ontologie der sozialen Gemeinschaften," in *Jahrbuch für Pholosophie und phänomenologische Forschung*, Vol. VI (Halle: Max Niemeyer, 1923), 1. In the first volume of the *Ideas*, whose index Walther prepared, Husserl deals with the question of ontology. He maintains, "Every concrete, empirical object inserts itself with its material essence into a higher material genus, in a region of empirical objects. A regional essence corresponds to a regional eidetic science or, in other terms, a regional science"—E. Husserl, *Idee per una fenomenologia pura e per una filosofia fenomenologica*, Vol. I, ed. by E. Filippini (Torino: Einaudi, 1982, 26). The question of ontology is a *vexata quaestio* because a minor or major determination of an object signals the divide between realist and transcendental phenomenologists. On this question of realist versus transcendental phenomenology, Walther follows her teacher, Pfänder, who understands formal ontology as a theory of the object and its properties. But this ontology serves also as the foundation for further

Edith Stein and Gerda Walther, though they share a phenomenological framework, describe community in different ways. Stein starts from I-experience to reach her understanding community, which is analyzed deeply and in all its constitutive elements, whereas Walther moves from the social self and, hence, from the background of psychic interiority in which the communal we moves and lives. The community is not an autonomous person in that it does not possess a center endowed with consciousness and will.

Community in Edith Stein and Gerda Walther

Stein reflects at length on community and connects it to the person. The idea of the person appears consistently throughout Stein's corpus, from *On the Problem of Empathy* to *Finite and Eternal Being*. In her 1922 text *Philosophy of Psychology and the Humanities*, Stein directly examines the question of community by asking: What is a community? Referring to Tönnies, she claims, "where a subject accepts the other as a subject and does not confront him but rather *lives with him* and is determined by the stirrings of his life, they are forming a *community* with one another."[20] Stein's definition is simple and clear: a community exists when an interior opening to others exists and, hence, a solidarity. She continues to develop this view of community in her *Aufbau der menschlichen Person*, in which she shares a position similar to Dietrich von Hildebrand's insofar as he defines a community as a social formation grounded in persons, their social acts and relations, and, above all, in the primary mode of a community of *humanity*. "Every human community, from the smallest to the 'largest,' is grounded in a more basic, encompassing community, namely, humanity."[21] Communities arise without any intervention of the will; they may arise from a shared life (for example, communities that are born out of classroom friendships

determination of content that can form material ontologies, which are more determined than formal ontologies, even though they need to follow certain laws. Walther maintains that, in Husserl, there is no individual essence, understood in the strict sense. One can speak of general essences to the point that one can achieve knowledge of an individual essence: "[...] jedes eidos [...] sich verkörpern kann [...] bei in jeder geistigen Person im Sinne Schelers, [...], bei jedem Grundwesen im Sinne A. Pfänders, auch das Wesen eines "Engels" oder einer einmaligen Kunstschöpfung" (Gerda Walter, "Zur Ontologie der sozialen Gemeinschaften," in *Jahrbuch für Pholosophie und phänomenologische Forschung*, cit. p. 5, note 3). Edith Stein takes up later the aforementioned question in her *Finite and Eternal Being*. In note 43 of chapter 3 she discusses Husserl's position as developed in his *Ideas*, which maintained that the *quid* of an individual thing could be seized by seeing the essence, but without actualizing a position from experience. Stein writes, "This concession only takes one side of reality into consideration, namely, the essential essence; it cuts the link to reality, a link that does not exist external to the essence, but which intrinsically belongs to it. It is precisely from the standpoint of this cut, made at the root that separates fact and essence, that one can understand how Husserl arrived at his idealist interpretation of reality, while his followers (Max Scheler, Alexander Pfänder, Adolf Reinach, Hedwig Conrad-Martius, Jean Héring, etc.) all guided by the full sense of essence, followed always more intensely as realist conception."

[20] Edith Stein, *Philosophy of Psychology and the Humanities*, 130.

[21] Edith Stein, *Der Aufbau der menschlichen Person*, 136.

or from living in a certain city or country). They may also emerge from some family bond, shared feelings, particular friendships, matrimony, or even from societies that share a common goal, as is the case with some learned societies.[22]

In *Philosophy of Psychology and the Humanities*, Stein tackles the difficult question of how one moves from the lived experience of an individual to the experience of community. She uses the example of the death of a beloved troop leader to explain the transition.[23] The sadness over the loss of the troop leader is content that is shared collectively by the community: all members of the community share the experience of sadness. But the communal experience can only be experienced by each individual member, in his or her own consciousness and only insofar as each individual experience himself or herself as members of the community who undergo the experience of collective sadness. In the individual I the sadness is lived as communal sadness: the community is sad, and as a member of the community I am sad with the community and the community is sad with me. Yet, the I grasps and lives the communal sadness. The collective sadness is an object and can be understood as such by individual members of the troop. Each member of the troop experiences his or her own sadness as well as the collective sadness of the community members. The collective experience of sadness is built, both the noetic and noematic elements, from the lived experiences of individuals who feel the collective sadness. If the communal sadness neither manifests itself nor is grasped by individual members, then no community exists. Yet, community remains possible if only one member grasps the communal sadness: "They all share in the assembling of the communal experience; but that which was *intended* in all of them came to *fulfillment* in the experience of this one alone."[24]

Stein claims for the individual a great autonomy: the community cannot and must not absorb the individual because she/he has a vast personal domain that remains distinct from the community, even though she/he may be a member of a community. Individual and community are never identical. Edith Stein is diffident to visions that view the human being only as social beings. In fact, in *Der Aufbau der menschlichen Person* she observes: "One finds today the widespread tendency to view human beings as solely determined by their membership in a social whole, thereby denying the reality of an individual personality."[25]

Walther follows, in part, Stein's view of community. In her definition of community, Walther proceeds in stages of analysis, adding diverse elements when called for to arrive at a comprehensive definition of community:

> We found a number of human beings that have, as a certain layer of their lives, the same intentional object. In principle, this knowledge deals directly or indirectly with the exchange

[22]Edith Stein, *Der Aufbau der menschlichen Person*, 137–138.

[23]This example is framed by the context of the WWI. Stein's own service as a nurse in a lazaretto near the front, where Stein attended to many sick and dying soldiers, and the death of her beloved teacher, Adolf Reinach. *Philosophy of Psychology and the Humanities* was written in 1919 and published three years later in Husserl's *Jahrbuch*.

[24]Edith Stein, *Philosophy of Psychology and the Humanities*, 137.

[25]Edith Stein, *Der Aufbau der menschlichen Person*, 134.

of individuals with one another, and from this exchange a communal life emerges ... [H]ence, each intention directed to the same object, immediately or mediately grasped, has been motivated in a unified sense."[26]

Starting her investigation by exploring the constitution of the inner experience of community, Walther proceeds to investigate the elements that constitute community and help distinguish one community from another. Communities can be either reflexive or iterative. The former only refer to the members themselves and they are permeated and regulated by a common sense given by the unity of the community itself, whereas in the latter members give a proper sense to their communal life though a common object. Every community possesses an intentional object that is communally obtained by all members. The object, broadly understood, may be the community itself or the intentional consolidation of the reciprocal union of its members. This union may be, and it would be better if it were the case, habitual:

> [The community] need not be constituted from the actual, present union of its members with others; rather, it can also be habitual: a unified, habitual resting of one member in another member, whether expressed, actually present, or even as an unconscious growing together, comes to be. Habitual union exists in all members, and it can act as the foundation or ground of a community.[27]

The consolidation of life through a habitual union is realized though the category of "humans, that also ...," which is always deeply present in the subject: these implied other humans are part of the individual, and together they constitute a communal we of which the individual is not always clearly conscious, but which is nonetheless unified in those layers that require the sense of community. "The humans, that also ..." are behind my egological center and they are always present in the background. Hence, the lived experiences of community are originary lived experiences.[28] The subject

> ... rests in the community and belongs to it, no matter how loosely or limitedly, and it belongs to him or her: together they build a we. The subject's life, insofar as it is communal, is not only his or her life, nor does community swell out of the subject alone, understood as a single individual; rather, community arises out of the union of the individual with others. The lived experience of the living, experiencing subject can be characterized not only as I *experience or live this*, but as *we live this, I and the others* with whom I am unified, live this lived experience together.[29]

Again, my lived experiences, insofar as they are communal lived experiences, do not solely arise from the personal I but also from others, from "Humans, that also," with whom I live and rest.

A problem arises in Walther's analysis: Does the possibility of communal guilt and responsibility exist or are they purely individual phenomena? For Stein the question of communal guilt and responsibility does not pose a problem, for they are localized

[26] Gerda Walther, "Zur Ontologie der sozialen Gemeinschaften," 29–30.

[27] Gerda Walther, "Zur Ontologie der sozialen Gemeinschaften," 69.

[28] Gerda Walther, "Zur Ontologie der sozialen Gemeinschaften," 69–71.

[29] Gerda Walther, "Zur Ontologie der sozialen Gemeinschaften," 7.

within the framework of the individual person. Stein remarks in the *Philosophy of Psychology and the Humanities*:

> Certainly the act of the community can also be culpable or meritorious. But whether the single member participates in them or withholds himself from them, this is a matter of his freedom and he himself has to answer for it. It's presupposed on this, of course, that we're dealing with a community of *free persons*—we could also simply say: [a community made up] of person, for freedom belongs to persons. This presupposition just isn't there with Scheler. [...] We'd just like to mention that in any community *with no members at all* who execute acts freely and on their own (insofar as something like that is conceivable at all) you can't discuss any responsibility, in the strict sense. You can't talk about the community's responsibility any more than that of the lone members.[30]

Walther raises the same problem as Stein on communal guilt. The problem is central for Walther insofar as she has a stricter, non-egoic view of community in which the community pre-exists in the individual in the background that allows communal experiences to be experienced precisely as communal. Although Walther posits a deep communal structure in the background of individuals, she still maintains the role of the I-center in actualization of the lived experience of community. She notes, "[The lived experience of community] can only be actualized by passing through the individual I-center of the individual members."[31] Walther affirms that, although the community is a psycho-spiritual unity, it does not possess the essential trait of a person (that is, a center endowed with its own consciousness and will [*das Bewusstseins- und Willenszentrum*]); therefore, "the community is reliant more on the I-center of its members as well as their bodies."[32]

Conclusion

Stein and Walther's positions on community are certainly very similar, especially in terms of some of their conclusions. Moreover, though they may differ on how they arrive at their conclusions, the differences between them are also relevant and substantial. Edith Stein simply makes use of Tönnies distinction, and she does not add or amplify its essential insight: a community exists when one can verify an interior opening among subjects to one another. Members could potentially have, then, neither a common, intentional object among them nor know one another in a reciprocal action nor be motivated in a unitary fashion by an intention, as Walther maintains. All that is needed is to accept one another as persons such that a community becomes possible. It is from this acceptance that community becomes possible. Stein makes an interesting claim in the *Philosophy of Psychology and the Humanities* when she maintains that a life community is possible even between two enemies that face one another on the battlefield because there is an opening of interiority: "Just such a

[30] Edith Stein, *Philosophy of Psychology and the Humanities*, 195–196.

[31] Gerda Walther, "Zur Ontologie der sozialen Gemeinschaften," 87.

[32] Gerda Walther, "Zur Ontologie der sozialen Gemeinschaften," 114.

'naïve' posture even exists in combat between hostile parties. Here the one is taking the other simply as a subject, and is leaving himself open to all the influences that are emanating from the other. Thus, they form a unity of life in spite of the chasm that exists between them, and it can be that one [party] fills the other with the power which then is directed against itself in the attack."[33]

The willingness for and openness to the other create relations and flows of experience that intersect, and when this happens one sees the passage of life, of sentiments, that ultimately make the community live. This view of interior openness as being foundational for community is very much in accord with the Christian position of unconditionally welcoming the other. Stein maintains that this is possible, even from an egological perspective—a position that is stronger in Stein than in Walther, though the latter also speaks of telepathy as demonstrating a great capacity for entering into the lived experience of the other. For Walther, it is possible for the other to feel what the other feels at a given moment, even though the other may not be visibly live before us. This position would have been hard to accept for both Stein and Pfänder because both of them argue that it is impossible to feel exactly what the other feels or lives. For Stein, subjects remain separate from one another: each has his or her own uniqueness or individuality, but this does not negate the possibility of subjects encountering and grasping one another as human beings. Despite the differences between the two philosophers, it is important to highlight that both Walther and Stein place great value on community, for it is for both of them the fundamental, common, and necessary terrain in which one can grow and be formed as human beings.

Anna Maria Pezzella was born in Naples. In 1989 she graduated from the Università degli Studi di Napoli Federico II, and in 1994 she completed her PhD at the Lateran University in Rome. Between 1995 and 1998 she served as an assistant to the Chair of Contemporary Philosophy at the same university. Since 1998 she has been a university professor at the Lateran University, and since 2003 she has taught the Philosophy of Education. Since 2009 she has also taught pedagogy. The manager of the *Centro Ricerche e Studi Edith Stein* (Rome), Anna Maria Pezzella also takes care of the website www.centrostudiedithstein.it. She is also a member of the International Research Area Dedicated to Edith Stein and Gender Theory in Rome. Her main philosophical interests lie in the history of 20th-century thought, especially the philosophy of Edith Stein, whose works she has translated (*Beiträge*, *Einführung in die Philosophie*, *Bildung*, etc.). Pezzella's papers have been published in various Italian and foreign journals. She also investigates the work of women philosophers like Maria Zambrano along with questions relevant to the philosophy of education and phenomenological pedagogy.

[33]Edith Stein, *Philosophy of Psychology and the Humanities*, 206–207. Here, one may also understand the Christian edict to turn the other cheek: I hate the other; I do not respond with hate, but with love. I offer the other cheek as a sign of this love.

Gerda Walther and the Possibility of a Non-intentional We of Community

Antonio Calcagno

Abstract Gerda Walther identifies the possibility of we-communities that are non-intentional and have no intentional object (for example, a community of lovers). What is expressed, shared, communicated, and understood between lovers need not necessarily manifest itself in an objective, social, or communal form, as is the case, for example, in a political party. I argue that this non-intentional we can be experienced at the level of habit or affect, a level that is lived but which is not fully grasped in terms of the consciousness of meaning and the relation between meaning fulfillment and meaning intention.

Keywords Gerda walther · We sociality · Non-intentional community
Reflexive community · Habit · Community

Gerda Walther (1897–1977), one of the early Phenomenological Movement's important thinkers, viewed her work as intersecting between phenomenology, psychology, and sociology. She took seriously Edmund Husserl's directive to examine things themselves to comprehend how it is that our own lived experience could yield understanding of objects as they present themselves to consciousness. Trained in part by Edith Stein in Husserl's "phenomenological kindergarten," Walther, like Stein, was interested in questions about social ontology and psychology. In her work, "Zur Ontologie der sozialen Gemeinschaften" (On the "Ontology of Social Communities"),[1] Walther defends the possibility of a strong we-consciousness, we-intentionality, and objective we-communities. A community, for Walther, is understood as a unity or oneness, a *Vereinigung*. Communities are marked by structures of habit, intentional we-consciousness, affectivity, and a meaningful consciousness of what it is to be and live as a unity or a we. Communities have both subjective and

[1] Gerda Walther, "Zur Ontologie der sozialen Gemeinschaften," in *Jahrbuch für Philosophie und phänomenologische Forschung*, Vol. 6, ed. by Edmund Husserl, Moritz Geiger, Alexander Pfänder, and Max Scheler (Halle: Max Niemeyer, 1923), 1–158. Hereafter parenthetically cited as OSG.

A. Calcagno (✉)
Department of Philosophy, King's University College, 266 Epworth Avenue, London, ON N6A 2M3, Canada
e-mail: acalcagn@uwo.ca

A. Calcagno (ed.), *Gerda Walther's Phenomenology of Sociality, Psychology, and Religion*, Women in the History of Philosophy and Sciences 2,
https://doi.org/10.1007/978-3-319-97592-4_5

objective sides, an *an sich* and *für sich*. Walther analyzes how certain linguistic formulations reveal we-objectivities (for example, formulations "in the name of ..." or "on behalf of ..." can bespeak or perform a certain we-reality). Curious in her analysis of the we is the fact that Walther also identifies the possibility of we-communities that are non-intentional and have no classical intentional object. Love is an example she focuses on as fulfilling the possibility of a non-intentional we: What is expressed, shared, communicated, and understood between lovers need not necessarily manifest itself in an objective, social, or communal form, as is the case, for example, in a political party. Yet, the lovers together live and experience each other as a unity, a we-community. The way she justifies a non-objectivated we-community is through the mutual grasping of the meaning or sense [*Sinn*] of the particular unity that lovers experience of being in a union without that meaning necessarily being objectivated in some social, communal externalized reality. Non-intentional communities were important for phenomenology as they were forms of sociality that resisted more positivistic sociological accounts that reduced the genesis of community to material, behaviorist, psychologistic, or historical factors. Moreover, the possibility of non-intentional communities could account for deeper affective structures of social life like love and friendship that were neither merely economic exchanges of a "tit for tat" sociality nor simply evolutionary structures developed for human survival.

Walther indeed makes a valid phenomenological claim about the possibility of a non-intentional we, a we that does not correspond to an intentional object at the level of an active, constituting (that is, sense-giving and sense-making) consciousness. But, in this chapter I would like to explore a possibility: if there exist non-intentional forms of we-communities, the meaning grasped, lived through, and constituted in the aforementioned type of community, understood as self-referential, need not be completely clear or fully present. I argue that the we of community can be experienced at the level of habit or affect, a level that is lived but which is not fully grasped in terms of the consciousness of objectivated meaning and the relation between meaning fulfillment and meaning intention. In this sense, one can speak of pre-conscious or passive presentation, in affect or habit, of a we that presents somewhat as an object, but this object, though it can register some form of meaning, is never and can never be fully formed, because the object itself is constantly in formation. In more practical terms, the reason why lovers can never fully objectify, and therefore make fully conscious or graspable, their love, to use more traditional, phenomenological terms, is that the love itself is a kind of object that is unlike other objects in that it is subject to the time of becoming and its essence is in constant formation. Love unfolds over time and can never present as a whole; rather, we only grasp aspects of the love. These aspects, perhaps like the different aspects of the house in Husserl's *Logical Investigations*, only are parts that we know point to a larger reality. I see habits and affects of love as parts of a whole that point to a larger reality called love. The parts have some objectivated presence, but the whole of love is never equal to the sum of its parts.

Gerda Walther on the Unity of Communal Oneness

Walther's work on community and psychology has been largely neglected. Yet, her work is important for presenting a fusional model of community that is rationally graspable both as sense [*Sinn*] and as a deep feeling or affect. In many ways, she extends Scheler's views, while developing her own view outside a largely personalistic and value-centered model. Her work also provides a critique of more egoic models of community that one finds in Husserl and Stein. Also unique is Walther's taking up of key insights (for example, the discussion of *Gesinnung* [attitude] by her teacher and mentor, Alexander Pfänder, who was a student of Theodor Lipps). The question of a non-intentional we or community is addressed by phenomenologists like Stein,[2] Scheler,[3] and Dietrich von Hildebrand.[4] In *On the Problem of Empathy*, for example, Stein says that love is a value that cannot be objectivated in the same way as other values.[5] Like Scheler, she claims that love (and hate, for Scheler) is a value that cannot be easily intentionally objectivated because the object of love exceeds what consciousness can grasp of it, largely because the object is usually a person with a distinct personality. Empathy cannot make fully present the whole mind and personality of the other *in se*. It can only analogically make present a part or aspect of what the subject intends about the mind of another through a comparison with the subject's own experience of himself/herself. Love as a value, indeed the highest value for Stein, cannot be fully presentified and analogically lived through as it is experienced in another. Love, then, is a unique phenomenon that can be understood as value, whose content is not fully objectivated in consciousness (E 102–105). Walther defends the aforementioned view of certain forms of community that have non-intentional objects. Yet, her understanding of the passive structures of consciousness, especially habit and affect, can be deployed to explain how we-communities may be partially conscious of an object, albeit an object that is not fully formed and in a state of becoming that may never be able to be fully realizable. In my view, we can find what Stein and Husserl describe as hyletic content dragging behind itself noetic content: the passive synthesis that we find in the hyletic sphere of genetic phenomenology first announces or manifests the possibility of an object that eventually may appear in the noetic realm.[6] Hence, although Walther defends the possibility of non-intentional we-communities, we must see them as not wholly

---

[2]Edith Stein, *Philosophy of Psychology and the Humanities* [*Beiträge zur philosophischen Begründung der Psychologie und der Geisteswissenschaften*], trans. by Mary Catherine Baseheart and Marianne Sawicki (Washington, D.C.: ICS Publications, 2000).

[3]Max Scheler, *The Nature of Sympathy*, trans. by Peter Heath with an Introduction by Graham McAleer (New Brunswick, NJ: Transaction Publishers, 2008); Max Scheler, *Formalism in Ethics and Non-Formal Ethics of Values*, trans. by Manfred Frings and Roger L. Funk (Evanston, IL: Northwestern University Press, 1973).

[4]Dietrich von Hildebrand, *Die Metaphysik der Gemeinschaft* (Regensburg: Habbel Verlag, 1955).

[5]Edith Stein, *On the Problem of Empathy*, trans. by Waltraut Stein (Washington, DC: ICS Publications, 1989), 102. Hereafter parenthetically cited as E.

[6]See Angela Ales Bello's masterful study, *The Sense of Things* (Dordrecht: Springer, 2015).

non-intentional, for in passive levels of consciousness some objectivation occurs, especially in Walther's analysis of habit and affect.

Before discussing Walther's analysis of community, we need to understand her view of what phenomenology is and how it achieves what it purports to do. Like Husserl, Stein, and Reinach, Walther maintains that phenomenology is the study of what appears in consciousness and how we live through [*Durchlebens*] such manifestations in consciousness (OSG 2). The lived experience of consciousness intentionally correlates to objects in the world; consciousness can objectivate what is given to consciousness, and in grasping the sense of what is given to consciousness, we also simultaneously grasp the meaning or sense of the object in the real world (OSG 2–3). The achievement of sense [*Sinn*] allows us to grasp the essence of an objectivated thing in consciousness, and this essence is what the thing is in its reality in the world. Walther, here, follows an earlier version of the phenomenological method, which Husserl later dismisses as descriptive or mundane while developing and defending the need for a transcendental phenomenology. Walther sees her work as fitting into a regional ontology (OSG 4) of social objectivities, and she sees phenomenology in non-transcendental terms:

> Das schließt nun freilich nicht aus, daß als Methode in der Phänomenologie die Wesenserfahrung eine große Rolle spielt, den die Phänomenologie will sich ja nicht mit irgendwelchen Tatsächlichkeiten des Bewußtseins und der empirischzufälligen Einzelerlebnisse abgeben, sondern ihr Wesen, ihr wesentlichen Unterschiede und Strukturzusammenhänge erforschen. Die Phänomenologie ist also selbst eine Wesenswissenschaft, die es mit dem Wesen des die Gegenstände konstituierenden Bewußtseins in weitesten Sinne zu tun hat (OSG 4).

Although Walther comes to phenomenology after Husserl's transcendental turn, she chooses to follow its more eidetic form as developed and taught by Stein and Reinach. I do not wish to deal here with the question of the relationship between and limitations of ideal, real, and transcendental approaches to phenomenology, as this would take us beyond the focus of our investigation here. It is important, however, to signal the importance of intentionality, the objective correlate of intentionality, and the belief in the possibility of achieving sense or sense-making—understood as manifesting the objective nature or embodiment [*Verkörperung*] of a real object (OSG 7, 9) in the world. It should also be remarked that contemporary analytic approaches to social ontology critique thinkers like Husserl, Stein, Scheler, and Walther as presenting a folk-psychological account of social mind and social objectivities.[7] What these critiques fail to recognize are the importance and power of the achievement of sense, through eidetic reduction (OSG 5), understood as the correspondence between or adequation of (OSG 6) meaning intention and meaning fulfillment. This early and

[7] Frédérique de Vignemont, "Drawing the Boundary between Low-level and High-level Mindreading," in *Philosophical Studies*, Vol. 144, 2009, 457–466; "Knowing Other People's Mental States as If They Were One's Own," in S. Gallagher and D. Schmicking (eds.), *Handbook of Phenomenology and Cognitive Science* (Dordrecht: Springer, 2010), 283–299; Alvin I. Goldman, *Simulating Minds: The Philosophy, Psychology, and Neuroscience of Mindreading* (Oxford: Oxford University Press, 2008).

important discovery that Husserl made in his *Logical Investigations* is rarely discussed by critics of the early phenomenological method.[8]

For Walther communities, like all social objectivities, manifest two aspects about themselves: first, they have an "outer" constitution (that is, they are organized and stand in specific relation to outer realities); second, they have an inner constitution (that is, the members of a community or social objectivity are conscious of a certain state of mind—in other words, the meaning of the lived experience of the state of mind) when they experience themselves living in a community or social community, including society or *Gesellschaft* (OSG 17). Community, understood as a particular form or type of sociality or social objectivity, is not to be understood as a society—in particular, as Max Weber understood society. Walther criticizes Weber's understanding of society because, although it shares similar characteristics to the phenomenological understanding of community, it lacks a robust inner account of the lived experience of community as a particular, shared, and meaningful experience of unity or *Vereinigung* (OSG 32–34). Weber, according to Walther, sees society as a particular ordered form of individuals who are motivated by an external goal or end (for example, a particular form of work).

According to Walther, communities are marked by a particular form of a lived experience of community or *Gemeinschaftserlebnis*. She describes the essence [*Wesenskonstituens*] or sense of community as a oneness [*Einigung*] (OSG 34–36). The oneness of community possesses both inner and outer aspects. I cannot here analyze all that Walther contributes to the discussion of oneness, but I will highlight important aspects relevant for the argument I wish to develop here about the possibility of non-objectivated communities.[9]

In terms of the inner aspect of the lived experience of community, Walther is aware that there exist both passive/unconscious aspects as well as more explicitly conscious ones (OSG 37). The oneness of community is described as touching upon various dimensions of the mental life of human beings: affectivity (psyche), the unconscious, passive structures (habit), and consciousness (intentionality and sense). No one dimension is privileged, and they all come with varying intensities of presence or manifestation.

Deeply influenced by the psychological work of Alexander Pfänder, Walther describes two psychic phenomena that correspond to the inner oneness of communities (namely, feeling/affect and habit). One can experience a feeling of oneness, of belonging to one community. The feeling of oneness can produce certain affects: joy, happiness, sadness, distrust, etc. She describes it as "[a] warm, affirming emo-

[8]Dan Zahavi has done much to draw attention to Husserl's contributions to the topic. See Dan Zahavi, *Self-Awareness and Alterity* (Evanston: Northwestern University Press, 1999); *The Phenomenological Mind* (with S. Gallagher) (London: Routledge, 2007); *Subjectivity and Selfhood: Investigating the First Person Perspective* (Cambridge, MA: MIT Press, 2008).

[9]For a fuller analysis of Waltherian community see Antonio Calcagno, "Gerda Walther: On the Possibility of a Passive Sense of Community and the Inner Time Consciousness of a Community," in a special volume dedicated to early phenomenology, ed. by Jeff Mitscherling and Kimberly Baltzer-Jaray, *Symposium: Canadian Journal of Continental Philosophy/Revue canadienne de philosophie continentale*, Vol. 16, No. 2, Fall 2012, 89–105.

tional wave of greater or lesser force suddenly flooding, more or less abruptly and violently or quietly and mildly, the whole subject or only a very 'thin' part of the subject" (OSG 34). The subject experiencing the feeling of oneness is an I that feels itself bound to the object-oneness [*Einigungsobjekt*] in a forceful, warm, and intensive stream of feelings (OSG 35). Walther notes that the feeling of oneness usually emerges from the background and not directly from the I itself, suggesting that I is overwhelmed or overcome by a feeling of oneness (OSG 35). The I does not produce the feeling, but undergoes it. Walther says that the I "has nothing to do with" (OSG 36) the feeling itself. There is a passivity of being overwhelmed by the feeling of the lived experience of community.

Walther notes that, although one can experience being taken up in the feeling of oneness, she cautions us not to think that this feeling arises out of nowhere and that it comes about all of a sudden *stricto* sensu. In fact, in all probability the feeling of oneness had been growing over time: she describes a *Zusammenwachsen* (OSG 36) or a growth of the feeling of oneness over time that is both unconscious or minimally or less conscious [*unterbewußt*] (OSG 36–37). She remarks:

> Zur Einigung im weitesten Sinne können wir aber doch jedenfalls dies unbewußte, unterbewußte Zusammenwachsen rechnen, es ist dann gleichsam ein Keimzelle, wenn auch nicht der notwendige Ausgangspunkt, aller anderen Einigung und Gemeinschaft. Bei ihm spielt das Ich, wie wir sahen, überhaupt keine Rolle, sei es aktiv oder passiv. Von einer Einigung im engeren Sinne kann mann aber wohl erst sprechen, wo es sich um ein aktuelles Ich-Erlebens handelt, das dann allerdings in ein habituelles Erlebnis übergehen kann (OSG 38).

Habitual forms of oneness are distinguished from unconscious or less conscious forms of oneness by virtue of memory (OSG 37). According to Walther, in the case of the latter one cannot presentify the role of the acting I and its role in experiencing oneness, whereas in the case of the former the acting I can be presentifed as remembering a habitual action in which it was present and in which it experienced a habitual feeling of oneness. But does this mean that experiences of oneness to which we are habituated are simply remembered lived experiences or memories? Walther distinguishes habits from remembered feelings of oneness by arguing that in memory one can observe that the I of the remembering person and the I of the remembered feeling of oneness are not always identically the same: they are separated by time and space. In habit one always returns to the same, identical I. She notes:

> So unterscheidet die habituell gewordene aktuelle Einigung sich von der erinnerten Einigung durch die Stellung zum Erlebnisquellpunkt—hier im Gefühlszentrum—, während es mit ihr die gleiche Stellung zum Ich-Punkt hat, —der ja sowohl im erinnerten, als auch im habituellen Erlebnis früher lebendig gelebt hat, aber mit dem wesentlichen Unterschied, daß es beim habituellen Erlebnis wieder dasselbe identische Erlebnis durchleben kann, während dies beim erloschenen, erinnerten Erlebnis wesensnotwendig ein-für-allemal ausgeschlossen ist. Anderseits unterscheidet sich die habituell gewordene aktuelle Einigung vom bloßen Zusammenwachsen durch die Stellung zum Ich, während es mit ihm die gleiche Stellung zum Erlebnisquellpunkt hat (OSG 43).

Habits of feeling of oneness are important for community: they help keep communities together, but the habitual feeling of oneness need not be marked by the full presence of the I, as is the case with intentional, fully conscious, and meaningful forms of community.[10]

Walther also describes habitual forms of *Einigung* as a particular category she calls "Menschen, die auch" (that is, "human beings, who also …") (OSG 69–70). There is an inclusive form of community, which may not always be fully intentionally present or its sense fully achieved, but which nonetheless contains within itself a oneness that lies in the background of a social unity. Walther gives the example of human beings, all of whom could be united in a common goal,[11] a goal in which they can all potentially take part:

> Bei Menschen, die gerade auf Grund ihrer Wesensverschiedenheit, die sich doch ergänzt (wie etwa manchmal bei Mann und Frau), sich einigen, liegt gewiß nur ein derartiges "auch" vor, ein "auch" allerdings, das vielleicht außserdem noch auf die höhere Einheit beider hinwiest, die potentiell in ihnen enthalen ist, die aber realisiert wird, wenn ist ein Gemeinschaft bilden (OSG 69).

Walther describes this wider form of belonging as intentional and the proper or foundational form of habitual oneness of the lived experience of community. The primary characteristic of this habitual and intentional form of unity is not constituted by an I that lives an experience, but a we that lives an experience as an "I along with others." She observes:

> Diese "Menschen, die auch" sind stets irgendwie, wenn auch noch so unbestimmt, im Hintergrund des Subjektes gegenwärtig. Es ist ihrer nicht nur dunkel inne, sondern es ist auch geeint mit ihnen, in den Schichten, in denen es eben der Sinn der Gemeinschaft verlangt. Es ruht in ihnen und gehört zu ihnen, sei es auch noch so lose und in einem noch so begrenzten Teil seines Gesamtlebens—und sie "gehören zu ihm"—, es bildet mit ihnen ein "Wir". Sein Leben, soweit es eben Gemeinschaftsleben ist, ist nicht nur sein Leben, quillt nicht nur aus ihm selbst, als Einzelindividuum, hervor, sondern es entspringt gleichsam aus seiner Einheit mit den anderen in ihm. Das Erleben ist hier für das erlebende Subjekt charakterisiert, nicht nur also "ich erlebe so", sondern als: "wir erleben so", "ich und die andern"— mit denen ich geeinigt bin—"In mir erleben so" und wir sind eins in diesem unserem Erleben (OSG 69–70).

Walther's analysis of intentional communities presents the fullest or highest form of the lived experience of community. It is here that we move from a more psychological account of community to a phenomenological one. Walther observes that communal experiences need not be only between persons, as her fellow phenomenologists believed; she broadened the sense of community in that she believed that

[10]See Emanuele Caminada, "Joining the Background: Habitual Sentiments behind We-intentionality," in *Institutions, Emotions, and Group Agents: Contributions to Social Ontology*, ed. by Anita Konzelmann Ziv and Hans Bernhard Schmid (Dordrecht: Springer, 2014), 195–212. See also Hans-Bernhard Schmidt, *Wir-Intentionalität: Kritik des ontologischen Individualismus und Rekonstruktion der Gemeinschaft* (Freiburg: Karl Alber, 2012), 135.

[11]Edith Stein argues that communities are not identical with societies, which are more goal- or purpose-oriented. Furthermore, communities, for Stein, are never experiences of fusion or what Walther calls *Verschmelzung*; rather, they are a building up in individual subjects of a shared coherence of sense or meaning of an experience of solidarity, where one lives in the life of another. Walther differs from Stein in her view of the lived experience of community.

there could be communities between people and objects as well, including structures of nature, landscapes, art objects, objects of science, religion, technology, God, etc. (OSG 49). In short, Walther extends the experience of oneness to include human persons and other non-human objects and domains. Intentional we-communities are multiple and their members are ordered in three different ways. Members can stand in relation to one another in three ways: (1) one member can be superior to or higher than another member (for example, the leader of a community); (2) members can be equal to one another (for example, they all equally work toward a common goal); (3) members can be subordinated to one another (for example, one occupies a lower position than another, say, in a religious community) (OSG 52–53).

The lived experience of belonging to the oneness of a community is constituted in the grasping of a certain (noetic) sense of a social objectivity. The oneness of a community is intentionally grasped when one understands that a person is one "with and in" others (OSG 99–100). Walther argues that feeling one with another is not the same as feeling the one of a community. There is a distinction insofar as the latter is a wider, more encompassing experience. The essence of community consists in the wider sense of oneness with a larger group of people or objects (OSG 63). Oneness is constituted in four primary layers. First, there must be a subject of unity [*Einigungssubjekt*] (OSG 64). The subject is necessary to experience and undergo the experience of communal oneness. Second, there is at the personal level an object of unity [*Einigungsobjekt*], an object that intentionally relates to and anchors the subject. The object fulfills the intention of the subject that is trying to make sense of what it is experiencing in the lived experience of community (OSG 64). Third, there must be a widening of the feeling of oneness that moves beyond the object and subject such that the oneness experienced must encompass others, thereby broadening the sense of the unity. Finally, the complete and full experience of the oneness of subject and object must come to "rest" and be "enrooted" or "anchored" in subjects (OSG 64). The collective or communalized subjects Walther calls "originary" or "first" subjects describe a new form of communal subjectivity or we-subjectivity that emerges which is distinct from the subjectivity of individual persons (OSG 65).

Thus far, I have discussed the inner aspect of community (that is, how it manifests itself from within psyche and spirit). But Walther recognizes that community is not only sustainable from within; community needs external, material, and historical reality to exist. The external reality that makes possible a community Walther calls the "life of the community" (OSG 66). How the community lives and acts *an und für sich*, how it externalizes or makes itself manifest, conditions the experience of oneness. There are two primary ways that we can grasp the life of the community: through knowledge and social acts. Knowledge is distinguished from the conscious awareness of the oneness that characterizes a community (OSG 95). Drawing upon Hegel and Weber, Walther argues that knowledge about a community consists of the particular super-individual traits that mark both the subjective and objective spiritual life of a particular community. For example, the life of a political party or a people, their histories, desires, wills, etc.—these all manifest a communal reality of a group:

> Es ist ein wesentlicher Gesichtspunkt in der ontologischen Klassifikation, wie in der historischen Entwicklungsgeschichte der Gemeinschaft, Grad und Umfang dieses Willens festzusetllen. Dieser Punkt ist von so durchgreifender Bedeutung, daß wir bei ihm etwas näher dieses Wissen erlangt. Es ist … eine eigenaratige, neu Gegenständlichkeit, eine synthetische, kollektive Gegenständlichkeit, die sich hier im Bewußtsein konstituiert … Die Verbundenheit der Menschen als solche und der Sinn dieser Verbundenheit ist es, der sich hier gleichsam von den Menschen, als ihre Trägern, ablöst, als neue, eigenartige Gegenständlichkeit sui generis, die ihrem eigenen Sinn, ihr eigenes Sein und ihre eigenen Gesetze hat, wenn sie auch andererseits unbestreitbar nur in den einzelnen Mitgliedern und ihrer Wechselwirking bestehen und erfaßt warden kann—sowohl von innen wie auch von außen … Erst wo dieses Wissen um die Verbundenheit, die Gemeinschaft als solche, als in gewissem Sinne übergeordnetes und alles durchdringendes Ganzes in einer Gemeinschaft bei inhren Mitgliedern auftaucht, können wir im engsten und vollsten Sinn von einer Gemeinschaft "für sich" sprechen (OSG 97–98).

The second and important way that a community manifests itself in the world is through its social acts. Walther concentrates her analysis on two social acts, which can be understood as collective speech acts, following Reinach, or even performatives, understood in the sense of Austin and Searle. When a community acts *Im Sinn* (for the purpose of, in accordance with the wishes of, in the interests of) or *Im Namen* (in the name of) (OSG 103), these speech acts manifest a collective intentionality and that a community is speaking or expressing itself. The aforementioned acts require individual persons to speak and pronounce them, but the private person speaking and performing these social acts becomes a communal speaker and articulates or promulgates a communal act. Walther gives the law and parliament as two examples of how social acts manifest themselves. She even discusses the debates in the Swedish parliament over whether the king should become a mere figurehead, ultimately making way for a republican constitution (OSG 105).

The Possibility of a Non-intentional Communal We

While Gerda Walther mentions both the affective and habitual sides of community, which presuppose a non-fully developed view of intentionality, understood as operating within the meaning framework of noesis and noema, she also posits strictly non-intentional communities (that is, communities who know they share a specific *Einigung*, but for whom there is no intentional object). Love communities are the classic example of such communities. The love between lovers can never be objectivated, albeit one sees the effects or traces of the love. For example, lovers buy for one another and exchange gifts as tokens of their love for one another, but the love for one another is not identical to the gifts exchanged. But how can there exist intentional communities that do not possess the traditional constituting noesis (subject-knower) and noema (object) structure of intentional consciousness, especially given that Walther discusses these kinds of communities just after her intentional analysis of community? Walther writes:

> Es ist jedenfalls klar, daß die intentionale Fundierung der Einigung und der gemeinsame Gegenstand in engsten Zusammenhang miteinander stehen, wenn sie auch vielleicht nicht immer ganz zusammenfallen müssen. Aber ist den überhaupt in der order neben der intentionalen Fundierung der Einigung und Wechseleinigung der Mitglieder eine gemeinsame intentionale Gegenständlichkeit nötig, die als Leitmotiv ihr gemeinsames Leben durchzieht? (OSG 66–67).

Walther calls communities that have no "external" intentional object (noema) reflexive communities (OSG 67). Examples of such communities include family, friendships, and marriages. She says that these types of communities have no externalized purpose or goal that bind their members, such as a banking society whose goal is to generate profit. Walther suggests that the members of a reflexive community are not unified according to a specific goal or achievable end. It seems that this claim is right: a family can intend or desire to achieve many goals or purposes, but it would be implausible to think that such goals alone define the unity of a family. The same can be said about friendship and marriage. Walther says that reflexive communities have in and of themselves their own purposes or goals, what she calls (*Selbstzweck*) (OSG 67). In particular, the goal they have is to live out their own lives and communal unities:

> Ziel des gemeinsamen Lebens ist es hier, die Einigung und Gemeinschaft der Mitglieder "auszuleben", zu erweisen, zu vertiefen, zu entfalten und zu erhalten. U.E. kann mann, weil die Gemeinschaft sich hier in ihrem Sinn auf sich selbst zurückwendet, jedoch nicht sagen, daß sie keinen gemeinsamen Sinn, keine Leitgegenständlichkeit hätte, dies ist nur hier kein äußerer, außerhalb der Gemeinschaft und ihrer Mitglieder als Person liegender Gegenstand oder Sinn. Solche Gemeinschaften, man könnte sie reflexive Gemeinschaften nennen, wegen ihrer Rückbeziehung auf sich selbst, haben eben nur einen derartigen Gegenstand von ganz besonderer Art (OSG 67).

Key in Walther's analysis are the self-reference and openness of purpose of reflexive communities. An example of a non-objective community could be a long-lasting friendship between old school mates: there is no one outward or external sign or social reality that fully embodies the sense of the friendship (that is, the friendship is not reducible simply and only to one act, convention, institution, or speech act that embodies the friendship). One can imagine an intense and long-lasting friendship in which there is no declaration of friendship: the parties involved in the friendship simply live it out in a very intimate way, perhaps at the level of sheer affection. The friends are friends insofar as they continue to relate to one another as friends in whatever form that friendship may take over time. The friendship is not embodied as the community of a political party with its formal declarations and institutional supports. The same non-fully intentional, non-objective sense could be seen to be true with family members. The love between brothers or sisters cannot always be necessarily demonstrated or understood through specific meaning structures and conventions. In a regular speech act (for example, marriage) the oneness of the couple as pronounced in the promise made by both individuals performs or effectuates publicly a unity: the speech act of the promise of marriage makes objective the unity of the married couple. But, in the phenomenological account of the relationship between lovers the whole of their unified relationship cannot be objectivated fully, for the sense of the union transpires over time and keeps evolving: every objective description of the meaning of that unity can never be fully objectivated by intentional consciousness. We have here what Jean-Luc Marion calls a saturated phenomenon. In her discussion of non-objective forms of community, Walther makes room for very intense and intimate communities that are not fixed or localizable in an external noetic or objective form: the oneness of these communities is not fully graspable or reducible to specific outward and intended objects that can be experienced meaningfully in conscious lived experience. But, is this always the case for the specific forms of non-intentional communities identified above? I believe that Walther's claim must make room for the possibility of some form of objectivity, albeit not a fully formed one, for without such an objective prefiguration one could never be aware of the very experience of non-intentional we-experiences like love and friendship. In other words, some objectivated form of friendship or love must come to manifest itself for us to recognize that we are living through some kind of communal relationship, even though we may not be capable of fully grasping the whole of the phenomenon and, therefore, unable to make present its full *Sinn* or sense.

Phenomenologically speaking, before the fullness of meaning or sense [*Sinn*] is achieved, we know that there are hyletic or passive structures (for example, *Empfindnisse* or sensory impressions like pleasure and pain) that enable meaning to form. Walther discusses habit and affectivity as key structures that help us understand the meaning of the lived experience of community. The feeling of oneness, we learned, is not only fully present as lived in the moment, here and how, but it builds over time: Walther says that there is an unconscious or passive building of the feeling over time. Affects, be it joy or sadness, for example, manifest in the body. Empathy can be deployed to understand the experience of the other (OSG 85). Presumably, through empathy we can bring into relief, to borrow Edith Stein's expression, the sense of a particular affect (for example, the loving gaze or the erotic attraction of a community of lovers for one another). Embodied affects and the grasping of them in the other can partially objectivate the love of one individual for another, albeit the affect alone cannot wholly objectivate the lived experience of a non-intentional we-community. We can call such objectivated affects moments of love constitutive of a we-community. Affects and their embodiment, as they are grasped in and through empathy, allow us to objectify the meaning of a lived experience of community.

But, affects alone do not only allow us to partially objectivate non-intentional we-communities. Habits also allow us to objectivate the social bond of love. In a love relationship, lovers form habits of togetherness which are conditioned by certain memories and expectations. A lover knows how to contort his or her body in order that lovers can lie together in a comfortable and usual way to enjoy watching a certain television program, for example. Lovers are familiar with the particular movements, heart beats, and comfort zones of one another. Lovers expect to or anticipate a certain habitual movement that marks their love relationship, a habitual behavior that is exclusive to them and no one else. Their body memory informs habits of being together and what is comfortable and regular. Lovers embody a certain habituated form of being together, especially around certain activities or events. Embodied habits between friends or lovers take on certain shapes, practices, and forms in the lived body, setting up certain expectations, bodily movements, and positions. One knows, then, depending on how people sit, stand, or lie together, that these persons are lovers—a knowledge achieved through the trading places of analogous experience in empathy. Habits can embody or make visible a behavior that objectivates the love-relation, thereby making it intentional and presentifiable as sense. Merleau-Ponty's discussion of the body schema and Husserl's work on passive synthesis can certainly be invoked here as giving credence to the aforementioned possibilities.

Furthermore, I argue here that there are particular speech acts, institutions, and institutional practices that can serve as objective correlates of reflexive communities in that they establish certain expectations, habitual behaviors, practices, and affective dispositions. In the case of marriages or friendships, for example, there are often particular speech acts (namely, declarations and promises[12]), which do objectively perform an intended communal oneness. For example, when one makes certain promises in marriage and when these promises are recognized by a community of witnesses, and when the promises impose certain habitual expectations on the part of the members of the marriage and call for certain actions or responses of one member to another, then one can objectively intend the sense of what a marriage could be. For example, if one pledges to be faithful and love the other person in both sickness and health, this creates certain obligations and expectations on both parties, especially when such declarations are made by members to a larger community in which the marriage can be situated (for example, a Church community). When others witness the practice or performance of the promise, and when one lives out the promise, one can intend the object that is marriage. This performance or execution of the promises of language is similar to the declarations of friendship. When friendship is declared and acknowledged by members in a friendship, then the living out or performance of this friendship can be recognized and understood as particular unity by the very enactment or performance of the habitual expectations and obligations of the declaration of friendship. For example, in the declaration of friendship one promises to love the friend and help the friend when in need. When situations arise where friendship is challenged or is called for the continual performing of what was promised and declared to be the case, always within the framework of a community of friends, this performance manifests an objectivity that can be seized and grasped as an intentional correlate of the intended sense of friendship. The friend who always habitually responds to the sickness of a friend (by helping her carry out the friendship) performs what is objectively entailed by a certain declared form of friendship (that is, helping another person in need can be considered an outward, objective sign of friendship): we understand the sense of the help as not only a state of affairs but as a social act that can be set within a repeated meaning structure called friendship or, more specifically, a reliable friend. The repeated and expected act of help itself can be an object, an object that embodies the friendship. The act, in this case, entails

[12]Both Adolf Reinach and John Searle take up and discuss the performative aspect of promises and the role they play in constructing social reality. See Adolf Reinach, "Die apriorischen Grundlagen des bürgerlichen Rechtes," in *Jahrbuch für Philosophie und phänomenologische Forschung*, Vol. 1 (Tübingen: Max Niemeyer, 1913), 685–847; John Searle, *The Construction of Social Reality* (New York: The Free Press, 1995).

the helping hand of the friend but also the receptivity of the sick friend who calls for help. Again, it should be remembered that the social act may be motivated by a genuine declaration of love between friends. This repeated declaration and performing of what the declaration or promise of friendship entails may be rationally motivated in the sense that one follows through on what logically the promise made entails one to do. The expectation of reliability and the habits associated with helping an ailing friend embody a certain sense of a we-community that is intentional.

Institutions and their repeated and expected practices also give reflexive communities an objective status in the world—albeit the objective sense of these reflexive communities may be limited, given the context in which such institutions and institutional practices play themselves out. In particular, I refer to specific frameworks and practices of the law, and specific cultural practices within any given society. The law, especially tax law, often will specify what constitutes a family. Certain deductions can be made from taxes, depending on whether or not one fits the given institutional criteria of a given nation's revenue agencies. Furthermore, certain religious or social events may also posit certain practices and rituals that help identify what constitutes a family or marriage in a given cultural context. For example, what a gay, lesbian, trans, Roman Catholic, Mormon, Muslim, etc. family might look like can be objectively understood through the intentional repetitive/habitual practices and laws of states, religions, and cultures, etc.

Walther's analysis of the non-intentional, non-objectivated reflexive communities is based on a view of families, friendships, and marriages as not being reducible simply to the performatives of speech or the habits stemming from the life of institutions and their practices. Yet, these speech and institutional frameworks also set limits or configure determinations, through habits, expectations, and affects, that help us understand what reflexive communities are: they provide and make objectivity of reflexive communities possible. Sometimes, friendships, marriages, and families actually follow the conventions performed in speech and live the institutional frameworks of a given culture or people: they are thoroughly objectivated and do not have the open, non-intentional structure that Walther sees as belonging to their essence.

Finally, Walther's discussion of non-intentional, non-objectivated reflexive communities challenges the whole constitutive possibility of sense or *Sinn*. The achievement of any sense implies the building up of perduring unity of cohesion (namely, the unity of parts and wholes) that helps constitute sense in and through time. The sense of community of family, marriage, and friendship is not capable of being achieved or fulfilled—at least, in an objective phenomenological sense. Yet, one can identify a specific sort of reflexive unity that belongs to the aforementioned social realities. Walther leaves open the possibility that reflexive communities in their self-reflexivity and self-purposiveness continue to have some unity of sense even though the unity lived in such relationships is never able to be fixed or essentialized fully. The sense that can be given or that arises from the habitual practices and affects of speech acts and institutions, however, is fixed and is capable of being fulfilled. Walther's analysis cannot exclusively leave reflexive communities as having no intentional objectivated sense; rather, it would be more accurate to say that sometimes the communal lives of friendship, families, and marriages are not reducible to a specific given sense, but at other times there are partially objectivated, intentional senses, especially in speech and institutions, in affects and habits, that can be grasped. It is having both of these possibilities, both intentional and partial non-intentional *Einigungen*, that can be said to typify reflexive communities.

Antonio Calcagno is Professor of Philosophy at King's University College, London, Canada. He is the author of *Giordano Bruno and the Logic of Coincidence* (1998), *Badiou and Derrida: Politics, Events and Their Time* (2007), *The Philosophy of Edith Stein* (2007), *Lived Experience from the Inside Out: Social and Political Philosophy in Edith Stein* (2014).

Human Beings as Social Beings: Gerda Walther's Anthropological Approach

Julia Mühl

Abstract This chapter focuses on Gerda Walther's early works on social communities and the ego to clarify the following questions: Why do individuals want to create a social community and why do they strive for connection with other human beings? To answer these questions, I start with the basic assumption that Walther understands human beings as social beings and I explain her concept of the human being. I demonstrate that the constitution of the human being, for Walther, consists of three parts: the ego or I-center, the self, and the fundamental essence of a human being. The analysis of the human being permits one to delineate which of the aforementioned constituent parts assists the individual to strive for social community and which parts are crucial for deciding to enter into social community. I argue that only by examining the essence of the individual is it possible to understand why persons wish to enter into community. Hence, this chapter will illustrate the Waltherian development of community that starts with the assumption that human beings are social beings who strive for being a part of a community and for being combined with other individuals. The development continues with the constitution of a human being, which consists of three parts, and it ends with the formation of a social community. In the end, I argue that Walther maintains the development from the individual to a community that is grounded in the assumption that human beings are both social and communal beings.

Keywords Social ontology · Social community · Social beings · Social drives Ego

Introduction

Gerda Walther (1897–1977) was a German woman phenomenologist who worked on such topics as the constitution of social communities, the ego, and mysticism. Her published works include her PhD dissertation *Ein Beitrag zur Ontologie der sozialen*

J. Mühl (✉)
Paderborn University, Paderborn, Germany
e-mail: julia.muehl@upb.de

A. Calcagno (ed.), *Gerda Walther's Phenomenology of Sociality, Psychology, and Religion*, Women in the History of Philosophy and Sciences 2,
https://doi.org/10.1007/978-3-319-97592-4_6

Gemeinschaften (1922), *Phänomenologie der Mystik* (1923), and her autobiography *Zum anderen Ufer* (1960). This chapter will focus on her two early works; however, it will also take a look at some of her unpublished manuscripts, which are part of her *Nachlass* at the Bayerische Staatsbibliothek in Munich, Germany. In her dissertation Walther investigates the essential characteristics of a social community. Walther identifies the elements that constitute a social community and she establishes how individuals are connected within a community. Her dissertation is an ontological analysis of social communities. Moreover, she includes a phenomenological analysis of social communities at the end of her work. Her second work, *Phänomenologie der Mystik*, written while she was working on her dissertation, presents Walther's investigation of mystical experiences. In this work she analyzes the constitution of human beings, especially persons, because Walther assumes that only persons can have mystical experiences. Therefore, she undertakes a detailed analysis of the ego. It is interesting to see that only one third of her book thematizes mystical experiences and the spiritual connection with God. The main part of her work is devoted to an analysis of the ego.

This chapter will deploy the aformentioned early works to answer questions that arise when we look at Walther's analysis of the ego and her theory of social communities. The questions are: What is the reason why individuals want to be part of a social community and why do they want to join with each other to create a social community? The present chapter provides an insight into the issue. In her book *Phänomenologie der Mystik* Walther writes that human beings are not able to live without other human beings. They cannot develop fully if they are not in contact with other beings and if they have no connection with them. In this case Walther describes these human beings as "feral children" who live isolated from human contact. In Walther's view, human beings exist in a physical and soul-spiritual world, which they share with each other (Walther 1976: 54). It is not possible to think of a world consisting of isolated human beings who live on their own. Walther claims that "Human beings are not windowless monads, as Leibniz says" (Walther 1976: 54). Human beings want to be connected with other beings. In light of this argument, this chapter wants to focus on the question why Walther states that individuals want to be connected with other beings and why they strive for this connection. What is the reason for individuals to create a social community? To clarify these questions, we begin with the assumption that Walther understands human beings as social beings. Section "Human Beings as Social and Communal Beings" presents Walther's views on this topic and demonstrates why this assumption is paramount for Walther's theory of social communities. Section "The Constitution of Human Beings" investigates Walther's concept of the human being. The constitution of a human being consists of three parts: the ego or I-center, the self, and the fundamental essence of a human being. In particular, I discuss the parts of the human being that make one strive for being a part of a social community, and I also explore which parts are crucial for making the decision to enter into a social community. Only by examining the individual can we understand why individuals want to be part of a social community. Ultimately, this chapter illustrates a progression, which starts with the assumption that human beings are social beings, who strive to be part of a community and be combined with other individuals. The progression develops with the constitution of a human being and it ends with the arrival at a social community. In the end we find the development from the individual to community justified by the assumption that human beings are social beings and communal beings.

Human Beings as Social and Communal Beings

> Humans are social not because they live in a society. Humans can live in a society because they are already and immediately social within their self-awareness. This means that they each bear an essential psychic similarity with other members of their species. In this way, the social is neither something between humans nor above them, but it is in them, such that the social relation [...] is already completely given in every individual consciousness[1] (Adler 1913: 6).

In Gerda Walther's view, human beings are social and communal beings. To obtain a clearer understanding of Walther's ideas on human beings as social beings, we should examine some of Walther's unpublished manuscripts, which are a part of her *Nachlass* at the Bayerische Staatsbibliothek in Munich, Germany. These unpublished manuscripts are very helpful in understanding Walther's theory of social communities. In one of her unpublished manuscripts titled *Zum Wesen der sozialen Gemeinschaften* (ANA 317, A III, 1.4), Walther refers to the quotation from Max Adler presented at the beginning of this section. She uses this reference to demonstrate that human beings are social and communal beings, who strive for connectedness with other humans. The reason why human beings strive for connectedness with others is itself the condition of the being of humans, as they are social beings.

As Max Adler wrote in his book *Marxistische Probleme* (1913), social behavior [*das Soziale*] is part of the individual human being (Adler 1913: 6). The social as a characteristic of human beings is engrained in every single individual. Hence, society is not the bearer of social life, but is in the individual as a socialized person [*vergesellschafteter Mensch*]. The socialized person is given to herself as a single individual among many who have the same essence. She is a being that is connected with other human beings to form a unity because they have the same kind of spiritual life[2] (Adler 1913: 6). Thus, the human being strives for unity with its psyche

---

[1]"Der Mensch ist sozial, nicht weil er in einer Gesellschaft lebt, sondern er kann in Gesellschaft leben, weil er schon unmittelbar in seinem Selbstbewusstsein sozial ist, das heißt auf die Wesensgleichheit des Psychischen mit seinen Artgenossen bezogen ist. [...] Auf diese Weise ist also das Soziale weder etwas zwischen den Menschen, noch über ihnen, sondern es ist in ihnen, so dass der soziale Zusammenhang, die Gesellschaft als Tatsache, nicht als Begriff, schon in jedem Einzelbewusstsein vollständig gegeben ist" (Adler 1913: 6; translation my own).

[2]"In Wirklichkeit aber scheint mir, dass wir das soziale Leben nirgends anders suchen können, als wo es allein real gegeben ist: und das ist nur im Einzelmenschen der Fall. Nicht die Gesellschaft ist der Träger des sozialen Lebens, sondern nur der Einzelmensch, aber freilich der Einzelmensch, wie wir heute allein noch verstehen können: nämlich der als Einzelmensch zugleich vergesellschaftete Mensch ist, das heißt der bereits aus seinem Ich heraus, aus seinem ganzen psychischen Sein, sich selbst nicht anders gegeben ist wie als ein einzelner unter wesensgleichen vielen, als ein durch

(Adler 1913: 8). The fact that Walther uses these references to Max Adler's work *Marxistische Probleme* clarifies that she has, similar to Adler, views on the constitution of human beings as social beings. Moreover, by referring to Adler's theory, it could be assumed that Walther employs his theory as the basis for her own theories aimed at the clarification of the question of how individuals strive for unity with other individuals. This assumption arises because of another unpublished manuscript by Walther (1917) titled *Soziale Triebe (Noema und Noesis)* (Ana 317, AIII, 1.6). In this manuscript she explains that human beings have a social drive [*sozialen Trieb*], which accounts for why individuals connect with others to form a social community. Social drives are the drives of unification, which aim at unifying different essences within other human beings. Walther describes them as follows, "[Social drives] looking for 'kindred souls'; [they] aim at similar essences in other human beings" (Ana 317, AIII, 1.6). Furthermore, she argues that the type of social community depends on the type of essence toward which the social drive is directed. With the help of these drives, individuals look for other human beings who have similar characteristics. As we will see later in this chapter, these social drives are the precursors of Walther's concept of inner joining or unification. Only by possessing these social drives is it possible for individuals to join with others and to be a part of a social community. This aspect will become relevant for section "The Development from the Individual to the "We"" in terms of understanding how individuals form a social community.

The Constitution of Human Beings

This section discusses Walther's concept of the human being, which is necessary to understanding human beings as social beings. In her work *Phänomenologie der Mystik*, Walther decides to analyze the inner structure of human beings. In her view human beings, especially persons, consist of three parts: the ego or I-center, the self, and the fundamental essence of a human being.[3] Persons also have a lived body, which, in Walther's view, is not something necessary for the essence of a person. Therefore, Walther focuses on these three aspects of a person.

(a) *Ego or I-Center*

Walther starts her exploration with the ego or I-center. The ego is something that lives and has lived experiences, it has consciousness, and it is directed, or it can be directed toward different objects. Every single object is experienced intentionally and has its own sense (Walther 1922: 2). The ego is the one who experiences. As Walther observes:

die gleiche Art des geistigen Lebens mit seinen Artgenossen zu einer Einheit verbundenes Wesen" (Adler 1913: 6; translation my own).

[3]In her book *Phänomenologie der Mystik*, Walther only focuses on persons. How Walther defines the concept of the person in this work is unclear. She does not extensively explain the concept. Although I deploy the term "person" in this chapter, I cannot here undertake a full exposition of the concept in Walther's corpus.

> [There] is a 'point-zero' [*Nullpunkt*] inside me, a point that radiates my experiences, which seems to be sitting inwardly in the head [...], which focuses on objects of any kind in a conscious way while I experience. We want to call this 'point' I-point or the I-center. [...] It is the experienced starting point of our consciousness, our aiming at objects in a conscious way, whatsoever nature this aiming may be (thinking, desiring, loving, hating or whatever)[4] (Walther 1976: 36).

According to Walther, the ego is capable of intentionality. Walther distinguishes two different kinds of conscious beings that are directed toward objects: namely, psychic and spiritual being. Both experience consciousness in different ways and the ego plays different roles in each form of being. Psychical beings, such as animals, experience lived experiences in a random way: The lived experiences occur, and the ego is directed to them, or the ego is directed at a lived experience and a new lived experience arises, such that the ego switches to the new lived experience (Walther 1976: 36–38). Spiritual beings, such as human beings, on the other hand, have more abilities. In Walther's view, spiritual beings use the moment of attention or concentration to focus on certain lived experiences. For example, someone looks out of the window and observes passing pedestrians indifferently and disinterestedly. Suddenly, this person discovers someone who could be an acquaintance, and she directs her attention to that person on the street. Walther observes, "Here it is, as if the ego draws itself together internally, draws its own forces [...] together from all directions in which its attention was fragmented, as it intensifies its inner gaze with which it is directed to the objects"[5] (Walther 1976: 38). The fact that the ego turns its attention in this example is a special act of the ego. It differs from the mere act of being directed to an object and from the circumstance of being flooded with a lived experience (Walther 1976: 38). This is the starting point for spiritual beings because the ego is performing a free action in that moment. It is the beginning of self-determination insofar as the ego is free and distinct from its lived experiences. It has the opportunity to choose an object that receives the attention of the ego. The conscious I can take a stand vis-à-vis the object. Walther remarks, "that the ego turns its attention in a deliberate manner is a seed of freedom, thereby a seed of self-determination of the ego towards the lived experiences and its contents. Therefore, it is a starting point of the spirit"[6] (Walther 1976: 39). The second and third differences between

[4]"[Da ist] ein "Nullpunkt" in meinem Inneren [...], gleichsam der Ausstrahlungspunkt meines Erlebens, der wie im Kopf innerlich zu sitzen scheint [...], der sich bei allem meinem Erleben bewusstseinsmäßig auf alle möglichen Gegenstände [...], richtet. Diesen "Punkt" wollen wir den Ichpunkt oder das Ichzentrum nennen. [...] [Er ist der] erlebte Ausgangspunkt unseres Bewusstseins, unseres bewusstseinsmäßigen Hinzielens auf die Gegenstände [...], wie auch immer dies innere Hinzielen sonst noch geartet sein mag (denkend, begehrend, liebend, hassend oder wie sonst)" (Walther 1976: 36; translation my own).

[5]"Hier ist es, als ziehe sich das Ich selbst gleichsam innerlich zusammen, ziehe seine eigenen Kräfte [...] in sich aus allen Richtungen, in die seine Aufmerksamkeit zersplittert war, zusammen, als intensiviere es seinen inneren Blick, mit dem es sich auf die Gegenstände richtet" (Walther 1976: 38).

[6]"[...] die absichtliche Aufmerksamkeitszuwendung ist ein Keim der Freiheit, damit ein Keim der Selbstbestimmung des Ich gegenüber den Erlebnissen und ihren Inhalten, damit ein Ansatzpunkt des Geistes" (Walther 1976: 39; translation my own).

psychical and spiritual beings lie in the concept of self-awareness and the idea that spiritual beings have a spiritual core, which Walther calls a spiritual essence. According to Walther, self-awareness is an ability of spiritual beings. It is the capacity to pull the ego out from its lived experiences to rise above them and to focus on these lived experiences in self-awareness. The action of being directed toward an object in self-awareness can happen in recognizing, judging, hating (self-hatred), loving, etc. Nonetheless, this ability for self-awareness is not sufficient for the ego in itself to be absolutely free of its lived experiences because it is conceivable that the ego thinks about the lived experience while experiencing it, becoming completely absorbed by the current of lived experience. Therefore, the ego needs the moment of will power [*Willensselbstmacht*] (Walther 1976: 42–44) to break the force of the absorption.

The last difference between psychical and spiritual beings is that the latter have a spiritual core, a spiritual essence, which can experience spiritual realities outside of itself. Walther states that spiritual objects can only be detected by spiritual beings, whereas psychical beings are not able to experience them. Walther maintains:

> To the human person, a being who is also spiritually determined, belongs an I-center, which can withdraw itself from the psychic, [...] [and] this inner psychological-spiritual area, which gives the ego a "solid ground" from which the internal psychic structure can be judged and evaluated, especially within the framework of higher values, can shape "itself"[7] (Walther 1976: 46).

The meaning of this spiritual essence will be discussed later when I take up the different fundamental essences of a person.

(b) *The Self*

Walther starts her analysis of the self with a comparison:

> If we compare the human person with an ancient lamp, the I-center is related to a burning wick, which turns its light outwards and illuminates the surroundings. The wick floats on the flammable liquid from which it draws its force to shine, [and] to burn. Within this liquid it can move more or less freely. This corresponds to the "subconscious," the inward psychic "embedding," the "self" [...]. If the flame is calm, the liquid clear enough, the light is able to shine into it, brighten it, so that one is able to see how it is arranged inside [...]. Everything is surrounded by a vessel, the lamp in a narrow sense, it resembles the lived body in which we are seated as psychological-mental beings[8] (Walther 1976: 47).

---

[7]"Zu der menschlichen Person, also einem Wesen, das auch geistig bestimmt ist, gehört neben dem Ichzentrum, das sich dem seelischen Getriebe entziehen kann, [...], zweifellos dieser innere seelisch-geistige Bereich, der dem Ich auch den "festen Grund" geben dürfte, von dem aus es das innere Getriebe beurteilen und bewerten, im Sinne höherer Werte "sich selbst" gestalten kann" (Walther 1976: 46; translation my own).

[8]"Vergleichen wir die menschliche Person mit einer altertümlichen Lampe, so ist das Ichzentrum dem brennenden Docht verwandt, der sein Licht zunächst nach außen sendet und die Umgebung erhellt. Der Docht schwimmt auf der brennenden Flüssigkeit [...], aus der er seine Kraft, zu leuchten, zu brennen, schöpft. Innerhalb dieser Flüssigkeit kann er mehr oder weniger frei sich bewegen. Diese entspricht dem "Unterbewusstsein", der innerseelischen "Einbettung", dem "Selbst", [...]. Ist die Flamme ruhig, die Flüssigkeit klar genug, so vermag das Licht auch in sich hinein zu leuchten, sie zu erhellen, so dass man zu erkennen vermag, wie sie im Inneren beschaffen ist [...]. Das Ganze ist von einem Gefäß umschlossen, eben der Lampe im engeren Sinn, sie gleicht dem Leib, in den wir als seelisch-geistige Wesen hineingesenkt sind" (Walther 1976: 47; translation my own).

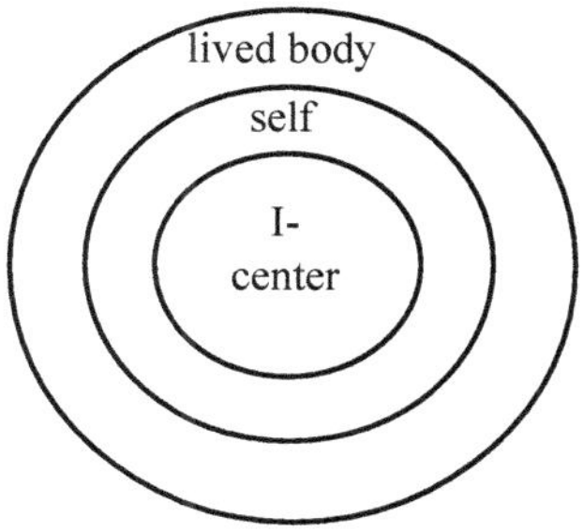

Fig. 1 Relation between lived body, self, and I-center

Walther demonstrates that the I-center takes its force from the self, which is an inward psychic background in which the ego is embedded (Walther 1976: 47; Resch 1983: 38). Usually, the I-center is directed to the external world, to objects, which lie outside the person, but it is also possible that the I-center is directed inward toward the self. According to Walther, "we have an experiencing ego in the foreground of consciousness that is embedded in an inward psychic background *a tergo* [from behind], in a manner that cannot be defined conceptually"[9] (Walther 1976: 51). Within this background various lived experiences flow to the ego. Within some spheres of this background, inner total settings are given, from which single lived experiences of the current of lived experiences rise[10] (Walther 1976: 51). Figure 1 illustrates the relation between the lived body, the I-center, and the self.

(c) *The Fundamental Essence of a Person*

In addition to the ego an d the self, there is equally a fundamental essence of a person. The essence is the soul-spiritual core of the personality of a person (Walther 1976: 49). The question that Walther wishes to answer is: How can we recognize or grasp the essence of a person? In Walther's view it is not sufficient to recognize or grasp the essence in an indirect way, for example, by investigating lived experiences and the objects toward which they are directed (Walther 1976: 49). Walther claims that there must be a direct way to grasp the essence of a person. The problem here is that not every lived experience arises from the essence of a person. Furthermore, the personal essence need not show itself in every lived experience. Since the essence is shown only in certain lived experiences, it can only be examined with the help of an analysis of its background [*Hintergrundsanalyse*] and an investigation of its source or foundation [*Quellgrunduntersuchung*] (Walther 1976: 51). This analysis demonstrates that not every lived experience that is immersed in the foundation of

[9] "Wir haben da ein erlebendes [...] Ich im Vordergrundsbewusstsein, das in einer nicht näher begrifflich festzulegenden Weise in einen innerseelischen Hintergrund "a tergo" eingebettet ist" (Walther 1976: 51; translation my own).

[10] "Aus diesem Hintergrund strömen dem Ich in verschiedener Weise alle möglichen Erlebnisse zu, in die verschiedenen Sphären dieser Einbettung scheinen die inneren Gesamteinstellungen eingesenkt zu sein, aus denen die einzelnen Erlebnisse des Erlebnisstromes sich jeweils emporheben" (Walther 1976: 51; translation my own).

the person [*Quellgrund*] leads back to the essence. To understand the concept of the fundamental essence in a better way, Walther compares it to the center of a sphere:

> If we illustrate the fundamental essence as the center of a sphere, as if they [the lived experiences] flowed out either from the center point as a radius that extends from the center to the periphery of the sphere or from any point that lies on the radius within this sphere, but not from the center itself, one might perhaps say that all these kinds of lived experiences can emerge from the fundamental essence, but not all individual lived experiences of this kind actually do in all cases[11] (Walther 1976: 94).

There exist other sources for lived experiences besides the fundamental essence, which is the reason why it is hard to delineate which lived experiences emerge from the fundamental essence of a person and which do not (Walther 1976: 52).

Walther proceeds to explain the various sides of a fundamental essence. The fundamental essence consists of three parts: body, soul, and spirit (Walther 1976: 94). Depending on the part focused on, the fundamental essence is represented in a different way (Walther 1976: 97). However, they are all interwoven and mutually imbricated (Walther 1976: 95). The essence as a body is the most concrete, most obvious [*sinnfälligste*], and the lowest aspect of a personality (Walther 1976: 100). The bodily side of the essence interacts intensively with the soul without being identical to the former (Resch 1983: 41). Along with the bodily side of the essence, there is the fundamental essence as a soul, which includes the area within a human being that can be situated between the bodily side and the spiritual side (Resch 1983: 41). The soul shows itself in lived feelings and emotional lived experiences, as well as in wishing and striving [*im Wollen und Streben*] (Walther 1976: 111). These lived experiences rise sensibly from below, as from the heart (Walther 1976: 112). The last side is the fundamental essence as a spirit. This side is a spiritual sphere of light, which is inside a human being. It points beyond itself to a spiritual, primordial source. The human being experiences himself under certain circumstances as a part of a spiritual world (Walther 1976: 122). This essence as a spirit enables a spiritual being to experience a spiritual reality that lies beyond the person's own being (Resch 1983: 40). With this explanation of the person and its particularities, Walther comes to the conclusion that a human person comes to full development when she strives for harmony between her body and her soul-spiritual existence (Resch 1983: 43). Even if Walther describes the spiritual aspect of the fundamental essence as something higher, which only human beings possess, it is not possible to grasp the fundamental essence only in terms of objective spirit. Spirit requires an object that arouses the lived experiences that emerge from the fundamental essence through which the ego attains its own recognition (Walther 1976: 131). Therefore, the existence of a non-

---

[11] "Es ist, wenn wir uns das Grundwesen als den Mittelpunkt einer Kugel veranschaulichen, als strömten sie aus dem Mündungspunkte eines vom Zentrum kommenden Radius in der Oberfläche, oder aus irgendeinem noch weiter innen auf einem Radius gelegenen Punkte im Inneren der Kugel hervor, aber nicht aus dem Mittelpunkt selbst. Man könnte also vielleicht sagen, dass alle diese Erlebnisarten aus dem Grundwesen hervorgehen können, aber nicht alle Einzelerlebnisse dieser Art das auch tatsächlich in bestimmten Einzelfällen immer tun" (Walther 1976: 94; translation my own).

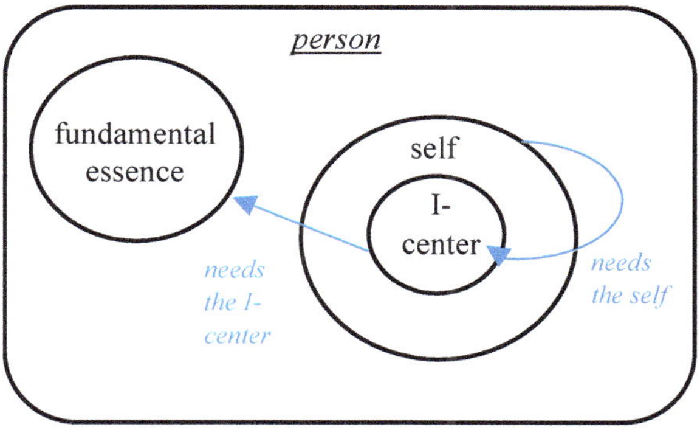

Fig. 2 Relation between I-center, self, and fundamental essence

ego is necessary to grasp the fundamental essence of a person. The non-ego serves as a contrast or a counterpart:

> First, the total dedication of human beings to a transcendent inner or external "otherworldly" object is necessary in learning, viewing, loving, valuing, [etc.] and [this object itself] is the first and supreme precondition for seeing its own fundamental essence[12] (Walther 1976: 133).

But, the presence of the non-ego, which can be other human beings or other objects of the external world, is only the essential genetic precondition for directly grasping the fundamental essence. Looking back at the fundamental essence as the source of lived experiences, a human being can see its fundamental essence in an unveiled and original way (Walther 1976: 133).

As we have seen in this section, Walther analyzes the constitution of a person and divides it into three parts: the ego or I-center, the self, and the fundamental essence of a person. In conclusion, it can be said that the I-center takes its force from the self, which is an inner, psychic background in which the ego is embedded. The fundamental essence, however, is the soul-spiritual core of the personality of a human being, which can only be grasped with the help of the non-ego. It requires self-awareness, and self-determination or self-power of the I-center, so that it can realize itself and become what it is supposed to become[13] (Walther 1976: 135). The I-center, however, is independent of the fundamental essence (Walther 1976: 137). Figure 2 represents the relation between the I-center, the self, and the fundamental essence of a person.

---

[12]"Zunächst ist [...] die völlige Hingabe des Menschen an einen transzendenten innerlich oder äußerlich "jenseitigen" Gegenstand in Wissen, Schauen, Lieben, Werten und dergleichen und damit dieser selbst die erste und oberste Vorbedingung für seine Erschauung des eignen Grundwesens" (Walther 1976: 133; translation my own).

[13]"Tatsächlich liegt die Sache so, dass beim Menschen als Person, als personalem Wesen, das Grundwesen eben der Selbsterkenntnis und Selbstbestimmtung, Selbtsmacht des Ichzentrums bedarf, um das zu warden, was in ihm angelegt ist, um sich selbst zu verwirklichen" (Walther 1976, 135; translation my own).

The Development from the Individual to the "We"

In Walther's view the development from the individual to the "we" takes place in the context of social communities. The individual enters into one or more social communities and becomes a part of the "we." As we have already seen, there are two reasons why individuals want to enter into social communities. The first reason is the predisposition of human beings for community: Human beings have social drives (*soziale Triebe*) that lead us to strive for the connection with other human beings who have similar essences. The second reason is the fundamental essence of a person: The human being needs a non-ego for developing and recognizing its own personality. It can do this by connecting itself with other human beings to recognize or grasp its own fundamental essence. Other human beings are perceived in terms of contrast, thereby rendering possible a comparison with other human beings. Let us now explore how a social community is created, and how individuals become a part of the "we."

Inner Joining or Inner Unification

The individual connects with others to form a social community through the concept of inner joining or inner unification. This concept is the essential characteristic of a social community. For the establishment of a social community, however, the following conditions must be satisfied. First, social communities must exist between human beings. Second, the members of social communities must know each other. Third, they are in an intentional correlation with each other. Finally, the members of a social community are related to an intentional object. These conditions form the basis of a life in common (Walther 1922: 29–30). If the conditions are fulfilled, the members of a community live together. Although these are preconditions for a social community, the essential characteristic is the concept of inner joining. It is a feeling of togetherness and belonging. It is a feeling and not an act of cognition [*Erkenntnisakt*] or judgment [*Urteil*][14] (Walther 1922: 34). Walther describes inner joining as a peculiar inner-psychological connection [*inner-seelisches Sich-verbinden*] with an intentional object:

> This unification is, at first, a present lived experience, an act emanating from the I-point in which it lives now. The I-point stretches toward its object of unification and connects with it in a more or less powerful, warm and intense stream of feeling that emerges from the background, enters into the ego, [...] and now brings it to the object of unification in

[14]"Ein Gefühl sagten wir, es ist also nicht ein Erkenntnisakt oder ein Urteil, wie wenn etwa jedes Mitglied der Gemeinschaft (innerlich oder äußerlich-ausdrücklich) feststellte oder behauptete, dass es nun diese anderen Mitglieder als zu sich gehörig betrachtet, sich mit ihnen für vebunden hält [...]" (Walther 1922: 34; translation my own).

> an intentional way. The ego persists, then, in a continuous calm as long as the unification lasts[15] (Walther 1922: 35).

This present unification is the starting point for creating a social community. Nonetheless, the individual's desire to join others is not sufficient for the constitution of a community. It is required that every subject wants to join with all the other members of a community so that there is a reciprocal effect of one member on the other (Walther 1922: 63; Calcagno 2012: 94). Thus, it can be stated that a social community is constituted by inner joining of individuals. Importantly, only the reciprocal effect of inner joining is what Walther calls a "social community." The special feature of Walther's concept, however, is that the present unification can become a habitual one. That means that the ego is no longer constantly directed to its intentional object of unification (Walther 1922: 38). But, how can the present unification become a habitual one? Walther explains:

> Something quite particular takes place there! It is as if the current of unification flowed back into the center of feelings, as though the current were objectively saturated [...] and this current is taken into the spiritual subject, behind the I-point, into the very sources of these lived experiences in the self[16] (Walther 1922: 39).

The lived experience of the unification takes its object mentally and intentionally into the self (Walther 1922: 41). Thus, the individual experiences the present unification with another individual and either enters into a social community or creates one. In the case of habitual unification the individual carries the other in herself such that she remains connected, even if the ego is directed to other objects. This act of inner joining, however, can be carried out because of the predisposition that human beings have for social drives. They are the reason why human beings strive for connectedness with others and they are the precondition for inner joining.

We-Experiences

The aforementioned concept of we-experiences is important for the continuance of a social community. Only through such lived experiences does the individual become a part of the social community. We-experiences arise by living in a social community, as well as by means of reciprocal inner joining between individuals. They derive from a

---

[15]"Es ist diese Einigung zunächst ein aktuelles Erlebnis, ein vom Ich-"Punkt" ausgehender Akt, in dem er jetzt lebt. Der Ich-"Punkt" streckt sich hier hin zu seinem Einigungsobjekt und verbindet sich mit ihm in einem mehr oder weniger wuchtigen, warmen und intensiven Gefühls"strom", der, aus dem Hintergrund auftauchend, in das Ich eingeht [...] und es nun intentional zum Einigungsobjekt hinträgt. In diesem verharrt dann das Ich seelisch in kontinuierlicher Ruhe solange die Einigung dauert" (Walther 1922: 35; translation my own).

[16]"Es ist etwas ganz Eigentümliches, das sich da abspielt! Es ist, als flute der Einigungsstrom wieder zurück ins Gefühlszentrum, als wäre er nun aber von einem Etwas an seinem Gegenstand durchtränkt [...] und dies würde nun mitgenommen in das psychische Subjekt hinein, "hinter" den Ich-Punkt, in die Quelle dieses Erlebnisses im Selbst" (Walther 1922: 39; translation my own).

common layer within a social community, which Walther calls *Gemeinschafts-Selbst* [the communal self] (Walther 1922: 74). We-experiences mean that every individual can receive experiences of others within themselves by inner joining. Walther gives an account of the way we-experiences operate:

> [M]y experiences are actually lived in my I-center, they stream toward it from my consciousness-background, from my self, in which my I is embedded. Though in this embedment, in this background, from which these lived experiences arise, I am not alone as "myself" [...] but I have taken the others inside into the background, I intentionally received them beyond my I-center in my self (or they grew up in it by themselves) and I feel myself at one, I feel myself joined with them (unconsciously, automatically or because of an explicit joining)[17] (Walther 1922: 71; Caminada 2014: 205).

Furthermore, Walther observes:

> I live and experience at the same time through myself and through them in me, through "us." Well before these experiences come to the fore of the I-point, before they are actualized, they are lived experiences of the community, because they already arise as motions [stirrings] from me and the others in me (Walther 1922: 71).[18]

To understand how present we-experiences arise from inner joining, Walther carries out a structural analysis, which consists of four steps that form the whole of we-experiences:

1. Experience of "A", who is intentionally directed toward an object;
1a. Experience of "B", who is similarly intentionally directed toward the same object.
2. Empathic experience of "A", who empathizes with the experience of "B" (1a);
2a. Empathic experience of "B", who empathizes with the experience of "A" (1).
3. Joining act of "A" with the act of "B" (or with him) whom "A" empathically experiences;
3a. Joining act of "B" with the act of "A" (or with him) whom "B" empathically experiences.
4. Empathic experience of "B", who experiences that "A" has joined his act (or him);
4a. Empathic experience of "A", who experiences that "B" has joined his act (or him) (Caminada 2014: 207; Schmid 2012: 132; Walther 1922: 85).

---

[17]"[M]eine Erlebnisse vollziehen sich aktuell in meinem Ichzentrum, sie strömen ihm aus meinem Bewußtseinhintergrund, meinem Selbst, in das es eingebettet ist, zu. Doch in dieser Einbettung, in diesem Hintergrund, aus dem diese Erlebnisse hervorgehen, bin nicht nur ich allein als "ich selbst"—bei dem Gemeinschaftserlebnissen, sondern ich habe die anderen ja mit in ihn hereingenommen, ich habe sie hinter meinem Ichzentrum in mein Selbst intentional aufgenommen (oder sie sind von selbst hineingewachsen) und ich fühle mich eins mit ihnen (unbewußt, automatisch oder auf Grund einer ausdrücklichen Einigung)" (translated by Emanuele Caminada, see Caminada 2014).

[18]"Ich lebe und erlebe aus mir selbst und aus ihnen in mir zugleich heraus, aus "Uns". Schon ehe diese Erlebnisse in den Ichpunkt eintreten, in ihm aktualisiert werden, sind sie also Gemeinschafterlebnisse, denn sie entspringen ja schon als Regungen aus mir und den anderen in mir" (translated by Emanuele Caminada, see Caminada 2014).

Walther seeks to show that each experiencing individual should experience inner joining with other persons as well as grasp empathically the lived experiences of another person so that everyone has the lived experiences of others inside themselves (Walther 1922: 85). However, only the habitual inner joining consolidates a community life. This inner joining is a habitual resting in one another as members of a community (Walther 1922: 69). This is the reason why social communities can exist for a long time. Through two aspects of social community (namely, inner joining and we-experiences) the individual enters or creates a social community and becomes a continuous part of it. But, only the habitual moment makes the social community a stable unit.[19]

Conclusion

The aim of this chapter was to demonstrate that Walther's idea of a social and communal being is the basis for her analysis of a social community. Walther understands the human being as a being who is social and strives to connect with other human beings. Her analysis of the constitution of human beings has shown that, on the one hand, human beings have a natural disposition, which Walther calls social drives, to be connected with others. On the other hand, human beings need a non-ego to develop and recognize their own personalities, and this non-ego can be other human beings. The section titled "The Development from the Individual to the "We"" explained the transition from the individual to the "we," which in Walther's view is only possible in the context of a social community. There exists the development from the individual to the social community, and thus to the "we," which is activated by the nature of human beings as social beings.

References

Adler, Max. (1913). *Marxistische Probleme: Beiträge zur Theorie der materialistischen Geschichtsauffassung und Dialektik*. Stuttgart: J.H.W. Dietz.

Calcagno, Antonio. (2012). Gerda Walther: On the possibility of a passive sense of community and the inner time consciousness of community. *Symposium, 16*(2), 89–105.

Caminada, Emanuele. (2014). Joining the background: Habitual sentiments behind we-intentionality. In A. K. Ziv & H. B. Schmid (Eds.), *Institutions, emotions, and group agents: Contributions to social ontology* (pp. 195–212). London: Springer.

Resch, Andreas. (1983). *Gerda Walther*. Innsbruck: Resch.

Schmid, Hans B. (2012). *Wir-Intentionalität: Kritik des ontologischen Individualismus und Rekonstruktion der Gemeinschaft* (2nd ed.). Freiburg: Karl Alber.

Walther, Gerda (1917). *Die sozialen Triebe (Noema und Noesis)*. Ana 317, AIII, 1.6. Munich: Bayerische Staatsbibliothek. Unpublished manuscript.

[19]For more information about the constitution of a social community see Julia Mühl (forthcoming). "Meaning of Individuals within Communities: Gerda Walther and Edith Stein on the Constitution of Social Communities", in R. Hagengruber and S. Luft (eds.), *Women Phenomenologists on Social Ontology: We-Experiences, Communal Life, and Joint Action* (Dordrecht: Springer).

Walther, Gerda. (1922). *Ein Beitrag zur Ontologie der sozialen Gemeinschaften. Mit einem Anhang zur Phänomenologie der sozialen Gemeinschaft*. Max Niemeyer: Halle.
Walther, Gerda (1976). *Phänomenologie der Mystik* (3rd ed.). Olten: Walter Verlag.
Walther, Gerda (n.d.). *Zum Wesen der sozialen Gemeinschaften*. Ana 317, AIII, 1.4. Munich: Bayerische Staatsbibliothek. Unpublished manuscript.

Julia Mühl is a doctoral candidate and works as a Research Assistant at Paderborn University. She started her studies in the teaching and research area of the History of Women Philosophers and Scientists. She is completing her PhD on Gerda Walther's dissertation *Ein Beitrag zur Ontologie der sozialen Gemeinschaften* (1921). She has given lectures and written papers on such topics as Walther's concept of a social community, inner joining, and the ego. She also specializes in early phenomenology and social ontology. From 2016 to 2017 she was managing director of the Center for the History of Women Philosophers and Scientists funded by the Ministry of Culture and Science of the German State of North Rhine-Westphalia at Paderborn University.

Körper, Leib, Gemüt, Seele, Geist: Conceptions of the Self in Early Phenomenology

Christina M. Gschwandtner

Abstract This chapter considers conceptions of the self in three early phenomenological thinkers: Hedwig Conrad-Martius, Edith Stein, and Gerda Walther. Although colleagues or students of Husserl and influenced by his phenomenology, they developed their own phenomenology of the human person in explicit opposition to Husserl's more "idealist" turn. They remain, however, virtually unknown today in philosophical circles. This chapter seeks to retrieve their philosophies of the human being and suggests that their particular phenomenological approach still has much to teach us, especially in the context of the conversation about the "self after the subject" and the question of inter-subjectivity.

Keywords Phenomenology · Person · Hedwig Conrad-Martius · Edith Stein Gerda Walther

The early phenomenological movement inspired by Edmund Husserl in Göttingen and Freiburg included several prominent women. Hedwig Conrad-Martius was the leader of a phenomenological working group in Göttingen, later joined by Edith Stein, who was the first person to receive her doctorate under Husserl just after his move to Freiburg. Gerda Walther originally studied with Alexander Pfänder in Munich and then came to Freiburg to work with Husserl, while Stein was his assistant. While other students of Husserl, such as Martin Heidegger and Eugen Fink have received far more attention, these female thinkers have been unjustly neglected, although they did not slavishly follow Husserl, appropriating his method with no less critique and

---

C. M. Gschwandtner (✉)
Fordham University, New York, NY, USA
e-mail: gschwandtner@fordham.edu

A. Calcagno (ed.), *Gerda Walther's Phenomenology of Sociality, Psychology, and Religion*, Women in the History of Philosophy and Sciences 2,
https://doi.org/10.1007/978-3-319-97592-4_7

creativity than Heidegger or Fink.[1] Walther and Conrad-Martius have barely been translated into English and Stein's phenomenological writings have been dwarfed by the religious interest in her conversion and martyrdom in Auschwitz-Birkenau. Yet, not only were they among the most active early phenomenologists—and taken seriously by Husserl, Max Scheler, Adolf Reinach, and Roman Ingarden—but all three also develop a unique phenomenological perspective on human subjectivity, analyzing it in far more detail than Husserl himself did, at least in his works published at the time. This chapter will lay out their phenomenological approaches to the human self and suggest that they provide important insights that may well complicate the—predominantly French—obsession with refiguring the "self" that "comes after the subject."[2]

Gerda Walther

We will begin with Walther because her analysis is the most straightforward.[3] She devotes several chapters in her *Phänomenologie der Mystik* to the human person, trying to ascertain its most basic nature (*Grundwesen*) to give an account of experience, including the ability to distinguish between self-generated experience and experience that comes from elsewhere. Walther treats the I (*das Ich*) as the center of experience (*des Erlebens*). We experience ourselves first in our experience of the world, which makes a core of the "self" separate from the world difficult to distinguish. Yet, the self-reference of experiencing assumes a basic, internal "zero point of orientation" (*Nullpunkt*) that is directed toward the experience and illuminates it. She calls this the "I-point" or "I-center."[4] We can distinguish between the *experience* of the I and the *I* having or undergoing the experience (that is, we can examine both

[1]It is hard to tell to what extent gender plays a role here, but it is revealing that Jean Héring, for example, who was instrumental in introducing phenomenology to France, extensively refers to Conrad-Martius in his explication of phenomenology and speaks of her in the most positive terms, yet only Scheler, Husserl, and later Heidegger find a voice in France; the women phenomenologists are entirely ignored. This is obviously just as true of the Anglophone appropriation, where Husserl and Heidegger play an outsize role and Stein, Walther, and Conrad-Martius are virtually unknown. Both Stein and Walther attempted to pursue *Habilitation* with Husserl, but he stymied both efforts, apparently supportive of the banning of women from professorships at German universities at the time.

[2]The title of an important collection edited by Eduardo Cadava and Jean-Luc Nancy, trans. as *Who Comes after the Subject?* (London: Routledge, 1991).

[3]Much of Walther's work is unpublished and languishes in archives. I rely here on her main work *Phänomenologie der Mystik* (Olten: Walter Verlag, 1955 [1923]). She was encouraged by Conrad-Martius to present a second revised edition.

[4]That is, the *Ichpunkt* or *Ichzentrum* (Walther, *Phänomenologie*, 36). She compares this "center of the I" repeatedly throughout the book to an oil-lamp with a burning wick (see Walther, *Phänomenologie*, 47 for first mention). Sometimes, one wick can be fed by the liquid of two separate lamps or the oil of two lamps can flow into each other if they become connected or two wicks can be found in one lamp. These metaphors illustrate various ways in which one consciousness can interact with another (through telepathy and mystical experience).

its noetic and its noematic pole). Experiences are both generated by this core of the self or come to it and affect it from the "outside." In various conscious acts, the I can exercise attention or effort, which point to its spirit (*Geist*) as a free experience of intentionality or self-determination. It can also suppress experiences or ignore them; thus, although it may not be able to generate certain experiences at will, it does have an influence over experiences that come to it, at least regarding the attitude with which it approaches them. Consciousness can direct itself intentionally toward experience in manifold ways. Consciousness has to be "present" in some way to what we experience (that is, it has to be "corporeal" to feel corporeal sensation, be "spiritual" to discern the movements of spirit; Walther, *Phänomenologie*, 45). The human being therefore has "ein geistig-seelisch-leibliches Grundwesen," unlike animals or other beings (Walther, *Phänomenologie*, 46). The human psyche can also be open to the experiences of others, which can be experienced within oneself as someone else's psyche intruding upon one's own. After establishing this possibility (of interacting with others, whether dead or alive, human or not), she goes on to examine more fully the basic being (*Grundwesen*) of the self: as *Leib* [body], as *Seele* [soul], and as *Geist* in Chaps. 8, 9, and 10, respectively.

Walther suggests that only some experiences come out of the ground of our being, from its source (*Quelle*) or core (*Kern*). To distinguish the kinds of experience that proceed from this core, she demarcates three aspects of the self, which belong together and are not easily separated.[5] The corporeal ground of being as *Leib* (not *Körper*) should not be understood either as a prison of the soul or as the only "real" self.[6] *Leib* is not pure material, but a living entity. Yet, *Leib* is only truly itself when it is thoroughly permeated by both soul and spirit. She suggests that this often happens naturally in children, while adults tend to withdraw the spirit into the head or mind and only send it out into other parts of the body on occasion. Something similar can occur with a soul confined to the heart rather than being poured out over the entire body. This leads to a battle between the three parts, in which each goes its own way and the *Ichzentrum* constantly has to alternate between them. Sometimes, one part is lost entirely, either suffocated or withered away (for example, if the *Leib* has become the only center of being, one becomes obsessed with food, sex, or bodily prowess as in sports). She also distinguishes between different ways of permeation: the soul permeates the body in terms of light (*Durchleuchtung/Durchseelung*), while the spirit "glows" (*Durchstrahlung/Durchgeistigung*).[7]

---

[5]Walther, *Phänomenologie*, 95. She tries several times to distinguish the human from the animal. She admits "soul" (that is, emotion, affectivity) for animals, but not mind or spirit (*Geist*). At the same time, she contends that whole eras or people might have lacked *Geist* entirely and that it only awakes slowly in young people (that is, it must be cultivated and is not there as a naturally occurring gift; Walther, *Phänomenologie*, 96). Although "spiritual" experience might be especially attuned to it, she does not seem to think of it as limited to such experience.

[6]That is, thinking of the soul as a mirage and the spirit as evanescent.

[7]She also contends that the Greeks and their ideas of beauty perfectly understood the way in which the soul permeates the lived body, but they ignored the higher permeation of the ensouled body by the spirit (Walther, *Phänomenologie*, 102). Beauty is the expression of such illumination of the body by soul and spirit: they are fully interwoven into the body (Walther, *Phänomenologie*, 103).

The second ground of being of the self is the soul, which refers to the "psychic" reality of the self.[8] This includes desire, emotion, affect, even rudimentary thinking.[9] Feelings like love or joy can ascend from the very depth of one's being, seemingly from the "heart" but certainly not from the body. This source of feeling is "essentially different" in the manifestation of its phenomenality from the physical heart.[10] Encounters with a beloved person or with something highly valued call forth distinct experiences in the "heart" (or soul). The self enters into the experience internally; she describes this as a sort of submerging into the feeling to its very core where one suddenly grasps its source and manner in consciousness in a kind of "flash" (*blitzartig*).[11] Although the object of this feeling need not be present to perception but can be imagined or remembered, the I is turned toward it, devoted to it, lies or even "rests" in it.[12] This is hence a living, bodily (*leibhaft*) experience of the soul as *Grundwesen*.[13] Such feeling can be colored by the particularity of the person experiencing it. It allows subject and object to coincide in a way that leads to the ground of the self as soul. She identifies this also as the source of the "aura" of a person in occult experiences (Walther, *Phänomenologie*, 117).

Finally, the self can be experienced as *Geist*. This "higher self" has to be distinguished from the lower self (the soul) or the bodily self. It is not identical to the *Ichzentrum*.[14] *Geist* is concerned with willing and valuing, hence not reducible to the intellect. She illustrates this notion of "spirit" with the sudden illumination of clarity when trying to resolve a difficult problem, whether this be purely academic or of a moral nature. After a crisis, the I might also experience itself in this special light without being focused on a particular object. This is an experience of one's own spiritual essence as such (that is, one experiences "seine eigene geistige Wesenheit gleichsam 'an sich'"; Walther, *Phänomenologie*, 121). The center of the self is no longer "embedded" into an I serving as the spectator of consciousness, but is freed into an inner realm of light. Experiences no longer call forth the I, but they are illuminated through the I. Although these streams of light have their source in the I

[8]This is also present in animals. (She admits that one might prefer using a different terminology for the two realities.)

[9]That is, experiences of feeling or affect (*Gemüts- und Gefühlserlebnisse*) manifest or point to the basic being (*Grundwesen*) of the soul.

[10]She appeals to telepathic experiences as phenomenological evidence for this, as well as experiences of prayer or meditation in various religious traditions. She cites several Sufi sources (Walther, *Phänomenologie*, 112–113).

[11]She argues that "*je mehr er sich seinem Gegenstand hingibt, desto tiefer versinkt sein Ichzentrum in den Quellgrund jener Gefühle*" (Walther, *Phänomenologie*, 114; emphasis hers).

[12]"Nur das Erlebnis, das Gefühl selbst muß leibhaftig und ursprünglich erlebt werden" (Walther, *Phänomenologie*, 115).

[13]This lightning flash of insight into the self (*Selbstschau*), generated by reaching the core or source (*Quelle*) of the experience, lasts only for a moment, otherwise it would become narcissism or insanity. She argues that self-love is only permitted as or through love of others or as the recognition of being created by a loving God who endows it with value (Walther, *Phänomenologie*, 116).

[14]"Die Welt des Geistigen ist eine Region für sich, der auch das geistige Grundwesen des Menschen angehört." Es "*ist aber streng zu unterscheiden vom Ichzentrum*" (Walther, *Phänomenologie*, 119; emphasis hers).

they are felt as coming from elsewhere and connect the spiritual source of the I to another source beyond it (that is, *Geist*).[15] This is an experience of the self as being the proprietor and source of this spiritual (albeit not necessarily religious) life and as participant in a realm or world of "spiritual" things. It is an individual and personal experience of the self, understood as having its own "coloration" or "light," its own manner of seeing spiritually or mentally. This aspect of the human *Grundwesen* is the most generally valid (*allgemeingültig*), and it does not lack individuality or particularity. The self is the source of these experiences and they take on the particular coloration of that individual and the particular extent or expanse of that person.

The desires, feelings, and mental attitudes of a person can proceed from either soul or spirit and are different depending on their source.[16] Although the three "sides" of the self can be clearly distinguished, they ideally operate closely together and flow into each other. Only when they permeate each other fully is a person "whole." Each of the ways of being has its own core and yet the three cores can combine into one and act as a unity or be wholly in harmony (Walther, *Phänomenologie*, 126). One can listen to one's heart or spirit and, hence, focus specifically on one of the centers. The goal, however, is always to penetrate their respective cores and to unify them as much as possible. Everyone has to find his or her own path to such unity or harmony (Walther, *Phänomenologie*, 130).[17] The concentrated power or insight of the I must not coincide with these basic ways of being; one can live in experiences that are peripheral rather than at the core of one's being. The I can even be scattered over a variety of experiences, can grow, develop, and live in ways that are not identical to the "core" of one's being. In traumatic experiences the I can even be entirely empty of world or soul or basic being. It experiences itself, and is fully conscious of this experience, without connection to its essential core. She concludes that the *Ichzentrum* serves as the "eye" to the *Grundwesen* rather than being identical to it (Walther, *Phänomenologie*, 141). Walther carefully distinguishes, then, between I, lived body, soul, and spirit. Although they form a unity and ideally operate in harmony, they are distinct aspects of the human being. Stein and Conrad-Martius use similar terminology, but they present a somewhat more complicated picture.

[15] "Sie leiten zu einer zentralen geistigen Lichtquelle hin, mit der jene Quelle im Menschen selbst gleichsam verbunden ist. Die Quelle in him scheint irgendwie von ihr abzustammen, mit ihr wesensverwandt, ihr freilich durchaus nicht gleich zu sein" (Walther, *Phänomenologie*, 122).

[16] *Geistige Liebe* [spiritual love] is different from love generated in the soul (Walther, *Phänomenologie*, 124).

[17] She gives as an example having just survived a moment of highest threat to life and describes how all three cores are active and yet flow entirely into each other in a higher unity that comprises all three elements (Walther, *Phänomenologie*, 127).

Edith Stein

Stein wrote extensively on the question of the human person.[18] In almost all cases, she draws distinctions between the phenomenological "pure ego" (*das reine Ich*), the notion of the human being (*der Mensch*), and the idea of personhood (*die Person*). The human being has a lived body (*Leib*), soul, and spirit, but none of these (or their unification) is reducible to the I or to the person. Even in her early lectures she distinguishes personhood from the pure I as the source of experience and the seat of consciousness. She defines the person as subject of an actual egoic life with a lived body, soul, and a developing character.[19] Human life has a core in a way that inanimate things do not; it has both an organic and psychic life-force.[20] The lived body of the person has the ability to express its inner life. She distinguishes soul (*Seele*) from psyche (*Psyche*) and both from the flow of consciousness (*Bewußtseinsstrom*) or their totality (*Gesamtheit der Erlebnisse*) (Stein, GA, 8: 124). Although character may seem to belong to *Geist*, it is actually connected to affective life and the realm of the will.[21] The lived body is formed by the soul, which she explicitly distinguishes from religious notions of the soul as a purely psychic concept. The soul is inextricably tied to the body and unable to survive without it.[22] The soul comprises the *Gemüt*,

---

[18]Stein's dissertation on empathy raises the topic, and she returns to it as a central concern in her introduction to philosophy, her early text on the philosophy of psychology, and on the state; she designed two lecture series, one on philosophical anthropology and one on theological anthropology, and both her attempts to bring together phenomenology and Catholic Thomistic philosophy, the unpublished *Akt und Potenz* and the posthumously published *Endliches und ewiges Sein* devote much space to this topic. Although some of Stein's work has been translated, for consistency's sake I rely here on the recent German critical edition *Gesamtausgabe* [*Complete Works*] (Freiburg: Herder, 2000–; 27 volumes expected). As I cannot examine all of her works here, I will make some brief remarks about her early lectures (1920–21) introducing philosophy, half of which are devoted to the topic of the human person, and look more fully at her main work *Finite and Eternal Being* (completed 1938 before her move to the monastery in Echt). This is therefore a necessarily brief treatment. For a much fuller account see Peter Schulz, *Edith Steins Theorie der Person: Von der Bewußtseinsphilosophie zur Geistmetaphysik* (Freiburg: Karl Alber, 1994). This is a slightly revised dissertation that considers most of Stein's works chronologically in terms of what they have to say about the topic of personhood. For a briefer (but less pedantic) consideration see Antonio Calcagno, *The Philosophy of Edith Stein* (Pittsburgh: Duquesne University Press, 2007), especially Chaps. 2, 3, and 5. Stein's works are cited by volume number, followed by page number.

[19]The person is "Subjekt eines aktuellen Ichlebens, das Leib und Seele hat, mit leiblichen und seelischen Eigenschaften, speziell mit einem Charakter ausgestattet ist, das sich bzw. seine Eigenschaften unter der Einwirkung äußerer Umstände entwickelt und in dieser Entwicklung eine ursprüngliche Anlage zur Entfaltung bringt." Stein, "Einführung in die Philosophy," ed. by Claudia Mariéle Wulf, in *Gesamtausgabe*, Vol. 8 (Freiburg: Herder, 2004), 103.

[20]"Es kann also nicht von einem Zusammenfallen von Ich und Kern die Rede sein, sondern nur von einer Einbettung des Ich in den Kern, einer Aufnahme in ihn" (Stein, GA, 8: 120).

[21]"Die eigentliche Domäne des Charakters ist der Bereich des Gemüts- und Willenslebens" (Stein, GA, 8: 128). "Charakter ist die Aufgeschlossenheit (eventuell auch Verschlossenheit) für das Reich der Werte und die Art, wie man sich für ihre Verwirklichung einsetzt" (Stein, GA, 8: 128).

[22]"Sie kann nur existieren in realer Anknüpfung an einen Leib und hört auf, sobald er seine Leiblichkeit verliert und als bloßer materieller Körper zurückbleibt" (Stein, GA, 8: 145). This is something that will shift in her later work, where she increasingly thinks of the soul as immortal.

understood as the ground of affect, the seat of emotion, and the ability to feel what comes to it. The soul takes "in" such feelings and is the "place" of the center of the person, where it makes its own what is given to it from the outside, but also has its own quasi-independent life in its *Grundstimmungen* (Stein, GA, 8: 137). She distinguishes between soul and spirit, although she refuses the popular association of *Geist* solely with the mind. Human *Geistigkeit* includes a kind of openness and awareness that suggests self-consciousness.[23] A person has freedom and hence the ability to act or not. Intentionality is a key element of the "basic form of specifically human soul-life."[24]

In her magnum opus *Finite and Eternal Being*, she explores the phenomenological I—moving from Husserl's pure ego to something like Heidegger's facticity—in conversation with Thomistic philosophy.[25] She begins with a summary of the pure ego, distinguishing between internal and external consciousness, and moves from there to the recognition of our finitude. Part II of her book proceeds in a phenomenological manner from my temporal being. She engages in an extensive phenomenological analysis, unfolding the being of the I and its experiences (*Erlebniseinheiten*) as pure I, distinguished from but always directed toward the content of experience. This being I find and analyze in my self is finite; I am not its source and cannot maintain it in being.[26] I therefore encounter the notion of another being who is not thus dependent or finite, which is not mine, but fundamental to it (that is, eternal being).[27] Part III of her book attempts to get to a notion of nature or essence (*Wesen*) that would be general, unchanging, and unified, able to give an account of singular instance but not reducible to it. Philosophy can get us to a first and simple being, but only revelation (especially notions of the Trinity and of creation) can guide fully to the first being.

---

[23] *Der Aufbau der menschlichen Person: Vorlesungen zur philosophischen Anthropologie (Münster 1932/33)*, ed. by Beate Beckmann-Zöller, in *Gesamtausgabe*, Vol. 14 (Freiburg: Herder, 2004), 78. These lectures on philosophical anthropology draw explicitly on phenomenology and, increasingly, on other sources to provide a pedagogically useful account of the human person. (She was still able to give these lectures before being barred from teaching after the Nazi takeover. Her subsequent lectures on theological anthropology remain incomplete and were not delivered, although the labor of thought she invested in them obviously finds resonance in her later writings.) She again distinguishes human from animal, arguing that both have a soul, but that the human soul responds in a way that animal souls do not and that it is self-reflexive.

[24] "… die Grundform des spezifisch menschlichen Seelenlebens: Die Intentionalität oder das Gerichtetsein of Gegenständliches" (Stein, GA, 14: 80). The analysis of capacities and of the moral dimension is also much stronger in this text than in the early lectures.

[25] Although she does not follow Heidegger entirely, she employs his account for a recognition of our finitude and anxiety toward death. In fact, the book has an appendix that provides a reading and a critique of *Being and Time*. She treats phenomenology as a "natural" approach in contrast to the approach from revelation, which relies more heavily on Thomistic philosophy.

[26] She refers repeatedly to Heidegger's analyses in *Being and Time* here, including the analysis of being-toward-death, although she is more critical of it in the appendix, based on her own experience with severely wounded and dying people in her stint as a field hospital aid during WWI. See *Endliches und ewiges Sein: Versuch eines Aufstiegs zum Sinn des Seins*, ed. Andreas Uwe Müller, in *Gesamtausgabe*, Vol. 11/12 (Freiburg: Herder, 2016), 471–481.

[27] (Stein, GA, 11/12: 60) She points to the traditional proofs for God's existence as another way of getting to the same insights.

After extensive discussion of Thomistic philosophy in Parts IV–VI, she returns to the being of the I as lived body, soul, and spirit (*Leib, Seele, Geist*) in Part VII.

In Part VII of her book, Stein distinguishes between "I," "soul," "spirit," and "person." *Geist* and *Vernunft* go together. Spirit refers to the innermost core of the person. She claims that it can be offered entirely without being lost. Like Walther, she compares the spirit to a light that illuminates the person. The I is the bearer of an individual and particular life, internal even without rationality.[28] As in her earlier treatment, the human being is always "leiblich-seelisch-geistiges Sein" (Stein, GA, 11/12: 310). Consciousness is not identical to life but assumes deeper layers of personhood. There is much we do not remember or that has escaped us and that we can no longer recall to conscious awareness. The "pure I" refers to the flow of experiences of consciousness that are unified in it and that can be distinguished from the person. Here, body and soul are operative (rather than spirit). All my experiences show me to be a "me," a self, rather than just a thing called "human person." The body is not simply a "thing" (*Körper*), but is experienced internally and intimately as *Leib*. The feelings of and pressures on this lived body are my own. What turns a *Körper* into a *Leib* is having a soul (that is, affect and emotion).[29] The soul is the center of the living being; it is the source of its being and its identity.[30] Because humans are conscious they have an inner life and are bearers of their life in a special way. We have freedom, although we do not always use it. We experience ourselves as given to ourselves and yet can also give ourselves to others. The three "parts" (body, soul, spirit) are not separate from each other, but are intimately interwoven, yet refer to different experiences of the self. She supports this with extensive phenomenological analyses of experiences, concluding that the I can be experienced to some extent as separate from the lived body, yet only in a certain sense; in other ways it is always connected to it. Similarly, the *geistig* life can be distinguished from that of the soul or the senses, but is still intimately connected to them. While the spirit can exercise a certain freedom over the lived body, it is still its material substructure and illuminates the self only through the body.

Stein argues that the soul is the center of or the "inner [part] within" the whole; it lives in the body, moves it, and has an impact on it, while the spirit can transcend the soul and view the world through consciousness. The personal I is "at home" in the soul.[31] Everything is gathered, all information from the senses and from the

---

[28] Only when accompanied by understanding and freedom do we have full rationality.

[29] Stein is clear that all living entities have a soul, including plants and animals; it is simply the designation for lived affect, although this is manifested differently in humans, animals, and plants, or even angels (who do not have bodies), respectively. To have "spiritual life" (again, nothing especially religious is implied here) means that the being has fully unfolded: "Geistiges Leben ist Wesensentfaltung als Betätigung eines in seiner Wesensart Vollendeten" (Stein, GA, 11/12: 314).

[30] She appeals here to Conrad-Martius, of whose *Metaphysische Gespräche* she provides an extensive review in Section VI of her unpublished *Akt und Potenz*, which she sent to Conrad-Martius for examination. *Potenz und Akt: Studien zu einer Philosophie des Seins*, ed. by Hans Rainer Sepp, in *Gesamtausgabe*, Vol. 10 (Freiburg: Herder, 2005), 153–270.

[31] One should note that in her earlier treatments she is much closer to Walther's analysis, where *Geist* is superior to soul (Stein, GA, 11/12: 317).

spirit. The soul cannot live without such receptivity; it lives off what it receives from spirit and body.[32] I, soul, spirit, and person are intimately connected, yet each has its own meaning. The I refers to the being that is its own life, both in terms of sensory perception and consciousness. It lives within the body and the soul. Not all corporeal life is *Ich-Leben*, but this life has to be experienced. For example, growth does not belong to it in the same way because it is not sensed. Similarly, the soul is not identical to conscious life, because it can be affected in various ways without consciousness. The I, in turn, can open up the soul through memory or recollection. The soul is the depth of the person (that is, what goes on "within" me without my always being aware of it). Turning toward our experiencing, becoming conscious of it, or deliberately reflecting on it reveal various layers of consciousness accompanying the I. We grow to know ourselves through our experiencing, even if no active self-reflection is involved. The soul as the bearer of this life only becomes "visible" (or evident) in such reflection, in self-conscious awareness. The person, as conscious and free, is able to influence soul and body. The conscious *Ichleben* is informed by the depth of the soul. We occasionally get a glimpse of it, but it usually remains hidden (Stein, GA, 11/12: 319–320). The I is the place of encounter where the deeper levels of the self break through the surface.[33] The person is not reducible to the "pure I" because it requires the entire fullness of life. Spirit is the most primordial form of being; it gives meaning to life and leads to "Seinsvollendung" [fulfillment of being] (Stein, GA, 11/12: 323). Stein is hence able to distinguish within the complex interplay of acts of consciousness aspects of the self that enable self-identity or make possible self-transcendence and directness toward others, as well as various conscious and unconscious dimensions of our experience of the self.

Hedwig Conrad-Martius

The human person is a central theme for Conrad-Martius, a topic she addresses in most of her writings.[34] In an early text composed in the form of a dialogue, she distinguishes the human soul from the animal soul, human body from all other lived

[32]"Es ist das Wesen der Seele mit den darin verwurzelten Eigenschaften und Fähigkeiten, das sich im Erleben aufschließt und dadurch aufnimmt, was sie braucht, um zu werden, was sie sein soll" (Stein, GA, 11/12: 318).

[33]"Das Ich ist gleichsam die Durchbruchsstelle aus der dunklen Tiefe zur klaren Helligkeit des bewußten Lebens und damit zugleich von der 'Möglichkeit' oder "Vorwirklichkeit' zur vollen gegenwärtigen Wirklichkeit" (Stein, GA, 11/12: 320). The soul, unlike the spirit, is always tied to the material; it is "form" of the body (in a quasi-Aristotelian sense). And yet this material (*Stoffliche*) is filled with spirit (*geisterfüllt*).

[34]Her early *Metaphysische Gespräche*, a phenomenological dialogue, has this as its main topic; several lectures focus on the question of the human soul or the distinction between human and animal, and her extensive writings on the question of being also frequently return to the topic. Hedwig Conrad-Martius, *Metaphysische Gespräche* (Halle: Max Niemeyer, 1921); *Bios und Psyche: Zwei Vortragsfolgen* (Hamburg: Claassen & Goverts, 1949); *Die Geistseele des Menschen* (Munich: Kösel-Verlag, 1960); *Das Sein* (Munich: Kösel-Verlag, 1957); *Schriften zur Philosophie*, 2 vols. (Munich: Kösel-Verlag, 1963); *Die Zeit* (Munich: Kösel-Verlag, 1954).

bodies, and human spirit from incorporeal spirits. This is written as a phenomenological conversation between two people in search of a definition of the human. The existence of incorporeal spirits is not assumed but merely used as a phenomenological tool of imaginative variation to ascertain the "essence" or "nature" (*Wesen*) of the human more fully. The following insights emerge from the dialogue: We experience directly in and on the body (*Leib*), although such bodily experience of the I can be distinguished from soul and body.[35] The states of the soul are expressed bodily.[36] Yet, the soul is not identical to the I; rather, it is its deepest expression.[37] Souls have weight, while spirit is expressed in terms of lightness or self-transcendence.[38] While the spirit understands or grasps, the soul experiences or participates more intimately.[39] She draws on the etymology of *Geist* to interpret it as the "breath" of the person (namely, the free essence that animates the *Leib* and is the fullness of the person).[40] While *Leib* constitutes the self, *Geist* allows for self-transcendence and self-givenness.[41] This self-emptying elevation of the spirit makes us a person.[42]

This is worked out further in various lectures in which she considers the biological substructure of the human and life as such as well as its psychic dimensions. A special concern in several of her works is the relation between soul and body.[43] She points to the fact that the unmediated lived experiences (*unmittelbaren Erlebnisphänomene*)

---

[35] Conrad-Martius, *Metaphysische Gespräche*, 28–34.

[36] She calls this a *Niederschlagen* of the *Seelenzustände* in the body (*Leib*) (Conrad-Martius, *Metaphysische Gespräche*, 36).

[37] Conrad-Martius, *Metaphysische Gespräche*, 40.

[38] Conrad-Martius, *Metaphysische Gespräche*, 44–54. She disagrees with the scholastic/Aristotelian account that the soul forms the body, but she argues that it is formed with and alongside it (*das Mitbestimmte, Mitgeformte, Mitformierte*) (Conrad-Martius, *Metaphysische Gespräche*, 56). Although the human lives "from" the soul, it is not "das die seinsmäßige Totalität schlechthin Gestaltende" (Conrad-Martius, *Metaphysische Gespräche*, 57).

[39] "Mit dem Geist nimmt oder faßt er nur auf, mit der Seele aber 'erlebt' er es. … Die Seele scheint also immer dort beteiligt, wo der Mensch mit seinem zentralen Selbst in das Erlebte miteinbezogen oder von ihm betroffen wird. Und weit bedeutungsvoller noch ist die umgekehrte Einsicht: weil und insofern der Mensch in sein eigenes Zentrum hineingesetzt ist, durch das er—in immanent beschlossener Selbstheit—Welt und Leben in sich und durch sich empfangen kann, hat er eine 'Seele'" (Conrad-Martius, *Metaphysische Gespräche*, 72). Later, the soul is described as a living mirror of one's experience of the world (Conrad-Martius, *Metaphysische Gespräche*, 78). A human being "without soul" is missing a central self (Conrad-Martius, *Metaphysische Gespräche*, 80).

[40] "So mag jetzt heraustreten, daß der spirituelle Leib oder wenn Sie lieber so wollen, die spirtuelle Leibhaftigkeit die in freier und immer aktueller Wallung und Wesung besessene und geinnerte Fülle des eigenen Seins darstellt" (Conrad-Martius, *Metaphysische Gespräche*, 144).

[41] "Das Leiben ist das Selbsten, das Geisten das Entselbsten. Im Leiben zieht die Wesenheit sich selber an, umkleidet sich mit sich, umgrenzt, beschließt sich, versiegelt sich in sich—konstituiert ihr von allem anderen abgeschiedenes, ihr monadisches, ihr *selbstiges* Wesen. Im Geisten aber bietet sie nun wieder dieses ihr geleibtes Wesen dar, verströmt sich, ist ganz und gar hinaus- und fortgegeben, außer sich, frei von sich und von bewahrter und umgrenzter Beschwerung des eigenen Selbst" (Conrad-Martius, *Metaphysische Gespräche*, 215–216).

[42] Conrad-Martius, *Metaphysische Gespräche*, 220.

[43] The second lecture series is entitled "Grundstrukturen des Leib-Seele-Verhältnisses" (Conrad-Martius, *Bios und Psyche*, 75–137). In several places she considers the question of the human spirit or soul (*Geistseele*) and its relation to the body one of the most difficult philosophical problems,

of psychosomatic illness have made the Cartesian dualism that thinks of the soul as inner subject and the body as mere external object untenable. Instead, body and soul are intimately tied to each other on a variety of levels.[44] The "entelechial" soul has four aspects: corporeal, psychosomatic, affective, and spirited.[45] Together with the "ground" of the soul itself, this provides five primordial realms of experiencing.[46] Thus, the ensouled human self is actualized in four directions: outward to the lived body (*Exkarnation*) and inward to the psyche (*Inkarnation*), with the psyche allowing for three possible movements: toward body, soul, or spirit.[47] Like Stein, she associates *Gemüt* with affect, grounding corporeal movements that express or manifest the soul. The movements of the *Gemüt* lie at the bottom of corporeal movements, work in parallel with them, or can also be opposed to them.[48] The *Gemüt* seems to function

insisting that the two belong together intimately and yet can be distinguished in terms of function and phenomenological experience (see Conrad-Martius, *Geistseele*, 9–10). In her *Metaphysische Gespräche* one of the speakers notes that it is absurd to separate body and soul artificially and then attempt to bring them back together. They are always experienced as an ontic unity (Conrad-Martius, *Metaphysische Gespräche*, 22).

44"... in vielfach wesensverschiedener Art und Weise miteinander verflochten sind und wechselseitig aufeinander wirken" (Conrad-Martius, *Bios und Psyche*, 80). She again ascends from plant to animal to human. Animal and human share in common the intimate link between soul and body. "Tier und Mensch greifen von der selbsthaften Innerlichkeit oder dem inneren Selbst her in den Leib hinein, bzw. zu den Gliedern hindurch" (Conrad-Martius, *Bios und Psyche*, 88). In the earlier dialogue she describes this as the human ability to emerge from the sphere of nature, while the animal is submerged in it (Conrad-Martius, *Metaphysische Gespräche*, 91). Yet, an animal owns its life and is able to be the "bearer of actions" (Conrad-Martius, *Metaphysische Gespräche*, 95).

45"... vierfache Ausgestaltung der entelechialen Seele: eine leibliche, eine leib-seelische, eine affektive und eine geistige," plus "den entelechialen Seelengrund selber" (Conrad-Martius, *Bios und Psyche*, 93). "Uns kann aber kein Beispiel so deutlich wie dieses zeigen, daß die vier Lebensbereiche der menschlichen Totalität, das leibliche, das leib-seelische, das affektive und das geistige, ein und diesselbe Einlenkungsstelle in der Gesamtstruktur des Menschen besitzen, nämlich das beim Menschen personal geprägte entelechiale Seelenselbst, das als virtueller Wurzelgrund in allen vier Bereichen zu selbsteigener Verwirklichung und Manifestation gelangt und deshalb auch über alle vier Bereiche, die Psyche mit ihren drei Bezirken und den Leib, wirkursächlich zu herrschen vermag" (Conrad-Martius, *Bios und Psyche*, 105).

46"Wir haben folgendes Ergebnis gewonnen: es gibt zunächst eine zweifache große Gabelung der grundlegenden entelechialen Seele: einerseits zur leiblichen Verwirklichung oder zu dem, was ich soeben Exkarnation nannte, und andererseits zur selbsthaften inneren Verwirklichung, die man im Unterschied zur leiblichen die psychische im allgemeinen Sinne nennen kann. Diese Psyche aber gabelt sich wiederum in drei Unterbereiche: den leib-seelischen, den affektiv seelischen und den geistig seelischen. Der leib-seelische ist von innen her zum Leibe hinausorientiert, der affektive in sich selbst hinein orientiert und der geistige ... über sich selbst hinaus zu sich selbst zurück" (Conrad-Martius, *Bios und Psyche*, 93).

47"Wir haben gesehen, daß sich das personalgeprägte menschliche Seelenselbst, die grundlegende entelechiale Seele nach vierfacher Richtung ausgestaltet und aktualisiert zeigt: zunächst mit der großen Gabelung: exkarnativ zum Leib hinaus und inkarnativ zur Psyche hinein; sodann in bezug auf die Psyche selbst: erstens von innen her zum Leibe hinaus oder leib-seelisch, zweitens in ureigener Entfaltung in das Selbst hinein oder affektiv seelisch und drittens in objektiv-subjektiver Selbstbegegnung oder geist-seelisch" (Conrad-Martius, *Bios und Psyche*, 134).

48Conrad-Martius, *Bios und Psyche*, 115. "Aber der Leib ist ja ohnehin das eigenste Inkarnations- und Manifestationsfeld der Seele" (Conrad-Martius, *Bios und Psyche*, 116).

as the place where *Leib* and *Seele* meet, where feeling or affect is translated into bodily response or expression. She vividly describes the various bodily manifestations of corresponding *Gemütsbewegungen*.[49] We can distinguish whether something begins in feeling and is expressed in the body or whether it proceeds from the body and impacts the affective soul. Only in the human does the soul lead to personhood.[50]

In her later work Conrad-Martius develops the distinction between animal and human into a distinction between *Sichheit* [selfhood] and *Ichheit* [I-hood]. The animal has a self, but is not self-reflective.[51] While the animal has a kind of subjectivity in which its body is its own and the body is self-directed through its self, only the human has the kind of self-reflexivity that allows for "Retroszendenz" (that is, an "*absolute* inner reverse-transcendency").[52] The personal I has a depth that other beings do not. Only such entering or deepening into the self allows for a psyche.[53] She also stresses that humans *have* a soul and body, rather than *being* a soul or body.[54] The "spirited" (*geistige*) nature of the human "grounds specifically and directly in its *ichhaften Seinsposition*."[55] Spirit is associated explicitly with inner self-reflection and self-transcendence.[56] A self that is an I cannot be conceived without a self-transcending self-foundation.[57] In her *Geistseele* she develops the notion of an *Ursprungsselbst*,

---

[49] She explicitly speaks of this as a "translation" from one language into another (Conrad-Martius, *Bios und Psyche*, 115). She does, however, in places assimilate *Gemüt* and *Seele*, even employing the expression *Gefühlsseele* (Conrad-Martius, *Bios und Psyche*, 116).

[50] "Die beim Menschen personhaft geprägte und geistig gestaltete entelechiale Seele ist es selber, die außerdem zum Leibe, zum affektiv Seelischen und zum Leib-seelischen ausgestaltet ist" (Conrad-Martius, *Bios und Psyche*, 123).

[51] "Das Tier hat wohl sein leiblich-seelisches Sein im Besitz, aber es hat diesen Besitz nicht wiederum in Besitz. ... Man kann auch sagen: die Ichheit springt da heraus, wo die Sichheit auch noch zurücküberantwortet ist" (Conrad-Martius, *Das Sein*, 120). "Die animalische Konstitution ist nur eine sichhafte, die geistige eine ichhafte" (Conrad-Martius, *Geistseele*, 59).

[52] Conrad-Martius, *Geistseele*, 10.

[53] Conrad-Martius, *Geistseele*, 19. She does think certain "higher" animals share such "inner space"; animals have "soul" in the sense of affect and emotion.

[54] "Der Mensch *ist* nicht Geist, er *hat* einen Geist. Das ist aber etwas völlig anderes" (Conrad-Martius, *Geistseele*, 11). Cf.: "... ich selbst *habe* einen Leib und eine Seele" (Conrad-Martius, *Das Sein*, 121). This mode of "possession" is important to her for several reasons. In this context, she also strongly argues against Heidegger's notion that Dasein's existence is its essence. Only in God are essence and existence identical. See also her review of *Sein und Zeit* in Conrad-Martius, *Schriften zur Philosophie*, Vol. I, 185–193.

[55] Conrad-Martius, *Das Sein*, 119.

[56] "Alle geistigen Akte, Erlebnisse und Zuständlichkeiten sind dadurch charakterisiert, daß sie primär in der inneren Retroszendenz wurzeln, mögen sonst was immer für Faktoren materialgebend und qualifizierend in sie eingehen. Dadurch grenzt sich das geistige Ich von dem leiblichen und seelischen aufs deutlichste ab" (Conrad-Martius, *Das Sein*, 122). "Mit der Ichverfassung ist eine Stelle absoluter innerer Rücktranszendenz gegeben" (Conrad-Martius, *Das Sein*, 123).

[57] "Wir finden überhaupt kein anderes aktualisiertes Sein und Sosein an der pneumatischen Substanz als die eigentümliche Ausgestaltung dieses ontischen Grundvermögens *selber*. Im 'Selber-Können' des eigenen Seins liegt das ganze Wesen dieser Seinsart beschlossen" (Conrad-Martius, *Das Sein*, 128); "Ein ichhaft Seiendes existiert überhaupt nicht ohne eine sich selbst übersteigende transzendentale Selbstbegründung" (Conrad-Martius, *Das Sein*, 137).

a primordial self, which refers to the particular kind of logos of the human in its "psycho-somatic realms of unfolding."[58] How can this general human self take on the particular characteristics of a specific person?[59] Here, she maintains the distinction between *Exkarnation* and *Inkarnation* further (and she carries it further than Stein): excarnation is a *selfless* formation of the primordial self toward the outside, while incarnation is a *self-adhesive* formation that moves the primordial self inward.[60] This enables the self to enter into itself, to deepen into itself; it creates an internal space for the self that exists only in humans and certain higher animals. While the spirit rises out of the self in self-transcendence, the soul sinks into it to attach the self to itself.[61] A full *physisch-leibliche Ausgestaltung* is necessary for complete human substantiality to manifest itself.

Conclusion

Several things are striking about these accounts. First, they do phenomenology in conscious interaction with the larger philosophical tradition and in explicit conversation with science. Scientific insights, understood as rooted in nature, are not simply set aside (through reduction, as in Husserl, or by ignoring them, as in many of the French thinkers), but are taken seriously, albeit not as determining everything that can be said about the essence of human beings. All three engage in an extended

[58]The German for this is *leiblichseelische Ausgestaltungsbereiche* (Conrad-Martius, *Geistseele*, 29).

[59]She lists several of the traditional views about the transmission of the soul (a soul pre-existing the body, genetic determination of the general human self, a specifically created soul as forming a particular body), but judges them unsatisfying. Materialistic options that would get rid of the soul entirely and reduce the human only to biology are similarly unsatisfying (*ontologisch völlig unbefriedigend*), because "the soul is neither a mere phenomenon nor a mere conglomerate of phenomena that can be characterized as 'soulful'" (Conrad-Martius, *Geistseele*, 35). Most of the other options are rejected because they treat body and soul as separate entities that have to be brought together artificially and think of the human as a composite of the two. She does want to maintain the soul as immortal, even if it has a beginning, and as having a qualitative particularity that it does not lose upon death (Conrad-Martius, *Geistseele*, 45).

[60]"Die Exkarnation ist die leibhaft selbstlose Hinausgestaltung des Ursprungsselbst in der Form einer arttypischen Stoffsubstanz; die Inkarnation ist die leibhaft selbsthafte Hineingestaltung des Ursprungsselbstes in sich selbst" (Conrad-Martius, *Geistseele*, 51).

[61]She distinguishes three kinds of *Geistigkeit*: "1. Geistigkeit als wesensentelechialer Logos, der mit dem Wesensstoff zusammen als Ursprungsselbst substanziell konkretisiert und individuiert ist; 2. Geistigkeit als das Urgeistige, durch das innersubstanziell werkzeuglich das Ursprungsselbst in seiner eigenen inneren oder, wie wir auch sagen können, materialen Selbsthaftigkeit zur Verwirklichung gebracht wird; 3. Geistigkeit als aktualisierter (teilsubstanzieller) Geist des Menschen" (Conrad-Martius, *Geistseele*, 53).

comparison of the human and the animal, distinguishing them from each other, but without denigrating or ignoring animality.[62]

Second, they all set accounts of the person in relation to human community. This is especially evident in Stein, who started out with a dissertation on empathy, followed it up with an account of community, and then wrote her own political philosophy. While I have not had the space here to consider their accounts of community (which are not simply accounts of empathy), just the fact that these philosophers are able to give substantive phenomenological analyses of plural selves (unlike the French) is telling. Stein's account of community, for example, makes full use of her body–soul–spirit distinction.

Three, although they use the language of "soul" and explore religious and paranormal experiences (the latter especially in Walther), these are genuinely phenomenological engagements. Their insights are derived from phenomenological reflection, imaginative variation, and extensive and detailed descriptions of concrete phenomena. Conrad-Martius especially employs these tools, including speaking of goblins, fairies, spirits, demons, angels, and the divine, not claiming any existence for them, but analyzing how their "being" appears imaginatively and how it is structurally different from that of humans or animals. Even her extensive analysis of plants and animals relies not primarily on scientific insight, but on eidetic variation.

Finally, by distinguishing between lived body and soul, rather than collapsing both into the flesh (which allows for a distinction only between *Leib* and *Körper*), they are able to escape some of the dualism that still haunts the French conversation. Falque argues that the body–flesh distinction in French phenomenology has led to "hypertrophy of the flesh," in which the Cartesian dualism of soul and body is now re-inscribed upon the distinction between body (*Körper*) and flesh (*Leib*).[63] Similarly, Marion expends intense effort in his *Descartes' Passive Thought* to distinguish the bodies of the world from my own body or flesh (*meum corpus*).[64] This distinction requires no such strenuous exercise with the German terminology, because it operates with a tripartite distinction of the lived aspects of the human being already distinguished from bodies (*Körper*) in the world. While for Henry, Marion, and to some extent Falque the flesh is the seat of affect and emotion, Walther, Stein, and Conrad-Martius attribute these to the *Gemüt* and/or the soul.[65] *Leib* is hence able to

---

[62]Besides the extensive discussions of animality in all three thinkers, Conrad-Martius also writes extensively on plants. In her *Metaphysische Gespräche* she includes a chapter on evolution, understood from a phenomenological perspective (Conrad-Martius, *Metaphysische Gespräche*, 167–241).

[63]He makes this argument in several places, as it is central to the "in-between" notion of the "*corps épandu*" (between *corps étendu*/Cartesian extended body and *corps vécu*/Husserlian lived body) he is trying to develop in his own work. See, for example, Emmanuel Falque, *The Wedding Feast of the Lamb: Eros, the Body, and the Eucharist*, trans. by George Hughes (New York: Fordham University Press, 2016), 12–15.

[64]Jean-Luc Marion, *On Descartes' Passive Thought: The Myth of Cartesian Dualism* (Chicago: University of Chicago Press, 2018).

[65]It is important to note that soul has no religious connotations, as these are attributed (together with many other elements) to *Geist*.

serve as a concept of the lived body (that is *neither* flesh nor soul) in a way that has become impossible for the French thinkers.

Obviously, the traditional terminology they employ is loaded and liable to be misunderstood. Yet, it may not always be necessary to reject old terms if they can be made subject to careful phenomenological analysis and articulation and, hence, retrieved more productively. We have here a cohesive and convincing account of the human person that is not a Cartesian subjectivity, not a controlling subject, but a healthy personhood in relation to others, characterized by both freedom and finitude. While more space would be needed to show all the ways in which they could address the questions of the subject raised in the past century, their account is at the very least a highly complex notion of the self that is as good a candidate for further conversation as Marion's *adonné* or Falque's "spread body."[66] Although Walther, Stein, and Conrad-Martius are certainly trying to reach for an understanding of "the human" or the (singular) person, this is never an isolated individual, but always a "being-with-others" (and in a more robust sense than in Heidegger). Hence, their accounts of self-identity and self-transcendence may also allow for a more genuinely phenomenological account of selfhood.[67] Obviously, far deeper engagement with their work is needed to explore fully all the riches they have to offer.

Christina M. Gschwandtner teaches Continental Philosophy of Religion at Fordham University. She is the author of several books and papers on the work of Jean-Luc Marion and contemporary religious phenomenology.

[66]Conrad-Martius, for example, gives an account of the givenness of the self that appears considerably more phenomenological than Marion's *adonné*.

[67]That is, a more qualified thinking of "oneself as another" than occurs in the French treatments (such as those by Ricoeur or Kristeva in response to Lévinas' account of alterity).

What Is the Condition for the Members of Social Communities to Be "Real" People According to Gerda Walther?

Manuela Massa

Abstract This chapter explores the notion of social community in the philosophy of Gerda Walther. I explore the essence of community to obtain the *inner* constitution of the community's members, as they become a "social community." This requires an understanding of the noematic and noetic sides of the lived experience of community to obtain the object of communal consciousness, and this understanding is identified by Walther as "we-intentionality." The community, as we will find, comes to be based on the mental state of its members and the profound similarity and union between every member through shared experience. I analyze Walther's understanding of community by considering the reason for its existence, in its passivity and activity. Ultimately, I demonstrate that, although community may be experienced internally, it may also present externally. In the case of the latter, empathy makes possible one's grasping of the lived experience of community in the other, which is to be distinguished from the unified we of the interior experience of community as a oneness.

Keywords Community · Society · Egos · Noema · Intentionality · Passivity Activity

Analyzing the Human Being: The Ontology of Social Community

To understand the philosophical significance of Walther's dissertation "Ein Beitrag zur Ontologie der sozialen Gemeinschaften," written in 1919 and published in 1922, we must first ask the following question: What is the meaning or sense of community? In posing this question, two further questions arise: (1) Is a community determined

M. Massa (✉)
Society and Culture in Motion,
Reichardtstraße 6, 06114 Halle (Saale), Germany
e-mail: manuela.massa@phil.uni-halle.de

A. Calcagno (ed.), *Gerda Walther's Phenomenology of Sociality, Psychology, and Religion*, Women in the History of Philosophy and Sciences 2,
https://doi.org/10.1007/978-3-319-97592-4_8

or defined solely by the sum or total numbers of its members? and (2) Is it possible for a plurality of living beings to create something like a community?

Many philosophers have taken up these two questions and most of them have offered a political response. According to Aristotle, for example, the human being is defined as ζῷον πολιτικόν [a political living being]. His view claims for human beings a political *communitarian* essence in the world, which unfolds most fully in the polis. The individual's political essence is concretized in his or her being-with-another or in the capacity to live with one another, understood as the telos of his κοινωνία [partnership or community]. The polis comes to determine the concrete life of its members. One contemporary philosopher, Matthias Kaufmann, in his *Aufgeklärte Anarchie: Eine Einführung in die politische Philosophie*, which studies the political meaning of community, emphasizes the role that the polis plays for Aristotle. He underlines how the polis comes into being "by nature" through human agency, giving the individual the ability to constitute the state. Moreover, at its base, the constitution of any state requires κοινωνία or the togetherness of its members.[1] Phenomenological analysis stresses this aspect, as the focus on the sociality of community becomes broader when considering consciousness and the intentionality of community members. For example, in his *Einleitung in die Ethik*, Edmund Husserl justifies the criticism of legal norms by "construct[ing] an idea of a social community as a pure idea of reason,"[2] in which aspects of the community are grounded on the self-consciousness of an autonomous subject, within the frameworks of subjectivity and inter-subjectivity. Also founded on this ideal limit is his idea of the state in which the constitution of society is grounded in a contract. For Martin Heidegger community also implies the idea of sociality. He refers to the πὸλις as the "possibility of human life," the expression of being-with-one-another. Heidegger notes that Aristotle sees the "ground of the being of human being" in the being of πὸλις, so Aristotle's identification of the human being as λογόν εχον must include the historical openness of the worldly constructed Dasein.[3] The reason for this is clarified in *Being and Time*. Here, the sociality of existence is interpreted through the fundamental meaning of "being-with." This reading results *mostly* from the fact that the everydayness in which existence is is not intended to express a negative sociological characteristic of a mass existence; rather, the sociality of existence affects every person in a normal "state of consciousness." Heidegger elaborates the essen-

[1] Matthias Kaufmann, *Aufgeklärte Anarchie: Eine Einführung in die politische philosophie* in Edition Philosophie No.? (Berlin: Akademie Verlag 1999), 72.

[2] "... die Idee einer sozialen Gemeinschaft als reine Vernunftidee zu konstruiren" (my translation). See Edmund Husserl, *Einleitung in Die Ethik: Vorlesungen Sommersemester 1920 and 1924*, ed. by Henning Peucker, in Husserliana Materialien Series No. 37 (Dordrecht: Kluwer, 2004), 57. For the concept of the state and his understanding of community see Karl Schuhmann, *Husserls Staatsphilosophie*, in Alber-Reihe Praktische Philosophie No. 29 (Freiburg: Karl Alber, 1988). For the meaning of law for Husserl see Sophie Loidolt, *Anspruch und Rechtfertigung: Eine Theorie des rechtlichen Denkens im Anschluss an die Phänomenologie Edmund Husserl*s, in Phaenomenologica No. 191 (Dordrecht: Springer, 2009).

[3] Martin Heidegger, *Grundbegriffe der Aristotelischen Philosophie*, ed. by Mark Michalski, in Gesamtausgabe No. 18 (Frankfurt: Vittorio Klostermann, 2002), 45.

tial principles constitutive of being-with's essence, which includes the nature of the average "rule state" of every individual. The social-philosophically decisive result of Heidegger's analysis, then, is his demonstration of the way in which Dasein not only opens a world in the everydayness of existence, whereby the handiness and the presence of nature are always already given, but also that this world of existence is always already "being-with," which also includes everything in the form of *in-Sein*.

Gerda Walther's analysis of community bears some similarity to Heidegger's notion of being-with. Given that social community requires real, actual human beings as its base, for community members *share* their experience with one another, she maintains that the essence of social community and its correlated phenomena maybe understood through empathy. In her dissertation she focuses on the experience of *sharing*, which becomes the foundation of her development of social community. This is the case because, without sharing, living beings cannot be socially involved with one another. Walther's analysis operates on two levels: the ontological and the phenomenological. The social community requires an ontological foundation, since ontologies involve "the essence in general," the *eidos*. But, it is only by following the principles of phenomenology that consciousness acquires the essence of an object through the adequation of meaning intention and meaning fulfillment. Thus, the task of phenomenology is to study the continuous flow of *experience* through a study of intentionality and by reflecting on the objects that populate our shared public and objective world. Walther shows how private *experience* can be understood as a methodological starting point for us to share the objects that populate the world; hence, the way of understanding social community becomes grounded in its external or internal constitution. Whereas the external focuses on a conscious subject facing the entire, objective social community, the interior explores how the conscious subject is *connected* to the community's other members. In this internal perspective, there has to be the same kind of intention, understood as something belonging to all members, since the community's foundation is given through shared experiences and the interactions of its members. So, by sharing experience the structure of social constitution emerges, which is based on the individual empathy of community members.

The Base of Social Community: Its "Emotional–Spiritual" Life and Its Relation to Intentional Content

When Walther speaks about the relationships between human beings and other essences, such as God, angels, and fairies, her aim is to show how this association, from an externally perceived perspective, is incapable of presenting the social community's *essential* meaning or sense. The connection between the community's members is expressed by the German word *Gemeinschaft* [community], which presupposes "one common factor" as its base. Hence, we must ask: What kind of common aspect is shared between different members in a human community? Walther argues that the common aspect cannot be anything related to members' *bodily* constitution, as she focuses on their emotional–spiritual life. The members of a social community are conscious of their *intentional* content and can communicate with one another. To understand what is shared by members of the community, Walther focuses on the noetic aspect of community.

Antonio Calcagno's analysis is very helpful for understanding better Walther's proposal. He points out that Walther "claimed that what makes us conscious of experiencing community is what she called a lived experience of '*Einigung*,' or oneness. What is proper to my mental experience of a community is the living experience of a profound similarity and unity of mind with an other."[4] According to his interpretation, we can distinguish roughly two phases of Walther's thinking about community. One phase concerns the community's real experience, characterized by the intended *experiences* of its subjects. The other is placed on the side of the we-experience (namely, the constitutive factor of the community). In seizing the peculiar real experience as *experience*, Walther uses the example of a group of children who pretend that they are the servants of a fairy and build a "community to serve this fairy."[5] The children are conscious that the intentional object of their community is not real, since the fairy does not exist, but reality arises from their intentional experiences, in which they understand the fairy and their consequent behavior towards it. Hence, the requirement for community need not be found in a real object or in real relationships; rather, the way to grasp community rises from the content of the same intention relocated on the noematic side of this reflexion, as a community's intentional object is required to be the same for the members of the community. Angela Ales Bello clarifies that, starting from a communal object, it is possible to obtain the intentional life of the subject by considering him or her as a being who possesses the very intentional content of his or her experience, which is similar to that of other members.[6] Drawing on this characterization of community as subjects' shared experience, we arrive at our second point, which concerns we-experience, which is grounded on the distinction Walther introduces between *Gemeinschaft* and *Gesellschaft* (that is, between community and society). This distinction may be understood by considering the example of a group of workers from different countries, such as Italy, Slovakia, and Poland; they are employed together on a construction site.[7] The workers' different linguistic idioms prevent mutual understanding. Furthermore, if they are employed together and doing the same kind of work, this implies a shared temporality and continuous work as a

[4]Antonio Calcagno, "Gerda Walther: On the Possibility of a Passive Sense of Community and the Inner Time Consciousness of a Community", in a special volume dedicated to early phenomenology, ed. by Jeff Mitscherling and Kimberly Baltzer-Jaray, *Symposium: Canadian Journal of Continental Philosophy/Revue canadienne de philosophie continentale* 16(2), Fall 2012, 89–105, 91.

[5]"Gemeinschaft der Diener dieser Fee." Gerda Walther, "Ein Beitrag zur Ontologie der sozialen Gemeinschaften," in *Jahrbuch für Philosophie und phänomenologische Forschung*, Vol. 6, ed. by Edmund Husserl, Moritz Geiger, Alexander Pfänder, and Max Scheler (Halle: Max Niemeyer, 1923), 25.

[6]Angela Ales Bello and Marina Pia Pellegrino, *Incontri possibili: empatia, telepatia, comunità, mistica* (Rome: Castelvecchi, 2014), 45.

[7]Gerda Walther, "Ein Beitrag zur Ontologie der sozialen Gemeinschaften," 30.

team. They share similar aims and needs, and in this sense they are a society. Because of their communal work they probably also live and cook together. Walther asks if this kind of togetherness is enough to build a social "community." Here, Walther claims that a social community can only be built between these workers if they have an inner connection [*innere Verbundenheit*] based on the *feeling* of their togetherness [*Gefuehl der Zusammengehoerigkeit*], which permits them to share their *Erlebnisse* [experiences], actions, goals, desires, and aspirations. The inner *Einigung* (namely, oneness), therefore, becomes the condition for distinguishing the community from society, since oneness represents a community's essence insofar as the oneness represents the "inner-soul self-connection with one intentional object."[8] The grasping of the oneness of community is to be understood as actual experience, as an act performed by the I, temporally located in the moment in which this very I lives. The seizing of the oneness occurs in the *Gefühl-strom* [the flow of feelings], which appears from the background and in which the I finds tranquility for the duration of the oneness. Hence, the awareness is fundamentally a *Keimzelle* [core or nucleus] in which the habitual lived experience of the community can localize itself.[9] Here, in habitual forms of community the conscious I does not play a primary role.[10]

This is the reason, as Felipe Léon and Dan Zahavi remark, that Walther's social community requires that it be given as shared experience, something that should not be grasped as purely mine or yours, for we are experiencing it together. "The We is not an experiencing subject in its own right. Rather the We-experiences occur and are realised in and through the participating individuals."[11] While Walther qualifies the consciousness of the community as intentional, we have two recognizable forms of experience, the "remembered" [*erinnerte*] and the "habitual," both of which are useful for understanding community life. These forms are marked by two different temporalities.[12] In the case of memory, the actual experience of remembering belongs to the intentional object in the self, located in the psyche/soul behind the I-point: here, the possibility arises that what is born in the mind with one memory may be reproduced as object, as noema. But, this kind of experience, as Walther clarifies, is *für immer abgelaufen* [always fleeting]. What is born in the mind, then, is given only as an afterimage [*Nachbild*] of past experiences.[13] In habitual awareness the content of experience is actually relived, whereas in unconscious experience it can only come to awareness in a present-now, but its background and constituting moments of past content remain hidden to an actual I.[14] Hence, the experience of community may

---

[8]"Jenes eigenartige innerseseelische Sich-Verbinden mit einem intentionalen Objekt," in Gerda Walther, "Zur Ontologie der sozialen Gemenischaften," 34.

[9]Calcagno, "Gerda Walther," 97.

[10]Gerda Walther, "Ein Beitrag zur Ontologie der sozialen Gemenischaften," 38.

[11]Felipe León and Dan Zahavi, "Phenomenology of Experiential Sharing: The Contribution of Schutz and Walther," in Alessandro Salice and Hans Bernhard Schmid (eds.), *The Phenomenological Approach to Social Reality: History, Concepts, Problems*, in Studies in the Philosophy of Sociality No. 6. (Dordrecht: Springer, 2016), 228.

[12]Angela Ales Bello and Marina Pia Pellegrino, *Incontri possibili*, 20.

[13]Gerda Walther, "Ein Beitrag zur Ontologie der sozialen Gemenischaften," 42–43.

[14]Gerda Walther, "Ein Beitrag zur Ontologie der sozialen Gemenischaften," 44.

be actually lived not only as a present moment, but also as an actual, habituated experience of oneness.

The Copernican Turn of Sociology[15]

What exactly does Walther mean by we-experience? Is she claiming that the social community is grounded only on the empathy of its members? According to Walther, empathy cannot be the only grounding factor of community because, as she points out, it is something different than the community's collective experience.[16] For example, let us consider the diverse experiences that a group of people have when viewing a beautiful film.[17] What happens when they see it? Each individual in the group—whom we will call A, B, C, and D—admire it. Here, the *einfühlend* [the object of empathy] of each member must be compared with the experience E (that is, the film), which is something different for everybody, since E remains for A, B, C, and D something experienced separately. Hence, to admire and enjoy E is something seemingly unique to each member, because each individual has his or her own experience (A, B, C, and D) of the film. However, at some point, what Walther defines as a *Zwischenraum* [an in-between space] manifests itself, and the common, collective view of A, B, C, and D emerges. For Walther such a factor determines the social community (namely, a we-experience emerges that belongs to A, B, C, and D and becomes part of their experience).[18] A, B, C, and D share a unified experience of living through the same film together.

Communal experience is distinguished from empathy. To grasp the lived experience of another person in empathy modifies the originary lived experience of the other and of oneself. For example, one may be able to grasp through words or any other phenomenon of expression the lived experience of another even though I myself may have never undergone such experiences. A gap exists between the I and the other, and union in empathy is impossible because the I and its objectivation of the content of the other's mind remain distinct. In communal experience the I and others experience the same thing and do so as a union or as a we: the gap between self and others of empathy means that the experience of both individuals remains distinct from one another, although one may understand another in a lived experience of empathy. Walther claims that community presupposes a *Wechseleinigung* [mutual oneness] in which there is a mutual exchange of the same, unified experience among the members of the group, who live the experience as one. Members of a community are capable of sharing the same, intense spiritual experiences. In a society whose members may

[15]Gerda Walther, "Ein Beitrag zur Ontologie der sozialen Gemenischaften," 98.

[16]"Dem Mitfühlen usw. gegenüber ist das Gemeinschaftserleben also etwa prinzipiell Verschiedenes." Gerda Walther, "Ein Beitrag zur Ontologie der sozialen Gemenischaften," 75.

[17]Gerda Walther gives a similar example of a beautiful panorama (Gerda Walther, "Ein Beitrag zur Ontologie der sozialen Gemenischaften," 75).

[18]Gerda Walther, "Ein Beitrag zur Ontologie der sozialen Gemenischaften," 75.

share a common purpose or end individuals mutually influence or affect one another: they may share a *Wechselwirkung* or mutual effect on one another. In a community, however, one may experience not only a *Wechselwirkung* but also a *Wechseleinigung* or the unity of one with others.

A community, then, must be understood as having its base in the life of its members, who share a feeling of unity or oneness that is simultaneously motivated by a shared object of experience. There are cases, however, in which a unity exists, but there is no shared object. What is primary is the union between members: the union itself may be said to be the object of the relation. These unions take the shape of intimate forms of sociality, including lovers, friends, and families.[19] Walther views these non-objectivated communities as reflexive. Walther also claims that there are iterated communities. Here, members of a large community are united by the structure of the community (for example, political parties).

The we form of sociality, for Walther, must not be viewed as something that lies behind or as surrounding an individual because community itself is grounded in the individual I-center of every individual: community is entirely grounded in members who are fully aware of its existence. Moreover, although members of a community may occupy different places insofar as some members may find themselves in subordinate or higher positions, they share, as Antonio Calcagno points out, an awareness of their unity, mutual reciprocity of exchange of experience, shared knowledge, and mutual affectivity.[20] But community also contains, as Husserl and Pfänder point out, a passive or "secondary"[21] level of constitution. If intentionality and affectivity are the active elements of a communal life the passive life of the community is deeply shaped by the unconscious, the subconscious, and habits. Walther, for example, distinguishes between the actual and habitual unions of a community. The actual union of a community's life is based on the spiritual union of the subject with the intentional object.[22] Community, here, is based on actual lived experience that arises from the background of consciousness and enters into waking consciousness through the I and its intending the object, which is union, along with a warm and intense "feeling of togetherness." Although the experience of community is constituted in the I-centers of individual members and is not an unconscious experience, Walther still admits that the experience does flow from a subconscious background in which there is no I or intentionality.[23]

In the habitual experience of community there exists a temporal gap between one's actions in the moment and the repeated memories that give rise to such actions. In other words, one may perform certain acts or live repeatedly certain experiences like community, but the originary source of such acts or experiences is not present.

[19]For more on these non-intentional forms of community see Antonio Calcagno's chapter in this book.

[20]Calcagno, "Gerda Walther: On the Possibility of a Passive Sense of Community and the Inner Time Consciousness of a Community", 96.

[21]Gerda Walther, "Ein Beitrag zur Ontologie der sozialen Gemeinschaften," 103.

[22]Gerda Walther, "Ein Beitrag zur Ontologie der sozialen Gemeinschaften," 34.

[23]Gerda Walther, "Ein Beitrag zur Ontologie der sozialen Gemeinschaften," 38.

When one is no longer conscious of the object of intentional experience or when one object replaces another in the flow of experience a distance between the I and its subject arises. In the case of community the union, understood as the intentional object, may no longer be conscious. It may, however, re-emerge through memory or by association with another act, person, or event.[24] Although the memory of community may not be actual (that is, it is "closed and dead") because it no longer has the living force of actual experience and because it is no longer present to the I as in actual experience, habitual community has its deep roots in consciousness. The source of the habitual experience of community lies in the recesses of memory, and when activated by consciousness it acquires some force that fortifies the communal experience, allowing it to persist. Although the I may not have an intentional object before it, as in actual experience, in habitual experience the passive source of the memory of the lived experience continues to structure the very fabric of our living and acting in community.[25] Additionally, it should be noted that if memories are intense enough the experience of habitual community can almost seem actual, in the moment, and living. Walther does not dismiss the possibility that the reactivation of habits may cause one to experience intense, actual experiences of community in which the intentional object of union is once again present.

Walther's understanding of communion "overturns" classical sociological positions, which describe community in more naturalistic or empirical terms as opposed to more intentional and phenomenological ones. Walther views her work as a "Copernican turn of sociology."[26] Although Walther takes a phenomenological view of community, she admits that the social life of community is still regulated by laws and norms, and that the community neither strictly depends on one individual member nor on the sum of individuals' relations. She does maintain, however, following Hegel, that a single, spiritual individual is able to express the existence of the community.[27] At this point one must ask: Where do the lived experiences of community of individual members reside? She maintains that they dwell and are actualized in each individual[28] member's I-center. This does not mean that the community arises out of each single individual, in "isolated selves"; rather, it surges in the I and in the other, in the we, understood as human beings whose I can become a unity.[29] The lived experiences are communal in and of themselves, even before they reach the individual: they arise in an I, but are of a we.[30] The presupposition of the full constitution of an objective and real community must always be the fulfillment of the intentions of every human being through their own *real*, direct, and indirect *experiences*. Hence, this real experience is the source of influence of one member on another.[31] Actions,

---

[24]Gerda Walther, "Ein Beitrag zur Ontologie der sozialen Gemeinschaften," 40.

[25]Gerda Walther, "Ein Beitrag zur Ontologie der sozialen Gemeinschaften," 42.

[26]Gerda Walther, "Ein Beitrag zur Ontologie der sozialen Gemeinschaften," 103.

[27]Gerda Walther, "Ein Beitrag zur Ontologie der sozialen Gemeinschaften," 81.

[28]Gerda Walther, "Ein Beitrag zur Ontologie der sozialen Gemeinschaften," 70.

[29]Gerda Walther, "Ein Beitrag zur Ontologie der sozialen Gemeinschaften," 71.

[30]Gerda Walther, "Ein Beitrag zur Ontologie der sozialen Gemeinschaften," 73.

[31]Gerda Walther, "Ein Beitrag zur Ontologie der sozialen Gemeinschaften," 82.

then, can be carried out in the name of the community because of this real, mutual influence of one member on another: once members are conscious of the sense of the unity of members they can properly assume a position in the world as a community.[32] Communal actions, then, cannot be understood, according to Walther, simply as a sum total of actions, for the mutual recognition of the members of community as real subjects, always through the I-centers of the members, is required for willed actions to be actualized. The existence of the community depends on the recognition of the union, and members feel and live the union as part of their being-in the community.[33] Walther claims that community may be localized in individuals in five important ways: in the true real, metaphysical, fundamental essence of its members; in the social self; in social acts; in the body and biological life of its members; and in an objective, material, and spiritual entity that is created for each member of the community.

The reality of the community is fundamentally dependent on the "social self" of its members, who are conscious of their communal essence as stemming from the we of a social self. This essence is "incarnated" and rooted in individual members. The lived experience is real and is not a *mere appearance*. It should be remarked here that, although one may live the deep union of community, as grasped by Walther, not all the lived experience of individual members in the community is reducible to the oneness of the social self; rather, individuals simultaneously experience themselves as private persons. If one experiences oneself only as a private individual or as belonging to another community, one may not experience the union, life, or objects of a given community. But, a private individual may also dwell in a community despite not living the union. A community, then, could be less than the sum of its members and their lived experiences.[34] For Walther, then, the most intense form of community requires that members live its true essence of oneness, which is not only lived and incarnated within individuals, but is also externalized in the communal behavior and actions of members. This form of community is understood to be real and absolute in the metaphysical sense of the term.[35]

Walther's understanding of community gives rise to an important question: What happens to the community when one individual member, for whatever reason, undergoes some kind of internal transformation or new development and no longer experiences himself or herself as belonging to the community? Walther argues that even though there may be a change of the noetic content of an individual member the community still persists as experienced by the other members.[36] This persistence is possible because the community dwells within a social or communal self, a we, that continues to exist through the social drives of others, who continue to affect and

---

[32] Emanuele Caminada, "Joining the Background: Habitual Sentiments behind We-Intentionality", in *Institutions, Emptions and Group Agents: Contributions to Social Ontology*, ed. by Anita Konzelmann Ziv and Hans Bernhard Schmid (Dordrecht: Springer, 2014), 195–212, 209.

[33] Ales Bello and Marina Pia Pellegrino, *Incontri possibili*, 55.

[34] Walther, "Ein Beitrag zur Ontologie der sozialen Gemeinschaften," 126.

[35] Walther, "Ein Beitrag zur Ontologie der sozialen Gemeinschaften," 127.

[36] Walther, "Ein Beitrag zur Ontologie der sozialen Gemeinschaften," 135.

influence one another. Each member's I-center continues to live the community in a real sense despite the change of one individual member.[37] Moreover, the habits of the other members may permit the community to continue to persist at a passive level.

Up until this point we have discussed the phenomenon of community as experienced from within lived experience. But, what about community as externally experienced? Walther points to the lived body and various phenomena of expression that communicate the life and essence of the community. But, to grasp from an external perspective what individual members are experiencing, empathy is required to understand the intended meaning of the individual members' own experiences of community.[38] Here, the traditional Husserlian framework of intentionality, noesis, and noema may be applied. Walther admits that, although one may deploy empathy to understand another individual's experience of community, empathy alone may not grasp the full experience of community because of its limited inter-subjective focus (that is, empathy as an act only allows one individual to grasp the lived experience of another individual, but it may not fully be capable of presentifying the collective experience of intimate union that is defining for Walther's view of community).

Conclusion

Walther's understanding of community is interesting not only because it draws from the work of Pfänder, Husserl, and Stein, but also because of its grasp of the particularity of we-experience. Admittedly, as Ales Bello[39] has pointed out, although Walther's analysis captures an important aspect of communal experience one must not be too quick to deploy her description to understand all forms of community, especially given that Walther's own views were deeply influenced by her own involvement in the Social Democratic Party and her Marxist thinking. Walther's analysis could have benefited from a stricter phenomenological understanding of the law and the state, and how these particular social objectivities condition community, especially in relation to judgment (about what is right and/or wrong, for example) and decision-making. Heidegger remarks that human beings are free and possess freedom of choice; they are *Sein-können*. A broader discussion of a community's experience of freedom, perhaps outside the narrow confines of acts of will, if this is even possible, may be viewed as extending Walther's analysis, especially at the level of social and political institutions. Moreover, although the foregoing consideration may have helped Walther extend her analysis of the objective life of community, it in no way takes anything away from her rich and provocative description of the interiority of community.

---

[37] Walther, "Ein Beitrag zur Ontologie der sozialen Gemeinschaften," 135.

[38] Walther, "Ein Beitrag zur Ontologie der sozialen Gemeinschaften," 156.

[39] Ales Bello and Marina Pia Pellegrino, *Incontri possibili*, 34.

Manuela Massa is a lecturer at Martin Luther University of Halle (Saale). She specializes in Heidegger and Wittgenstein. She is the author of various essays including "Selbstbestimmung und 'Daseinsbefreiung': Annäherungen an einen Rechtsbegriff in Heideggers Frühphilosophie", in *Perspektiven mit Heidegger. Zugänge—Pfade—Anknüpfungen*, ed. by Gerhard Thonhauser, 2017; "*Logos* und *Nomos* bei Heidegger und Schmitt", in *Regelfolgen, Regelschaffen, Regeländerung. Die Herausforderung für Auto-Nomie und Universalismus durch Ludwig Wittgenstein, Martin Heidegger und Carl Schmitt*, ed. by Manuela Massa, Stefan Knauß, James Thompson, and Matthias Kaufmann, 2018; "The Reinstatement of the Phenomenon: Hedwig Conrad-Martius and the Meaning of 'Being'", in *Women Phenomenologists in Social Ontology*, 2018. Until 2013 Manuela worked on a project financed by the DFG (German Research Foundation) called "*De Iustita et Iure* of Luis de Molina", which she transcribed. With a scholarship from the Landesgraduiertenförderung des Landes Sachsen-Anhalt, she began work on her Ph.D. thesis, "Sprache, Ethik, Leben bei Heidegger und Wittgenstein". From September 2016 until June 2017, with a DAAD (German Academic Exchange Service) Scholarship, Manuela was a visiting scholar at the Husserl Archive in Leuven where she studied the connection between Husserl and Wittgenstein. Manuela completed her doctoral thesis with the help of a FAZIT Stiftung Scholarship, which she defended in July 2018. Her areas of philosophical interest are early phenomenology, political philosophy, and philosophy of law.

Part III
Religion and Mysticism

Phenomenology of Mysticism, Introduction and Chapter One

Rodney K. B. Parker

Abstract Gerda Walther considered her *Phänomenologie der Mystik* to be her main philosophical work. Informed by her own alleged mystical experiences, this work attempts to show how spiritual beings are distinct from merely psychical beings, and that mystical lived-experiences and their objects can be distinguished from other forms of experience. Included here is a translation of the Introduction and Chapter One from the 1976 edition of *Phänomenologie der Mystik*, which outline her phenomenological approach to the study of mystical experience and her concept of the ego.

Keywords Mystical lived-experience · Ego-center

Translator's Preface

Alhough it has received far less attention in recent philosophical discussions than her dissertation "Zur Ontologie der sozialen Gemeinschaften," Gerda Walther considered her *Phänomenologie der Mystik* to be her main philosophical work. She began writing it in early 1920 upon returning to Munich from Freiburg to finish writing her dissertation. It first took shape as a manuscript titled "Ein Beitrag zur (bewusstseinsmäßigen) inneren Konstitution des eigenen Grundwesens als Kernpunkt der Per-

[1] This manuscript can be found in Walther's *Nachlass* in the Bavarian State Library in Munich under the signature Ana 317 A.III.2.1—*Die innere Bewußtseinskonstitution des eigenen Grundwesens als Kern der Persönlichkeit.*

Gerda Walther: deceased.
Translated and edited by Rodney K. B. Parker.

R. K. B. Parker (✉)
Center for the History of Women Philosophers and Scientists/Department of Philosophy, Paderborn University, Paderborn, Germany
e-mail: rodney.k.b.parker@gmail.com

A. Calcagno (ed.), *Gerda Walther's Phenomenology of Sociality, Psychology, and Religion*, Women in the History of Philosophy and Sciences 2,
https://doi.org/10.1007/978-3-319-97592-4_9

sönlichkeit (und Gottes)" (A.III.2.1), which she presented to her teacher Alexander Pfänder in honor of his 50th birthday.[1] As the title suggests, the original manuscript was a reflection on the ego and the self (and the experience of other egos), and is only tangentially concerned with the Divine. However, this evolved into the phenomenological investigation of religious and mystical experience presented here. This was a drastic move away from the naturalistic and historical materialisms that she had dogmatically accepted growing up as an atheist and Marxist.

There are three editions of Walther's *Phänomenologie der Mystik*. The first was published by Max Niemeyer in Halle in 1923. The second and third editions were published by Otto Walter in Olten and Freiburg in 1955 and 1976, respectively. As Walther explains in her short Preface to the third edition, the changes between the second and third are minor—corrections of typographical errors and some improvements to the notes. The changes between the first and second edition, however, were significant. Between 1923 and 1955 Walther attended lectures on psychology and psychiatry, worked in a state mental hospital, began studying parapsychology, and had a number of what she believed to be genuine mystical experiences. All of this led to an extensive reworking and expansion of the later chapters of the book. However, what I take to be the core philosophical theses remained the same: (1) that the capacities for free-will, self-consciousness, and empathy distinguish spiritual beings from merely psychical beings[2]; (2) that mystical experiences and their objects are distinct from both sense perceptions and the representations of dreams, imagination, memory, and hallucination; and (3) that the purported phenomenological equivalence between mystical experiences and the experiences of the mentally ill is not as great as some would claim.[3] Points (1) and (2) are dealt with in the Introduction and Chapter One, which remained nearly identical in all versions. Those are the sections translated here.

What follows is not the first attempt at an English translation of *Phänomenologie der Mystik*. That distinction goes to none other than Walther herself. The unpublished manuscript, "On the phenomenology of mysticism" (A.III.2.2),[4] is a rough translation of the Introduction through to the first pages of Chapter Four of the 1923 edition of Walther's book. The text bears no date, and could have been written at any time between 1923 and 1955, since we know that Walther was all but fluent in English since childhood.[5] However, the text presented here is not merely a transcription of

---

[2]Unfortunately, Walther's discussion of empathy does not arise until Chap. 3 and as such is not included here.

[3]For a detailed overview of Walther's book see Henry Corbin's review (in French) of the second edition, published in *Revue de l'histoire des religions* 153(1), 1958, pp. 92–101.

[4]Ana 317 A.III.2.2—*Englische Übersetzung von* "On the phenomenology of mysticism." The manuscript consists of 63 handwritten sheets—a 61-page first draft and 2 pages of a second. There appear to be pages missing, since the final page from the first draft cuts off mid-word ("It is as if the ego was here precipitating itself into an endless abyss where there is no embodiment and no ob-...").

[5]In a letter found in the *Nachlass* of Herbert Spiegelberg housed at the Bavarian State Library, Walther writes: "As you were wondering whether I can read English, I guess I must show you I can! Indeed, I have been talking, writing, reading, thinking in English ever since my childhood, as my

A.III.2.2. It is my translation of sections from the third edition of *Phänomenologie der Mystik*, using Walther's unfinished draft translation of the first edition as a guide. I often rely on her translation to determine how to render certain technical terms and complicated sentences into English. That said, I do not follow her at every turn.

Throughout the text, I have translated *Gegeben* and *Gegebenheit* as "given" and "givenness." I have also attempted to render consistently *Erleben* as "lived-experience" and *Erfahren* as "experience," although it is unclear if Walther means something different by these two terms. *Grundwesen* has been translated as "basic essence," but it is worth noting that in A.III.2.2 Walther translates the occurrence of *Grundwesen* on <34> below as "entelechy." Throughout A.III.2.2 Walther switches between translating *Gott* as "the Divine" and "God." I have opted to translate always *Gott* as "the Divine." She also often uses "intellect (or reason)" to translate *Verstand*, and I have employed this convention throughout my translation. I have chosen to translate *Seele* as "psyche" rather than "soul," and on this point the reader should see Note 30. In A.III.2.2 Walther translates *Ich* as both "I" and "ego," sometimes even writing "the I, the ego." I use "I" and "ego" interchangeably here. I have also translated *leibhaftig* alternately as "bodily" and "in the flesh." Finally, whereas Walther translates *Ichzentrum* as "central ego," I have translated this as "ego-centre". The pagination from the 1976 edition of *Phänomenologie der Mystik* is indicated throughout using <angle brackets>, and in a handful of cases I have included the original German in [square brackets].

Where there are noteworthy deviations from the first edition of *Phänomenologie der Mystik*, these have been indicated in the translator's footnotes. One change of particular interest is the removal of references to August Faust in the later editions. This choice on Walther's part was no doubt due to Faust's affiliation with the Nationalist Socialist Party. These references have been restored in my translation, since they were as a matter of historical fact sources for Walther's work. However, in the footnote on <23>, Walther did not include a complete reference in the 1923 edition, and so I was unable to add a book or paper title.

It may also be of some interest to the reader that the copy of the first edition of *Phänomenologie der Mystik* that I used for comparing the texts came from the personal library of Herbert Spiegelberg, now part of library holdings of Washington University in St. Louis. Walther herself had sent the book to Spiegelberg in 1954,[6] and a number of notes and deletions marked in the text were written by Walther herself. For example, from the second edition onward the reference to theosophy and the anthroposophy of Rudolf Steiner on <33> were omitted. This same passage is

---

father was the owner of an international sanatorium for consumptives in the Black Forest, and about 1/3 or 1/2 of the patients came from the British Commonwealth or the United States" (Ana 387 E.II—*Brief von Gerda Walther* (24.XI.1953)). It should be noted here that the translation presented in A.III.2.2 is far from perfect. Walther consistently makes grammatical errors and mistranslates certain words into English. This sometimes results in ambiguous and nonsensical passages.

[6] The dedication inside the front cover reads: "*Herrn Dr. Herbert Spiegelberg in Erinnerung an die gemeinsamen 'geistigen Ursprünge' mit herzlichen Grüßen! Dr. Gerda Walther, München 1954.*" The common "spiritual origins" referred to here likely relate to their mutual teacher, Alexander Pfänder.

crossed out in the copy of the first edition that Walther sent to Spiegelberg. Most of her handwritten changes are minor, but there is no doubt that the handwriting is hers.

Phenomenology of Mysticism

Gerda Walther

Introduction: Limitations of Our Method and Objects of Inquiry

<21> It appears imprudent to undertake an attempt to grasp the mystical phenomenologically, to analyze that which is completely obscure, irrational, and in the opinion of many absolutely ineffable and unknowable with the help of a scientific method of reasoning. Nevertheless, if we attempt to do so, then we need to offer some justification for and be aware of certain limitations of such an undertaking. Let us begin by briefly clarifying what a phenomenology of mysticism can and cannot accomplish.

What a phenomenology of mysticism *cannot* and *will not* attempt to do is give a possible natural, causal explanation or reduction of mystical facts according to the principles of natural science. If something of that sort were at all possible—and I am convinced that it is *not* possible—it is certainly not the task of a phenomenology of mysticism to provide it. Neither can it be to prove definitely or refute certain opinions about the mystical on the basis of logical conclusions and suppositions about the nature of reality, nor can a phenomenology of mysticism prove the possibility or impossibility of something being accessible to human beings according to prejudices about the nature of human understanding.[7] For the mystical is an irreducible, primordial phenomenon, a basic, primordial givenness that cannot be traced back to or derived from some other phenomena, such as colors, sounds, values, and so on. And these basic, primordial phenomena are what we want to examine here without prejudice, just as they present themselves in lived-experience to those who have had mystical lived-experiences. In these investigations we want to remain as close as possible <22> to these mystical lived-experiences, doing nothing other than highlighting that which is essential in them, by sharply distinguishing and characterizing all the essential aspects of these lived-experiences, so that they can be grasped according to their sense and the originality of their essential qualities, and, as far as possible, to distinguish them from givens that are seemingly similar, but which are essentially different.[8] Likewise, by way of our investigations we will attempt to contribute to the solution of the question of whether mystical lived-experiences truly

[7] An important book dealing with these and other problems is Edith Landmann-Kalischer, *Die Transzendenz des Erkennens* (Berlin 1923).

[8] See Edmund Husserl, *Ideen zu einer reinen Phänomenologie*, Vol. I (Halle 1913), p. 96ff., and August Faust, "Der dichterische Ausdruck mystischer Religiosität bei Rainer Maria Rilke," *Logos*, Vol. XI (1922), p. 226.

are or can be what they claim to be (namely, real, "bodily" lived-experiences of the Divine).[9] Here, we will count among mystical lived-experiences only those lived-experiences that claim to be direct, bodily (though perhaps imperfect and one-sided) experiences of the Divine *itself*. For if there is any experience of the Divine at all, if our opinions about the Divine and our relations to it are not based on pure phantasy, or, as opponents of religion claim, on "blind" belief in traditional dogmas (which, again, if there were no bodily experience of the Divine, would be based on phantasy, or at best upon mere improvable conjectures and conclusions), then surely it must be a real experience of the Divine, even if it is not complete.[10] For the objection that we merely have to believe the revelations of the Divine handed down to us by the churches only shifts the question of an original, bodily experience of the Divine without resolving it. Certainly, if *we* are not able to have such immediate experiences of the Divine, then we must believe in the revelations that have been told directly or handed down to us. But, what about these revelations themselves? Those who communicate them to us, and those from whom they are ultimately <23> transmitted to us, assert that those individuals who have had mystical experiences have received them directly from the Divine. But, then there *must* also be an immediate, original, bodily lived-experience of the Divine, if not experienced by us, then at the very least by a "medium," back to which our knowledge of the Divine may ultimately be traced. Thus, we cannot avoid assuming an immediate experience of the Divine, and this according to the statements of all mystics is found with the greatest perfection and certainty in mystical lived-experience.

For example, Brother Aegidius (Giles of Assisi) once said, "I know a man who saw God so clearly that he lost all faith." Brother Andreas (Andrew of Burgundy) said, "If you do not have faith, what would you do if you were a priest and had to celebrate High Mass? How could you say, 'I believe in one God'? It seems that you would have to say, 'I know one God.'" Then Brother Aegidius answered with a joyous countenance and sang in a loud voice, "I know one God, the Almighty Father."[11]

---

[9]On the concept of "bodilyness" see E. Husserl, *Ideen zu einer reinen Phänomenologie*, Vol. I (Halle 1913), p. 43ff., 70ff., 79ff., 209ff., 283, and Hedwig Conrad-Martius, "Realontologie," *Jahrbuch für Philosophie und phänomenologische Forschung*, Vol. VI (1923), p. 165ff. [7ff.], Sections 8 and 9, and pp. 188ff. [30ff.], §29, and most importantly her remarks on p. 189ff. [31ff.] in Sect. 29. Incidentally, I do not agree with the view expressed here that "God in the full and strict sense cannot be given bodily to any earthly creature" (p. 165 (resp. 7), Sect. 9), that "God in a final sense is not to be encountered by anyone," as I have indicated above. I hope that this will be further strengthened in the course of these investigations. Only for completely adequate knowledge of God would I admit this, but not for bodilyness. For something can very well be given bodily without being given completely and "from all sides." For example, when the moon shines unobscured in the sky, it is given to us bodily in perception (not in imagination, memory, or merely in thought), yet it is not fully given to us because of its distance from us and because we only see it from one side.

[10]See also E. Landmann-Kalisher, *Die Transzendenz des Erkennens* (Berlin 1923), Chap. 1, and p. 273ff.

[11]See Martin Buber, *Ekstatische Konfessionen* (Leipzig 1921), p. 69; p. 136 (Angela di Foligno) and p. 141 (Catherine of Genoa). See also August Faust, *Logos*, p. 20 and Teresa of Ávila, *Die Seelenburg* (Regensburg 1922), V. 1. 10.

We want, therefore, to investigate those lived-experiences which, according to their own inner sense, claim to present the Divine, although imperfectly, in true givenness, in which, according to their inner quality, a *direct* manifestation, revelation, or appearance of the Divine comes to givenness. All and only such lived-experiences, as has already been said, are to be counted as mystical lived-experiences. By no means are we to understand by mystical lived-experiences only mystical ecstasy (that is, a complete possession by or immersion in the Divine), although such lived-experiences come nearest to the sense and purpose of mystical lived-experience (that is, the most complete and adequate givenness of the Divine that any created being can possibly attain). However, communion *in the sense of the Catholic Church*, as the bodily presence of Christ, may also be connected with mystical lived-experiences.[12]

<24>In order to approach mystical lived-experiences in a truly unbiased way, one must first of all beware of two prejudices. One is based on the opinion that it is impossible for a human to experience the Divine "in the flesh"; what mystics experience in such lived-experiences is only a manifestation of their own psyche, their own deepest, basic essence. During ordinary, everyday life, this basic essence generally remains hidden in the depths of one's inner being, and when it suddenly enters into conscious awareness it is mistaken for a revelation of the Divine.[13] This view is the late offspring of the obsolete *psychologistic* theories of knowledge, which have partial roots in Kant. This view has survived in other areas[14] and apparently continues to go unchecked in our domain of inquiry. It is high time that it is finally here overcome. The second prejudice is inherited from British *empiricism*, culminating in the assertation that whatever is the object of consciousness, whatever can be experienced by us, is transmitted to us, directly or indirectly, only through the aid of *the outer bodily senses* and their "data" (colors, sounds, tastes, smells, tactile sensations). According to this view, it is impossible that something could be experienced that is not founded on the "categorial formation" and "meaning-giving tinging" of *these* sense data, even though it may be so by virtue of many detours and stratifications.[15] The first of these prejudices can only be completely refuted in the course of our investigations and on the basis of their results (see especially Chaps. 18 and 19). The second seems to be confirmed by the fact that in the writings of mystics one can find many references to such sense data (of fragrances, pleasant tastes, sweet feelings, light, warmth, sounds, and so on). However, these are certainly only analogies. For how could mystics even convey a vague approximation of the "absolutely other" to those who have<25>not experienced it, if not by referring to the familiar givens of everyday life? The fact that these are and can only be grossly imperfect analogies must be emphasized repeatedly in the strongest terms. (Time and again mystics have asserted that only those who

---

[12]See, for example, Lucie Christine, *Geistliches Tagebuch (1870–1908)*, 5th edn. (Mainz 1975).

[13]Even M. Buber in the Foreword to his *Ekstatischen Konfessionen* comes to this same view. See also Ernst Gundolf, *Nietzsche als Richter unserer Zeit* (Breslau 1923), p. 43.

[14]See, for example, H. Conrad-Martius, "Zur Ontologie und Erscheinungslehre der realen Außenwelt," *Jahrbuch für Philosophie und phänomenologische Forschung*, Vol. III (1916).

[15]Otto Gründler as well was unable to free himself from this prejudice. See his *Elementen zu einer Religionsphilosophie auf phänomenologischer Grundlage* (Munich 1922), especially p. 5.
In A.III.2.2 Walther cites Husserl here instead of Gründler.—Translator's note.

know from *their own* lived-experience what these analogies symbolize can completely understand such analogies.[16] But, of course, such a person no longer needs them.) Imagine that four fifths of humankind were born blind, and only one fifth were able to see. Suppose that the one fifth tried to convey to the other four fifths even the slightest idea of what they experience when they see colors. How should the "seers" do so if not by referring, as well or poorly as they can, to what is familiar to the other four fifths? To do so, they would have to translate, as it were, the colors into another domain (for example, that of sounds). There would be no other way. And then, perhaps, they would refer to the feeling that bright, "harsh" colors arouse in them and compare it with the sensations they experience when listening to "bright" major chords and high, treble notes, and perhaps compare the deep, dark, warm colors with certain minor chords and bass notes. (Some people, who are capable of experiencing such relations, claim, for example, that they always "see" liquid silver when listening to the music of Brünnhilde's awakening in Wagner's *Siegfried*.) Perhaps they would succeed in establishing here a fixed system of relations, which is connected to a certain something that these two otherwise different spheres have in common (perhaps one could call it the metaphysical essence), and which justifies precisely these analogies and comparisons (in contrast<26>to any other ones, which may at first seem possible but are simply arbitrary). One could then speak of greater or lesser degrees of "correctness" and "adequacy" in using these analogies for translating from one domain to another. And there would be, so to speak, better or worse, or even completely wrong use of analogies, which everyone who would give the color blind an idea of colors in the language of sounds must take as a model for judging the correctness of their translations. If there really were essentially fixed relations here, then everybody able to see would have to use the same tones and sounds for the same colors as other color-seers do, even without knowing it. But those who only ever hear sounds and tones could have but a very faint and unclear picture of the colors being presented to them. Only if they were suddenly able to "see" could they fully comprehend what was meant, and they would then realize that the use of certain sounds and tones as a symbol for certain colours was entirely appropriate based on an inner lawfulness and truth regarding the relations between sounds and colors. If they were only capable of seeing one color, or a group of colors, at first, even if they were still partially color blind, then they would have already been given the key to the whole world of colors and its representation in the world of sounds.

It is exactly the same in the case of mysticism. All that the mystics say about light, sweet feelings, and fragrances, or darkness, black clouds, and so on, is nothing other than a translation of purely spiritual lived-experiences into the sphere of sense perception. This is shown by the strange consistency in the application of certain identical symbols for the representation of certain mystical<27>lived-experiences. However, the fact that only a small part of humankind has so far experienced the purely spiritual givens of mysticism that are symbolically represented in this way is no more a proof against the correctness of the information given above than it would

[16] See Teresa of Ávila, *Die Seelenburg* (Regensburg 1922), VI. 5. 5, p. 194ff.

be in other domains.[17] Only a fraction of all people are able to understand the most advanced levels of mathematics, such as analysis, function theory, set theory, and so on. Nevertheless, we do not consider the mathematicians who do research in these areas to be engaged in mere arbitrary phantasy, lies, or self-deception with respect to these objects and their relations. On the contrary, one would regard it as a sign of great ignorance and arrogance if someone who did not understand these things were to dismiss or object to the assertions of such researchers simply because they lacked any knowledge of them. Why, then, is mysticism not afforded the same just treatment?

I have spoken above about the "*spiritual* givens" of mysticism. Evidently, I do *not* mean purely *intellectual* givens or phenomena, although the intellect (or *reason*) has again and again been confounded with the spirit, to the great detriment of both.[18] By intellect (or reason), we mean here the whole domain of consciousness that engages in analyzing, associating (comparing, distinguishing, separating, and so forth), systematizing, and defining (but not the intuiting of metaphysical essences). In short, thinking in the strictest sense. Insofar as it is related to particular objects (be they real or ideal in nature, be they human beings or animals, and so on, or coordinate systems of analytic geometry, etc.), the intellect (or reason) is dependent upon<28>other modes of consciousness, which provide it with the concrete (in the widest sense) material upon which it then carries out its investigations. Without these other modes of consciousness (for example, sense perception), the intellect (or reason) is entirely helpless, has no foundation, and hangs in the air, without them it cannot even "think" [*spintisieren*] properly. These other modes of consciousness, upon which the intellect (or reason) depends, can be among other things external, sensual, supernatural [*übersinnlicher*], psychical, or purely spiritual in nature. For example, the sensory perception of colors, sounds, smells, etc., and the experience[19] of bodily objects that are based on these (and not merely belonging to the intellect or reason), such as humans, animals, plants, rocks, and so on, belong, on the one hand, to those modes of consciousness upon which the intellect (or reason) is absolutely dependent for all concrete "material" statements, investigations, and knowledge. On the other hand, purely "spiritual" data and the experiences founded upon them are just as fundamental for the intellect (or reason), and it is precisely these data and experiences that one generally chooses to overlook, ignore, or confound with other things. But just as little as the intellect (or reason) is capable of carrying out a valid investigation of the external world, of nature in the broadest sense of the word, without basing it on bodily sense perceptions and the experiences founded upon them and without strictly adhering to what is given in them, in the same way it is not possible

[17]See also E. Landmann-Kalisher, *Die Transzendenz des Erkennens* (Berlin 1923), Chap. 1, and p. 277ff.

[18]Thus, for example, among other things, Ludwig Klages' attacks on the "spirit" and "spiritualization" seem to almost consistently be attacks on intellect [*Intellekt*] and intellectualization, but not the spirit in the strict sense. See my paper, "Ludwig Klages und sein Kampf gegen den Geist," *Philosophischer Anzeiger* III.1 (1928).

[19]It has been called "categorial intuition," but we will avoid this word here, since certain epistemological and metaphysical views are typically associated with it that we will not discuss here.

in the domain of the psyche and the spirit if the intellect (or reason) does not adhere closely to spiritual perceptions and the experiences founded upon them.[20]

Apart from sense perceptions and the experiences founded upon them, along with merely "empty" thoughts, there is now a great deal of talk about memories, representations [*Vorstellungen*], and<29>beliefs [*Meinen*] (without an intuitive representation) in psychology and epistemology. These memories, representations, and so on are often described as something purely psychical, or purely spiritual in comparison to sense perception. So, it seems reasonable to believe that what we mean by "spiritual" data and "spiritual" experience is nothing other than imagined representations and so on. However, what we mean is an essentially different, independent given, which stands over-against these representations in spiritual perception, just as in sense perception. This follows already from the fact that memories, representations, mere beliefs, and so on, may be *of both sensual* perceptions/experiences and *spiritual* perceptions/experiences. So, these representations, etc., cannot be identified with the latter.

For example, we can have a vivid memory of the house we grew up in, the furniture, the colors and patterns of the carpets in its rooms and the like, without having it before our eyes (perhaps it does not even exist anymore), or we can think of it without having it clearly before us in our mind, or we can imagine/represent something more or less vividly without ever having perceived it. (For example, the glass mountain on top of which the princess's castle lies and that the knight must ride up on horseback, which is mentioned in so many fairy tales.) Without any doubt, all this is given to us in a fundamentally different way from when we perceive something with one or more of our senses, which stands now before us and is bodily given to us in outer perception. If we look at a flower that is standing in front of us, it is given to us in a fundamentally different way than when we merely remember it, merely<30>imagine it, or think of it. Likewise, when we hear a sound or a piece of music, when we smell the scent of roasted coffee as we pass by a café, or when we stroke a piece of velvet and feel its distinctive softness, and so on. In all these cases we have, purely due to the givenness of these objects to consciousness in their bodily presence, the real objects themselves in full self-givenness, in contrast to mere imagined representations, memories, and so on, which, no matter how intensely we concentrate on them, never give us an original perception of the objects themselves, but only their inner givenness, according to the manner in which the things stand before us. (No logical conclusions, proofs, etc., are needed to see that the difference lies in the givens themselves.)

However, the same occurs with the relation between imagining/representing, remembering, and "mere" thinking, on the one hand, and psychical and spiritual perception and experience, on the other. One may clearly imagine the light of the Divine spirit that is experienced in the *unio mystica*, or the particular psychic radiation (the aura) of a human being, or one may intensely work oneself into the phantasy

---

[20] See Teresa of Ávila, *Die Seelenburg* (Regensburg 1922), IV. 3. 2, p. 85; V. 1. 10, p. 107; and M. Buber, *Ekstatische Konfessionen* (Leipzig 1921), p. 46 (Jalāl ad-Dīn Muhammad Rūmī); p. 51 (Plotinus).

of mystical ecstasy (to the point where one believes one has had a lived-experienced of it), or one may remember such a lived-experience, or intend it in thought. Yet all this is fundamentally different (according to its inner lived-experiential character) from those cases in which a psychical or spiritual experience originally presents its object "in the flesh" to consciousness.[21] All of the mystics who have commented upon this problem fully agree on this point. They have continuously emphasized that only those who have never had such genuine, bodily mystical lived-experiences, those who have never had the *tertium comparationis*—the possibility of comparing the <31> different modes of lived-experience—can confound their unique manner of givenness.[22] This consciousness of the bodily presence of mystical objects (insofar as one may be permitted to call them "objects" in a loose sense) in these spiritual experiences does not, as one might think, always coincide with a simultaneous experience of something "in the flesh" given in outer sense perception, such as the perception of a Divine messenger in the form of a human person.[23] However, such a simultaneous givenness of one and the same object in spiritual as well as outer sense perception, or some other combination of the two, often occurs. But, this connection is by no means *necessary* for the spiritual experience to present its content in bodily givenness. On the contrary, even with the complete lack of any outer perception (sometimes even precisely because of this) it can present itself as being absolutely certain and real.[24]

Lastly, one might be inclined to think that the spiritual perception of which we have been speaking is the same as what the occult and theosophical circles refer to as "higher senses," "paraphysical phenomena," and so on.[25] If these things are genuinely real, and not merely expressions of the subconscious (see Chaps. 4 and 5), then such givens will most likely contain some of the data referred to as "supernatural," but also what we may refer to with the collective noun "spiritual data," which includes their perception.[26] However, one must not therefore lump everything together, as if all *spiritual* perceptions and experiences must always be about *these same* data and experiences, only differing slightly in intensity. On the contrary, although they belong to the same species, supernatural data and perceptions <32> are no more equivalent to spiritual data and experiences than they are to outer sense perceptions. And just as it is not the case that because a person has had one kind of perception in the realm of outer sense perception, and they have therefore already experienced or are therefore capable of experiencing all other kinds of outer perceptions, it is likewise not so here either. Let us imagine a person who has lived their entire life since birth in a coalmine, having only seen things under artificial light. Such a person would certainly

[21] See Teresa of Ávila, *Die Seelenburg* (Regensburg 1922), IV. 3. 3, p. 83ff.; IV. 3.10–17, p. 92ff.; V. 1. 3ff., p. 100ff.; VI. 3. 10ff., p. 169ff.

[22] See Teresa of Ávila, *Die Seelenburg* (Regensburg 1922), IV. 3. 12; VI. 3. 12, p. 172ff; and her letter to Father Rodrigo Alvarez (see M. Buber, *Ekstatische Konfessionen* (Leipzig 1921), p. 145ff.).

[23] See Teresa of Ávila, *Die Seelenburg* (Regensburg 1922), V. 1. 9ff., p. 106ff.

[24] See Teresa of Ávila, *Die Seelenburg* (Regensburg 1922), V. 1. 10, p. 106ff; VI. 8. 3, p. 224ff.

[25] In the first edition Walther adds the following sentence: "We know too little about the apparitions of 'ghosts' and the like to be able to say anything about them".—Translator's note.

[26] In his famous work on *Die christliche Mystik* (Regensburg 1879/80), Joseph von Görres, unfortunately, does not distinguish between supernatural and mystical lived-experience in the true sense.

know many colors and have some knowledge of the nature of light. Yet, what they perceive would be limited and dim in comparison to what they would experience if they were to suddenly step out from this dark, dull shaft into the bright sunlight of a brilliant day and behold what might be seen there—the sparkling water, the colorful flowers, the green forests, and so on. Perhaps in that moment they would feel as if they had only just then learned to see properly, even though they had seen light and colors before. The same is true of those occult lived-experiences in comparison to what the mystic sees. To be sure, occult lived-experiences, insofar as they really are spiritual perceptions, are more closely related to mystical lived-experiences, both being *spiritual* experiences, than to outer sense perceptions. Nevertheless, religious experiences are by no means always connected with an occult lived-experience; they are only approximately so. It is quite possible that somebody who has had many occult experiences has not the slightest idea of the bodily religious experiences that matter to us here. Conversely, there are certainly mytics who have or have not had occult lived-experiences. This seems to be overlooked or<33>underestimated by many occultists.[27] Such people are, therefore, in danger of being so captivated by their own spiritual lived-experiences and the spiritual lived-experiences of others that they neglect their own religious life. Above all, the psychologistic prejudice that confounds the mystical lived-experience of the Divine essence and its emanations with the lived-experience of one's own basic essence (or that of others), contributes greatly to this (see Chap. 16).[28] It seems that there is too much talk of human beings and their hidden powers in some of these modern movements, and too little about the Divine and the light of its grace, which sometimes radiates into the interior of human beings. To be sure, those who are capable of psychical–spiritual lived-experiences will be able to grasp it very well; yet, it can never be called forth *solely* by training those "higher faculties of perception," since those Divine emanations are a gift springing from and given by the free will of the absolutely free, eternal Divine person and its grace (see Chaps. 16 and 19).

Nevertheless, experiencing the Divine essence and its emanations, despite all essential differences, possesses a certain affinity with some parapsychic givens, as well as the lived-experience of one's own innermost basic essence (and that of others), both with regard to its inner content and the way in which it is usually attained by the person in mystical lived-experience. Therefore, let us begin by examining these lived-experiences—though, we must emphasize, they are *not yet religious*—to be able to grasp the truly religious lived-experiences later on, and to distinguish them from other types of religious experience.

If we do not confound the spirit with the intellect (or reason), then the Divine is, as we have already suggested, spiritual.<34>But, the innermost, essential core of human personality, its *basic essence*, so to speak, is equally spiritual. Therefore, we must sharply distinguish the intellect (or reason) from the spirit in this sense. If

[27] In the first edition Walther states that this has not only been overlooked by many occultists, but also "theosophists and anthroposophists (perhaps even Rudolf Steiner)".—Translator's note.

[28] In the first edition Walther adds: "This is already shown by the replacement of the word *theo*sophy with *anthropo*sophy".—Translator's note.

we want to elucidate what we understand by spirit in general and by Divine spirit in particular in the most appropriate way possible, then the best way to proceed is by way of examining the basic essence of human beings, if only because, according to the opinion of all theologians and mystics, among all other things given in the real world, this has the greatest affinity with the Divine essence. And, also, because one of the main paths leading to a bodily intuition of the Divine leads from the inner depths, the basic essence of the person, through and beyond it. We will therefore look for a way to grasp our own personal basic essence, and then to grasp the essential grounding of this basic essence (that is, the Divine). <35>

Chapter One: The Ego as Centre of Lived-Experience[29]

If we know anything at all about human beings, it is that we find ourselves in both an inner and an outer world, but we are first and foremost entangled in the outer world, as if enchanted by it. An urban or a rural world surrounds us: with our eyes we plunge into it, hear its noises, take in its smells. In part, it stands before us "in the flesh," and in part it reminds us of earlier lived-experiences, and these earlier lived-experiences are either more or less vividly placed before us, or are thought in only an abstract way. Other human beings also significantly belong to this outer world. We know about ourselves that in this world we like this and not that, that we like to do this and not that, that this or that is pleasing or unpleasing, and so on. Here too we are grasping ourselves, above all, in our relationship to the outer world, and in our opinions of it. It is mirrored, so to speak, in us: we experience ourselves in the first place in terms of our reactions to these mirror images. But how do we actually find ourselves independent of these reflections, independent of the external world? Should we not do as little Alice from the fairy tale did, who stepped into the mirror and discovered on the other side a new, undreamt-of "Wonderland"? Undoubtedly, we must likewise seek the new, wonderful world of the psyche, of the spirit.[30]

---

[29]The title of this chapter in the first edition is "The Inner Givenness of the Psychical and the Spiritual" [*Die innere Gegebenheit des Seelischen und Geistigen*].—Translator's note.

[30]This paragraph replaces the following from the first edition: "The human being is not only a spiritual being, but is, above all, an ensouled being or, since we want to reserve the term 'soul' for a particular aspect of its basic essence, a *psychical* being. And among all the natural givens of the world, it is again the psychic that has the greatest inner affinity with spirit. Indeed, this affinity is so great that it is often said that there is only the psyche, and that the so-called spirit is only a variant of it. (On the distinction between the "psyche" ("soul") and spirit see H. Conrad-Martius, *Metaphysische Gespräche* (Halle 1921).) What is the psyche and where do we find it?

Undoubtedly, we, first and foremost, grasp the psychical in our own "mental life" [*Seelenleben*] when we look at it "from the inside." But, when we plunge into our "interior," we find all sorts of bodily [*Körperliches*] feelings as well, so we need to be more specific about what the psychical is before we go further. In addition to humans, we also consider animals to be psychical beings, while plants are not psychical, and stones and other "inorganic" substances are even less so. But, what is it that distinguishes animals from plants? Certainly, it must be consciousness (that is, the ability to know something, to experience something, the ability to think, to know, to want, to value, etc.,

The first thing we are always confronted with, and without which we could not know or state anything at all, is that we are always "intending-something," "thinking-about-something," or inwardly "referring-to-something,"[31] all of which emanates from us, from *our I*. *I* see, I see *something* (the thing seen); *I* love, I love *something* (the beloved); *I* hate, I hate *something*, and<36>this occurs in all lived experiences. This *I* from which the lived-experience emanates is always in me, with me. The I is also perhaps the first thing I find in this turning back, still in the looking glass, but no longer part of the mirror image. *I* experience ... what does this mean? It means that there is a "zero point" in my inner being, so to speak, the point from which my lived-experience emanates, which seems to be inwardly situated, as if in my head (at least I seem to immediately experience it as such), and which in all my lived-experiences consciously directs itself to the objects of experience.[32] We will call this point the *I-point* or the *ego-center*. To begin with, we cannot say much more than that we experience it as the starting point of our consciousness, from which the inner direction of our minds, our intentions with respect to objects, issues, however else this inner direction may be characterized (as thinking, desiring, loving, hating, etc.).

If we examine everything we discover in our conscious lived-experience, we find as I have said not only that *I* experience something, but that I *experience* something in various ways. Quietly looking out my window at the street below is quite different from when I am looking down at that same street with expectation because I am waiting for someone who has yet to arrive. It is again different when I look at the same street and am overjoyed at its delicate beauty in the glow of the evening sun. It is true that here I am always looking out onto the same street, but my lived-experience is at the same time always different—sometimes joyous, sometimes sad, sometimes indifferent, sometimes searching. At one time I may look at the street with strained attention, at others I am thinking of everything else, I am inattentive, absent-minded.

---

to be inwardly directed at something and this 'self-directedness at' itself, which cannot be reduced further, that we all more or less know by the name "consciousness"). But, consciousness has always been regarded as something essentially spiritual, as the most essential aspects of spirit, even if one does not confound it with intellect or reason. How then can the merely psychic be distinguished from pre-psychic life? Or is the moment of knowing only psychical and not yet spiritual? Even in loving, esteeming, valuing, etc., we find that moment of "intending-something," which we call consciousness, although all these impulses are not purely intellectual or rational, and so cannot be peculiar to reason alone. But what about spirit? Undoubtedly, animals are also capable of intending something. One could not possibly imagine any psychical being in which there is no sense of aiming or "intending-something," "thinking-about-something" broadly understood, that we call consciousness. *Here* then we have the essential difference between psychic and pre-psychic life, for certainly we must expect consciousness to be something psychical unless we want to count animals too among the spiritual beings. (The moment of consciousness is, then, the essential characteristic of the psyche. Nevertheless, as we shall see, the moment of consciousness already contains the essential germ for the emergence of the spiritual from the psychical.) But, what does this psyche look like? What do we experience when we grasp ourselves as psychic beings?"—Translator's note.

[31] Husserl calls this intention, intentionality [*Intentionalität*], the most important "primordial phenomenon" of consciousness. See E. Husserl, *Ideen zu einer reinen Phänomenologie*, Vol. I (Halle 1913).

[32] In the first edition the following sentence is added: "Incidentally, this inner 'self-awareness' of consciousness has been called 'intention' [*Intendieren*]".—Translator's note.

All of this is surely to be distinguished from the ego that "looks," even though these ways of looking seem to emanate from the I and are not<37>separated from it in any way, spatially or otherwise. And among these too such lived-experiences are obviously quite different; the inner lived-experience of love is entirely different from that of hate, or of mere perception, thinking, imagining, and so on. We must therefore differentiate lived-experiences from the ego, and, also, the different kinds of lived-experiences from each other. But, how is it that the lived-experiences emanate from the I? Do we really have the inner feeling of experiencing as if the lived-experience emerged from the ego? As long as we are examining a lived-experience into which we (our ego) have already inwardly entered, in which we are living, this seems to be the case. But, what about when we are entered into by an experience, when we are seized by an experience, so to speak, do we also have the feeling that it springs, so to say, from the ego-center? Let us examine this by way of an example. Suppose we look around our street outside the window again. Suddenly, some problem flashes across our mind, and we begin thinking about it intently. Is it not as if the thought of the problem emerged, as it were, from some darkness directly behind the I, the ego-center, as if it seized us, pulled the ego out of the outer self, drew it into itself, so that it now seems to be drawn back inwardly from its seeing, curled up in itself, in order now to ponder the thought *in itself*? Or when a profound inner joy emerges within us, is it not as if something in us, under the I, as if in the heart, were radiating through an inner space in the head in which the ego's inner spirit rests, from which it engages with that which is outside? As if the joy flows through the ego in this space, is drawn into the I, and flows back out into the world through it? And similarly in every case: so long as the ego lives in an experience the experience seems to spring from it, but if we consider what is going on in us when the I<38>passes from one lived-experience to another, we experience how the lived-experience emerges, as it were, from a definite direction in the inner-spiritual background, in the psychical embedding of the ego, and now the I is drawn into itself, until the I and its starting point melt together and become ever more indistinguishable.[33] We will therefore *distinguish* between these, without confusing this distinction for a real, possibly spatial, *separation*. All of this is psychical and is also found in spiritless animals. Let us now see how we might proceed from here to reach the first germs of the spirit and finally the spirit itself.

In addition to the different kinds of lived-experiences, we may distinguish in both the same lived-experience as well as in different lived-experiences degrees of attention and concentration, with which the ego experiences itself as having a lived-experience of something; they may be quite different in one and the same lived-experience, but can also be the same in different lived-experiences. If I look out of the window again, I may be at first quite indifferent, uninterested, and rather absent-minded concerning all the people who pass by down below. Suddenly, I see someone

---

[33] For this and what follows see the fundamental investigations of Alexander Pfänder in "Psychologie der Gesinnungen (Erster Artikel)," *Jahrbuch für Philosophie und phänomenologische Forschung*, Vol. I.1 (1913), p. 75ff., and II, p. 67ff., his *Seele des Menschen. Versuch einer verstehenden Psychologie* (Halle 1933), and the investigations connected with this in my "Zur Ontologie der sozialen Gemeinschaften," *Jahrbuch für Philosophie und phänomenologische Forschung*, Vol. VI (1923), p. 11ff., and especially p. 55ff.

who could be an acquaintance of mine, and now "I fasten my gaze upon him," "direct all my attention to him," "concentrate myself" on him. Here it is as though the ego is inwardly drawing itself together, drawing together its own forces (that is, not the forces of the different lived-experiences flowing into from the background) from every direction in which its attention had been diverted, as if intensifying its inner gaze, with which it is directed at objects. This shifting of its attention is, therefore, the *greatest achievement of the I*, which differs from the mere aiming at an object as well as from its being filled with a lived-experience that flows through it. However, any external object or event in the lived-body (such as toothache) <39> can purely by itself draw the attention of the I, can as it were compel or pull it. But there are also cases where the ego directs its attention at an object or withdraws its attention on its own, by its *own* spontaneity, so to speak, with nothing necessarily changing in the object or the stream of lived-experience (though this is also very often the case). However, *here* we have the first, though still germinal, starting point of the *spirit*. For here we have something like a free "action" of the ego. We thus stand, quite unexpectedly, at one of the first boundary points between the psychical and the mental, one of the main differences between man and animal. We have here, namely, *the first beginnings of self-determination, of a freedom of the I* over-against its lived-experience. For the ego can intensify its lived-experiences through concentration. In the case of several simultaneous lived-experiences (for example, thinking about an object while at the same time listening and seeing something else), it can strengthen the one by paying attention to it, thereby weakening the other by withdrawing its attention and thus its conscious power of experience until this lived-experience perishes from internal weakness until it dies. Thus, we maintain that the intentional turning of attention is the germ of freedom, the germ of the self-determination of the ego over-against its lived-experiences and their contents, and is thus *one* starting point of the spirit.

One must be careful not to confuse or equate this freedom of the ego-center with the emancipation and detachment of the intellect (or reason) from lived-experiences, or even more so with the suppression of lived-experience by the intellect (or reason), which has been so disastrous in our time. This phenomenon, however, is not a necessary (albeit possible) consequence of the freedom of the I. <40> Rather, it is an abuse, a fall from grace of the I, which is self-inflicted and unnecessary. For this one-sided intellectualization of the entirety of psychical (and spiritual) life and experience stems from the fact that the ego gives preference to the impulses of the intellect, and above all allows them to take priority over all other impulses that flow into it. Moreover, because the ego is one-sidedly anchored in them, as if internally clinging to those lived-experiences that originate from the intellect (or reason), in the end only the lived-experiences that are subjugated by the intellect (or reason) find a right to access the ego and enter into it. But, this is by no means necessary. The ego can just as well use its freedom in another direction (for example, by granting access to its inner being, above all to the impulses of its basic essence or to Divine inspirations to grasp *their* basic source). We will come back to this later on in detail.

But, it is not only through intensifying and strengthening, withdrawing and weakening its attention that the I acts freely with respect to lived-experiences. It is capable of much more. There can be impulses that are kept from emerging in inner lived-experience, either by supressing them (anger, for instance), repressing them, or "killing" them through some other means of rational analysis. In the case of repression the impulse of lived-experience does not quite reach the conscious threshold of the I. Here, the ego has placed an inner "gate keeper" on the path between the source point of lived-experience and the I, so that the impulse before it can reach the vicinity of the I is already pushed back to its source. In the case of suppression, on the other hand, the impulse seems to have been already noticed by the I and must now be pushed back by a conscious forcing on the part of the ego itself. This is above all the case with analysis. Here the lived-experience flows<41>out from its source and penetrates the I, but without properly flowing through the entire ego. It is accompanied by disintegrating analyses and ethical devaluations that the ego lives through *simultaneously*, and is gradually drowned in their stream. This is, of course, the "healthiest" path if the annihilation of the lived-experience in question is justified.

The freedom of the ego consists only in its ability to act with respect to those lived-experiences that appear as impulses in it, but it seems to have no direct influence on their emergence. But, this is not the case. In the case of outer perception and all other lived-experiences that are dependent on the self-givenness of objects that are *independent of the I*, the ego is not in a position to bring about the occurrence of these lived-experiences directly by its own power (with the exception of external actions, such as the locomotion of lived-bodies in space, through which this indirectly occurs). Here it can only prepare itself for lived-experiences that may come, or their possible refusal. (The I can listen into the distance, in case something calls out to it, but it cannot itself produce the call; or it can close itself off inwardly from lived-experiences, shutting its "inner" and outer eyes and ears.) At best it can as far as possible look for its object. On the other hand, in the case of those lived-experiences that flow out from an inner source, it can at least encourage their arrival. For example, the I can keep an inner "feeler" held out in the direction of the inner psyche, from which the impulses of its conscience (its basic essence) tend to flow, and it can as often and as willingly obey these impulses, despite all inner inhibitions, as if there was already a clear path from the I to their source point. Similarly, it can also aspire to give rise to certain lived-experiences<42>, as, for example, by internally presenting everything that usually attends to a certain lived-experience (such as joy). Finally, if it had a lived-experience of a certain kind, it can remain, so to speak, in constant contact with its source, so that this connection (for instance, with the "heart" from which the impulse of love arises) becomes a permanent (habitual)[34] attitude. Here the ego is certainly not entirely free. It is dependent upon the lived-experiences that arise in it, on the sources of these lived-experiences, the conditions of the body (a blind person can never be given a lived-experience of seeing), the original givenness of some partially independent object, a particularly strong lived-experience may "take it by surprise" (quick to anger), its strength may fail, and so on. Nevertheless, in the manner outlined above, it has the possibility to exercise a certain inner autonomy, and

---

[34]See my "Zur Ontologie der sozialen Gemeinschaften," *Jahrbuch für Philosophie und phänomenologische Forschung*, Vol. VI (1923), p. 38ff.

the power to execute this autonomy grows with increasing exercise.[35] According to contemporary psychology, all of this is absent in most animals, and they are therefore merely psychical, and not spiritual, beings. (The most primitive beginnings of the spontaneity of attention can be ascribed to them. Even if animals were to be granted more than this, the essential distinction between spiritual and merely psychical being would not be effaced. There would only be a shift in assigning some group of real living beings to one domain or the other.)

A second essential point of distinction between spiritual and merely psychical consciousness is *self-consciousness*. As we have discussed, all lived-experience has the form "I experience something." We have just now explored the meaning of the "*I* experience something," as well as the meaning of "I *experience* something."<43>Now, what remains to be investigated is the meaning of "I experience *something*," and here further essential points of distinction between psychical and spiritual beings will be made clear. They consist in the possession of *self*-consciousness, and in the possession of a *basic spiritual essence*, which enables the spiritual being to have a lived-experience of spiritual objects, which the purely psychical being in spite of its consciousness is absolutely incapable of doing.[36]

With the ability to withdraw voluntarily from or enter into its lived-experiences, as we have seen, the ego has provided us with the first point of departure for *mastering and regarding its lived-experiences*. For the ego bears within itself the ability to direct itself toward something, to be conscious of something. This is not given to it by the lived-experiences which enter into the I and through which it lives, but only by the content, the object, to which "knowledge of" is directed.[37] Similarly, the lived-experiences lead the I to the stream, as it were, in which it is swimming (whether thinking, loving, hating, valuing, willing, wishing, and so on). By the force of its independence over-against the various lived-experiences in which it lives, and due to the fact that the moment of consciousness of (the intentionality) pertains to itself, not to individual lived-experiences, the ego is capable of directing itself upon itself in self-consciousness (self-awareness, self-esteem, self-hatred, self-love, and so on). And this again enables the I to affirm, suppress, strengthen, weaken, etc., its impulses. But, taken in isolation the capacity for self-consciousness, the ability to have knowledge of the lived-experiences of the ego, would not yet guarantee the freedom of the I. For it is conceivable that in the lived-experience of reflecting on its lived-experiences the ego appears to grasp its lived-experiences, but then is completely unfree and at the mercy of their automatic stream.[38] The moment of relative freedom of the will<44>is therefore something other than that of self-consciousness. The latter,

---

[35] See Dietrich von Hildebrand, "Sittlichkeit und ethische Werterkenntnis," *Jahrbuch für Philosophie und phänomenologische Forschung*, Vol. V (1922).

[36] See A. Pfänder, *Philosophie der Lebensziele* (Göttingen 1948), p. 111ff.

[37] In the first edition this sentence continues: "... the special 'something' by which consciousness is the 'consciousness of something'".—Translator's note.

[38] This seems to be the case at times with hypnosis. See, for example, B.J. Björkhem, *Die verborgene Kraft* (Olten 1954), p. 186.

however, requires the former: the higher, later, spiritual part of the two is perhaps the moment of inner self-will.

We now come to the last essential distinction between psychical and spiritual beings, which relies both on *the object of experience* and on the inner condition of what can be experienced, and consists in the fact that the spiritual being has a *spiritual core*, a *spiritual basic essence*, which, among other things, allows it to have a lived-experience of realities outside of itself, something which purely psychical and not yet spiritual beings are incapable of (be it animals or human beings at a lower spiritual level, which, of course, has nothing to do in the least with intellectual education or lack thereof). Even in Plato's philosophy we find the basic idea that like can only be recognized by like, or things of a similar nature (*idem per idem*); that, for example, we ourselves have a body and it is only through having this body that we can possibly grasp the physical world; it is only through our psyche that we have access to psychical beings existing outside of us.[39] The same is also true of the spiritual: only insofar as we are spiritual beings can we grasp spiritual things (be it other spiritual beings, their auras, or spiritual objects they have created). And, the more we are spiritual, the higher our spirituality and the more and higher the spirituality we are capable of receiving. Just as we might imagine some being who can only perceive things in the physical world, such as a physical body having a physical color and form, but not the full spectrum of the colors of white light or colors irrespective of their attachment to a physical body, one might also imagine that a spiritual being could grasp only the lower degrees of the spiritual and the supernatural, while the higher spiritual beings would be beyond its grasp. As is the case with certain mediums, <45> who though "blind" to the religious domain, cannot help but recognize all kinds of ghosts: *Du gleichst dem Geist, den du begreifst* [you are like the spirit you comprehend] (and vice versa, it is only the spirit that you comprehend which is more or less like you). This applies at least to the lower levels; since the higher levels clearly encompass the lower ones, one can presumably survey and understand all lower levels of spirit from a higher level, but not vice versa.

Thus, if we attend to our lived-experiences, we notice how they flow from the different inner spheres to the ego, and how the I directs its gaze to the objects and contents corresponding to them, but that only certain kinds of lived-experiences "connect" with certain kinds of objects, and enable the ego to perceive them. It is only when we consciously exert our outer senses that we are able to have a lived-experience of the external physical world and the worlds constructed upon it, only when we are "inside" our lived-body that we can be conscious of its inner bodily processes (see also Chap. 8), only when we enter into our inner psychic realm that we are able to have a lived-experience of what is specifically psychical (for example, memory, phantasy, etc.). And it is only when we enter into the spiritual realm of

---

[39]This appears to be an allusion to the affinity argument in Plato's *Phaedo*. "Gleiches durch Gleiches" is a view attributed to Empedocles and criticized by Aristotle in *De Anima*.—Translator's note.

our inner being, into our spiritual basic essence, that we are able to have a lived-experience of the spiritual.[40]

Some have also spoken of a basic essence of animals, the entelechy of these living beings. This has led them to understand, first, the original type of essence (real being) that is realized in them, the "idea" (*eidos*) they instantiate: living being in general. Second, they have grasped the real force in them (and its real basic source), which causes these beings to be a specific type of living being. (The cause is already in the plant, <46> such that from the acorn comes the oak, not a fir, from the grain of wheat comes a stalk of wheat, not a beanstalk, and so on.) In this sense, we can speak of the "metaphysical real essence" of a being.[41] Finally, from here we can distinguish the beings that are themselves fully developed by this force in accordance with the idea. Here, therefore, we have in plants a purely physical ("vital") basic essence, in animals a psycho-physical basic essence, and in human beings a spiritual–psycho-physical basic essence.[42] Whether and to what extent these different kinds of basic essences are only particular radiations, emanations, of one and the same eternal, super-spiritual being—the Divine basic essence in the sense of Plotinus' theory of emanation—we cannot investigate here.

To the human person (that is, to a being that is also spiritually determined) belongs not only an ego-center, which can escape and not blindly succumb to psychic drives, but also an inner psycho-spiritual realm. This provides the ego with the firm ground upon which it can judge and evaluate these inner drives, and *shape itself* in accordance with higher values.[43] But where must we begin, into which sphere of our inner being must we delve to get hold of this basic spiritual essence?

---

[40] On the difference between the spiritual and the psychical see M. Scheler "The Idols of Self Knowledge" in *Abhandlungen und Aufsätze*, Vol. II (Leipzig 1915), and H. Conrad-Martius, *Metaphysische Gespräche* (Halle 1921).

[41] See my "Zur Ontologie der sozialen Gemeinschaften," *Jahrbuch für Philosophie und phänomenologische Forschung*, Vol. VI (1923), p. 7ff., as well as "Entelecheia" in H. Conrad-Martius, *Der Selbstaufbau der Natur*, 2nd edn. (Munich 1961).

[42] See A. Pfänder, *Philosophie der Lebensziele* (Göttingen 1948), p. 28ff.

[43] See, for instance, Edith Stein, *Endliches und ewiges Sein*, p. 336ff. (Freiburg 1950); H. Conrad-Martius, *Metaphysische Gespräche* (Halle 1921); and A. Pfänder, *Philosophie der Lebensziele* (Göttingen 1948).

The Sense of Mystical Experience According to Gerda Walther

Angela Ales Bello

Abstract Interest in mysticism is present in the writings of the Phenomenological School of Philosophy, which was founded by Edmund Husserl. Edith Stein and Gerda Walther, for example, are phenomenologists who investigate mysticism. The former is better known for this kind of investigation, but it should be remarked that the only book dedicated to the topic was written by the latter. Walther connects mysticism with telepathy, but she also distinguishes the objects of the two experiences. In mysticism Walther claims that the object of investigation is the exceptional and direct encounter with God. To describe this encounter, Walther, like Stein, examines the human being, ultimately comparing it to a lamp. Through this image, Walther allows us to grasp what it is like to experience the live presence of God that invades our being. This type of mystical experience can be found in all religions, thereby demonstrating that it is a real possibility given by God to human beings.

Keywords Phenomenological method · Hyletics · Noetics · Telepathy Mystical experience

The theme of mysticism is found throughout the philosophical explorations of phenomenology. This is due to the fact that phenomenologists, especially the early women phenomenologists, devoted much attention to the phenomenon of religion. Furthermore, interest in the structure of human beings also led to an exploration of religion because of the spiritual constitution of the human person. Gerda Walther can be rightfully viewed as the phenomenologist who carried out the most sustained and focused research on the phenomenon of mysticism. Edith Stein, though deeply interested in the question of mysticism, certainly explored it, but largely through the specific writings of Teresa of Avila and John of the Cross. Walther focused on the topic itself, making illustrative references to mystics from a variety of religions. To grasp Walther's unique position I will analyze her *Phänomenologie der Mystik*

Translated by Antonio Calcagno.

A. Ales Bello (✉)
Pontifical Lateran University, Rome, Italy
e-mail: alesbello@tiscali.it

A. Calcagno (ed.), *Gerda Walther's Phenomenology of Sociality, Psychology, and Religion*, Women in the History of Philosophy and Sciences 2,
https://doi.org/10.1007/978-3-319-97592-4_10

[*The Phenomenology of Mysticism*].[1] I argue that, for Walther, mystical experience presupposes an accurate understanding of the structure of the human person, which includes both hyletic and noetic dimensions.

Moreover, it should be noted here that, following Husserl, phenomenologists, from Stein to Heidegger, from Conrad-Martius to Max Scheler and the Munich phenomenologist Alexander Pfänder (who did not directly belong to the Göttingen and Freiburg Circles), who were often cited by Walther and Stein in their own studies, carried out philosophical anthropological studies to grasp the genesis of all expressions of a human being, a point with which I have great sympathy. These phenomenologists taught us that we cannot understand human attitudes, cultural works, and actions without grasping the essence of the human being.

The type of investigation Walther carries out is admittedly circular: what we encounter are human expressions and productions, and if we seek to understand their meaning and origin we inadvertently have to ask about their authors. Certainly, this is not the first time in philosophy that we encounter such circular thinking. The novelty of Husserl's phenomenology consists of a deep archeological excavation, which not only draws from psychology, especially Brentano's,[2] but which also is deeply philosophical and specifically gnoseological and anthropological. It inspires the members of the phenomenological school to investigate and rationally explain the deep, complex folds of a human being. As Husserl, citing Heraclitus, reminds us: "Whatever path you choose to follow, you will never find the limits of the soul, for its depths are most great."[3]

The presence of women in Husserl's school could be justified by observing that he was certainly open to their participation in the group and that phenomenology proposes a type of analysis that is very congenial to a "woman's" thinking. An immediate objection to this line of reasoning lies in the claim that philosophical research is not conditioned by gender differences. For many years, however, and not only at the personal level[4] but also in conjunction with other women philosophers[5], I have sought to demonstrate the particularity of philosophical research carried out by women.

Edith Stein was the first philosopher to take up at length the difference between male and female, though she did not extend her treatment to a discussion of how the two genders contributed to philosophy itself. I draw upon Stein's analysis to extend her treatment in the direction mentioned above. Her position on this theme is particularly important because she never opposed male rationality to female feel-

---

[1] Gerda Walther, *Phänomenologie der Mystik* (Olten: Walter Verlag, 1955).

[2] I treat the connection of phenomenology to psychology in my book: Angela Ales Bello, *Il senso dell'umano: Fenomenologia, Psicologia, Psicopatologia* (Rome: Castelvecchi, 2016).

[3] Heraclitus Fragment, as cited by Husserl in his *Crisis of the European Sciences and Transcendental Phenomenology*, trans. by David Carr (Evanston, IL; Northwestern University Press), Sect. 49.

[4] Angela Ales Bello, *Fenomenologia dell'essere umano: Lineamenti di una filosofia al femminile* [*The Phenomenology of the Human Person: An Outline for a Philosophy by Woman*] (Rome: Città Nuova, 1992).

[5] See the work of the group of Italian feminist philosophers at the University of Verona called *Diotima* as well as the work of University of Rome philosopher Francesca Brezzi.

ings, as many have done, including certain feminist thinkers; rather, she shows that women, and not only men, have theoretical capacities and interests that she defines as "metaphysical" and as possessing their own unique characteristics. She, along with Hedwig Conrad-Martius and Gerda Walther, are concrete examples of people who possess exquisite, profound capacities for theoretical work.

The descriptor "exquisite" came to mind spontaneously, and I believe that it demonstrates the particular quality of women phenomenologists' theoretical capacities. These capacities are accompanied by a sensibility that is not opposed to intellectual research; rather, they permit Gerda Walther to investigate aspects of reality that often escape standard research practices and methods. Stein claims that each individual human being possesses both male and female characteristics.[6] One should not see male and female as opposites; rather, they are tendencies found in both genders that appear in various forms.

As discussed above, a reading of the early women phenomenologists as well as female philosophers, in general, allows us to see these particular forms in relation to certain themes already investigated or questions to be raised. All of this is most clear in Gerda Walther's work. Let us recall that general tendencies that can be individuated in a "universal" way are articulated in each human being in a non-repeatable way, and this must be the object of philosophical reflection.[7]

I have written about the three phenomenologists together; however, they are three distinct personalities. Hedwig Conrad-Martius is more rational–scientific and Edith Stein is more rational, theoretical, and metaphysical. Gerda Walther is a rational type of person, though she investigates what is beyond the rational (namely, the paranormal and the occult). These different personalities show how universality articulates itself in singular, human forms.

Walther's concern with what lies beyond the purely rational can be found in her work, *Phenomenology of Mysticism*, first published in 1923 and in a subsequent edition in 1955. She states that the work is the fruit of her research into the nature of the Divine and, in particular, mystical experience. Her analysis of the Divine is like Edith Stein's, who precedes her investigation of mysticism with a reflection on religious experience, as lived by *homo religiosus* (the religious human being), who is not always mystical. Stein, following Teresa of Avila, distinguishes the experience of faith from mystical experience.

Walther also draws inspiration from Saint Teresa of Avila, but she is struck by the particular nature of the deep contact with the Divine, understood as mystical experience. An atheist, she describes opening herself up spontaneously to the Divine though a reading of the works of Saint Teresa of Avila, books about Saint Teresa, and the writings of other mystics. To understand Saint Teresa, Walther focuses her inquiry on the paranormal and the supra-rational.

---

[6]I have often returned to this argument and I have synthesized these tendencies in my latest book: Angela Ales Bello, *Tutto colpa di Eva. Antropologia e religione dal femminismo alla gender theory* [*It's All Eve's Fault: Anthropology and Feminism from Feminism to Gender Theory*] (Roma: Castelvecchi, 2017).

[7]I treat this theme in one of my first books, *Fenomenologia dell'essere umano. Lineamenti di una filosofia al femminile* (Rome: Città Nuova, 1992).

Walther's turn to the mystical must not be read as esoteric or light. On the contrary, she presents a rigorous phenomenological description in Husserlian style. Husserl wrote a letter to Walther, which could be read as a book review of sorts and which is preserved in the Husserl Archives at the University of Louvain. He does not criticize the manner in which his former student proceeded to describe paranormal phenomena; rather, he expresses, as Walther records in her Introduction to the text, his doubts about the object of mystical experience (that is, God). He raises his doubts not because he does not believe in God, but because he did not think that what the mystics described could serve as a valid foundation for attaining God. In other words, according to Husserl, mystics are guilty of a kind of a personal exaltation, an "ardent love," that pushed them to affirm mystical union. Again, Husserl does not reveal himself as a skeptic in his letter; rather, in my opinion, he shows himself as a possibilist, because he affirms that there exist depths in the human being that are not accessible, depths in which the Divine reveals itself. The descriptions of depth by mystics, however, are only "ideal possibilities." On one hand, the letter reveals that mystical experience possesses a certain typicality, a habitus that is identical in sense, understood as a structural sense, in all human beings. Every subject has his or her own particular world, with its own depths. On the other hand, Husserl hypothesizes the fullness of possible experiences that open new ways and perspectives, thereby establishing a double movement of descent into the "profound depths" and ascent out of the greatest depths; "... which moves in the profound depths and which comes from the greatest depths."[8] We know that what is "possible" for Husserl is also "realizable,"[9] even though in fact it may not be realized. Hence, Husserl's observations contained in his long 7-page letter have led me to postulate that perhaps he could have viewed mysticism as a way to God, not because the object is reached by moving outside of oneself, but because one can always enter more deeply into oneself, so deeply that one may reach the point where God dwells.[10]

Let us now focus our attention on Walther's text. Prior to discussing mysticism proper, she analyzes other experiences (for example, telepathy). To be able to investigate such experiences, one requires an understanding of the complex structure of human beings. To do this she deploys her "venerated teacher" Husserl's method. Although Walther examines her own personal experiences, she is able to extract important elements from them. Walther is different from Husserl in that she starts from very specific experiences that are clarified through Husserl's method. By using his method, Walther identifies closely with her teacher, but Husserl, rather than starting with specific experiences, looks to the human being and all that happens to him/her at the everyday level: perceptions, memories, imaginings, reflections, empathy, and

[8]Edmund Husserl, "Entwurf eines Briefes als Antwort gedacht an Frl. Walther" ["Thought Sketch for a Response Letter to Miss Walther"] (Ms. trans. A.V.21, p. 7.).

[9]See Angela Ales Bello, *The Sense of Things: Toward a Phenomenological Realism*, trans. by Antonio Calcagno (Analecta Husserliana No. 118) (Dordrecht: Springer, 2015), Sect. 5.2.1.

[10]Angela Ales Bello, *The Divine in Husserl and Other Explorations*, trans. by Antonio Calcagno (Analecta Husserliana No. 98) (Dordrecht: Springer, 2009).

many other kinds of lived experiences [*Erlebnisse*], which Walther will draw upon to analyze both telepathy and mysticism, as we shall see.

Neither Husserl nor Stein nor Conrad-Martius were attracted to the study of the paranormal and the occult, but they all maintained that no phenomena were to be excluded from phenomenological study. Hedwig Conrad-Martius pushed for a second edition (1955) of Walther's work on mysticism, and one finds in it numerous references to Saint Teresa's *Interior Castle* and Edith Stein's *Science of the Cross*. In my view, this indicates a profound intellectual collaboration between the women phenomenologists.

Research Method

In addressing the question about the characteristics and cognitive validity of the mystical lived-experience, Walther carefully uses the phenomenological method, as previously mentioned. The first step of the method is to deploy the epoché to suspend prejudices about our natural beliefs about phenomena. Husserl maintained that the epoché was essential for all phenomenological and philosophical investigation. In Walther's Introduction one finds the specific object of her inquiry delineated as well as two prejudices that must be bracketed. First, God cannot give Himself to human beings as He is standing before us in "flesh and blood." If one experiences God, then it must be considered an illusion of psyche. This prejudice stems, according to Walther, from the rampant and dominant psychologism found in German culture in the early part of the 20th century. The second prejudice extends from the legacy of British empiricism that maintains that all knowledge must pass through the senses; the senses are the only acceptable instruments of cognition.[11]

Concerning this second prejudice, Walther affirms that both telepathic and mystical knowing are not based in the senses, even though mystics will often describe physical sensations connected with the body. Many mystics, however, will lodge these sensory descriptions in metaphorical language. Moreover, although they use the language of sensation, mystics will also note a great difference between what is experienced or sensed in the body and what is being lived spiritually in the presence of the Divine. For example, Angela of Foligno felt the passion of Christ in all of her limbs, and she received the stigmata as a sign of Christ's presence. Certainly, her sensations were not received though physical contact with the Divine. In this sense Walther's claim about the second prejudice may be viewed as correct. I view these sensations as belonging to the "hyletic" aspect of knowledge. Let us briefly consider the hyletic sphere to show how it is present and active in mystical experience, which human beings live from within and not from without.

[11] Gerda Walther, *Phänomenologie der Mystik*, 24–25.

The Role of Hyletics and Noetics in Mysticism

The meanings of Husserl's terms "hyletic" and "noetic" can be clarified by tracing the flow of our lived-experiences. Consciousness shows us that all lived-experiences are dual in nature insofar as they consist of a noetic, intentional moment and a hyletic, material one. *Hyle* and *noesis* are Greek words that denote "matter" and "thought." However, they are used by phenomenologists in different ways than their Greek etymology would convey. They indicate two kinds of cognitive processes. The hyletic refers to a "material sensory" process, whereas the noetic refers to the fact that our cognition is intentional and always seeks a sense or meaning. The description of this doubleness can be seen in the analysis of our bodies that we feel as living [*Leib*]. This lived-body not only has localized in it the sensations delivered by our senses, which play a constitutive role in the constitution of objects in space, but also other kinds of sensations, which are often called sensual feelings (for example, the sensations of pleasure, pain, the well-being of the body as well as the discomfort of the body caused by some bodily condition or sickness).[12] This last point is important for understanding religious and mystical experience.

Edith Stein's example of a block of granite is particularly illustrative here. When we seek to know what the block of granite is like we know that we are dealing here with a formation of matter that has sense or meaning. Its form is full of sense because it is constituted according to a structural principle in which its weight, consistency, and hardness all participate. We can even say that part of knowing what granite is involves us grasping that it presents itself in "enormous blocks" and not in small grains or pieces.[13] What is important for us is that we are "affected at the level of the senses" by the granite, for as we touch and see it "it draws our attention in a unique way." In fact, its seemingly immovable consistency and its massiveness are not only things that fall under our senses and that reason may observe as real, but the senses and reason are also struck from within. The senses and reason reveal something to us, and we can grasp something about what the senses and reason present.[14]

The hyletic, then, is particularly connected to both the bodily and psychic dimensions of human beings. It is the sphere of sensibility revealed by Husserl in his analysis of passive synthesis, which looks at layers of perception as well as lived-experiences of psyche.[15] For example, a particular color may elicit a sense of well-being or feeling unwell, which may be seized consciously by "living through" such experiences. However, intentional functions, which are noetic, are connected with the aforementioned layers of sensations. This means that the material content of experience takes

[12]See Sect. 39 of Edmund Husserl's *Ideas Pertaining to a Pure Phenomenology and a Phenomenological Philosophy*, Vol. 2, trans. by R. Rojcewicz (Dordrecht: Springer, 1990).

[13]Edith Stein, *Der Aufbau der menschlichen Person. Vorlesungen zur philosophischen Anthropologie*, newly ed. by B. Beckmann-Zöller (Edith Stein Gesamtausgabe Vol. 14) (Freiburg: Herder, 2004), 116.

[14]Edith Stein, *Der Aufbau der menschlichen Person*, 116.

[15]Angela Ales Bello, *Hyle, Body, Life: Phenomenological Archaeology of the Sacred* (Analecta Husserliana No. 57) (Dordrecht: Springer, 1998), 63–74.

on a spiritual function. This is also the case for sense experience, which forms part of perceptions upon which perceptual judgments are based (for example, the judgment "This is a book").[16] Here we are dealing with another aspect of human beings, who not only physically feel but also react psychically, value, judge, and decide. Certainly, this aspect is specifically human because it is a unifying aspect. The human being must be considered in all its complexity, in a hierarchy of functions that move from the sensible-sensory sphere to the intellectual-voluntary sphere, from the hyletic to the noetic.

Both spheres are present in mystical experience. Edith Stein characterizes mystical experience as the manifestation of the Divine, understood as presence; we can also grasp something of the Divine in mystical experience. The whole of the human person is involved in a mystical experience, even though the sphere of the sensible may be privileged. In mystical experience one finds a sensible presence or even the deprivation of sense experience because all the senses are involved, although they may not all act autonomously. Whereas "faith concerns the intellect," "contemplation is an affair of the heart or the intimacy of the soul and, therefore, involves all of the faculties."[17] The presence of God is accompanied by interior sensations of happiness or intense nostalgia. Here the intellect and the will "stand and watch." They are not activated even though they may be seized by mystical experience. The Divine presence grips and burns with love, penetrating, following the description of Teresa of Avila, the "interior castle," which is like the heart of the Andalusian palm, the intimate center where the soul is truly at home.

Examining the texts of John of the Cross, whose poetic force successfully expresses a whole range of interior reactions, Edith Stein insists that diverse levels of the human being participate in such reactions. In particular, she traces in John of the Cross's *The Living Flame of Love* a series of "sensations" of the soul: "The activity of the Holy Spirit in the soul produces an inflamed love in which the will of the soul becomes one single love in union with the Divine flame."[18] The flame *touches* and *injures*, and in the deepest center of the soul it carries out a substantial and most pleasing action, which consists of a manifestation of the beatific vision. "The soul can only act itself with the help of the corporeal senses, and in this state it is totally free and far removed from them," and so "it limits itself to one thing which is receiving from God. He alone can move the soul and complete his work in the depths of its being... without the mediation of the senses." So, all movements of the soul become Divine, are acts of God, yet also acts of the soul. "For God works them in it and with it, insofar as it gives its consent and agreement."[19]

One thinks here of Bernini's statue of *Saint Teresa in Ecstasy* and how he succeeds in expressing the saint's rapture in being seized by God, which involved her whole person and in which all of the senses participated, even in their passivity. This union of

[15]Angela Ales Bello, *Hyle, Body, Life: Phenomenological Archaeology of the Sacred*, 63–74.

[17]Angela Ales Bello, *Hyle, Body, Life: Phenomenological Archaeology of the Sacred*, 206.

[18]Edith Stein, *The Science of the Cross*, trans. by Josephine Koeppel, OCD (The Collected Works of Edith Stein No. 6) (Washington, DC: ICS Publications), 187.

[19]Edith Stein, *The Science of the Cross*, 188.

the saint with God reveals something about the nature of God: one grasps in Teresa's hand that God is both one and three. Edith Stein suggests that the mystery of the Trinity is revealed not through rational reflection (which will never be successful), but through direct contact. It is through being burned that the hand and the caress of the Father, Son, and Holy Spirit are revealed. We are not dealing here with metaphors and symbols, for these are real presences and actions. "All three Divine persons take up their dwelling in the soul."[20] This dwelling of the Trinity produces extraordinary delight. The experience, as recounted by mystics, prevalently remains in the soul, but in certain cases, Stein says, "the internal wound also manifests externally in the body. John of the Cross recalls here the stigmata of Saint Francis."[21] As we shall see, Gerda Walther, in describing mystical experience, speaks of the rigidity of the body that accompanies mystical experience, though she does not explicitly mention the hyletic dimension.

The Structure of the Human Being According to Gerda Walther

The analysis of the hyletic and noetic dimensions helps us to understand the structure of the human being. Gerda Walther claims that body, psyche, and spirit are the three components that form the human individual, and she dedicates a significant portion of her work on mysticism to an essential description of them.[22] The three aspects are real and coordinated by the I-center, which Walther describes in a personal and original manner, although she follows in large part Husserl's analysis of the pure I. All lived-experiences ultimately refer to the I-point or I-center. It has the autonomous capacity to self-determine and to act freely through the power of spirit and the lived-experiences of spirit. The I is the most noble part of the human being. The conscious I is distinguished from the subconscious, which must not be understood as the unconscious of Freud, for Walther's subconscious is the source of determined lived-experiences.[23]

Walther describes the subconscious as *Einbettung* or embedment. The root sense of the word (namely, bed) denotes a place that contains or encloses something. It is the deepest aspect of the human being though unconscious. We can understand the subconscious with the metaphor of an ancient oil lamp. The combustible liquid is the deepest part of the lamp and may be viewed as the subconscious. One also finds in the lamp the layers of the psyche and spirit. The I-center is the wick. The container of the lamp is the body. We are conscious of the lived-experiences that emerge from

[20] Edith Stein, *The Science of the Cross*, 195.

[21] Edith Stein, *The Science of the Cross*, 197.

[22] Gerda Walther, *Phänomenologie der Mystik*, Chaps. 8–10.

[23] Gerda Walther, *Phänomenologie der Mystik*, Chap. 2.

this lamp, and all lived-experiences are ego-centered[24] (that is, they always refer to the I).

The I-center must not be confused with the fundamental essence of the human being, in which lie human autonomy and self-consciousness. Here, one could view Walther's I-center as being similar to Stein's notion of "core" or the "soul of the soul." Stein says the core is where the singularity of the human resides and where the Divine manifests itself. For Walther the fundamental essence of the human is placed behind or, more precisely, beyond the aforementioned embedment.[25]

Characteristics of Mystical Experience According to Walther

To arrive at the essence of mystical experience Walther begins by making a series of general claims, which can be read as a series of concentric circles. One moves through the various circles to arrive at the specific object constitutive of mystical experience. Two circles are of primary importance (namely, telepathy[26] and the particular form of emptying of the I).[27] Walther's analysis of telepathy draws upon her own and others' experiences of it. Her phenomenological descriptions display both critical distance and acute objective analysis.

In telepathy the origin of lived-experiences becomes important. As ego-centered beings we are conscious that the source of our lived-experiences is in ourselves and that some of those experiences may be deployed to understand what lies inside and outside us. Walther describes the lived-experience of telepathy as having within oneself the very same lived-experiences of another person without us causing such experiences to happen. We note here that the mystical lived-experience is related to the "other person." Whereas in telepathy the other person is human, the other person in mystical experience is Divine.

Empathy allows one to grasp the lived-experiences of another while knowing that the source of these lived-experiences lies in the other. Husserl and Stein describe empathic experiences as non-originary or non-primordial. Ego and alter ego never identify with one another in empathy. We grasp the sense of the other's lived-experiences and we can share what is universal about them. For example, the joy I experience also contains within itself the essence of joy in general, which I can recognize as being present in the joy of the other. In telepathy, by contrast, Walther asserts that one lives fully the experience of the other, as lived by the other. Walther gives the example of living the experience of a friend. The source of the experience

---

[24]For a more detailed description of the oil lamp metaphor see my *Fenomenologia dell'essere umano. Lineamenti di una filosofia al femminile* as well as my book with Marina Pia Pellegrino, *Edith Stein–Gerda Walther, Incontri possibili. Empatia, Telepatia, Comunità, Mistica,* ed. by Angela Ales Bello and Marina Pia Pellegrino (Rome: Castelvecchi, 2014). See also Marina Pia Pellegrino's chapter in this book (Chap. 3).

[25]Gerda Walther, *Phänomenologie der Mystik*, Chap. 12.

[26]Gerda Walther, *Phänomenologie der Mystik*, Chap. 4.

[27]Gerda Walther, *Phänomenologie der Mystik*, Chap. 12.

does not lie with the I, but in the other. Such experiences are not usual, nor do they fall outside the norm, and hence may be considered paranormal.

As we shall see, telepathic experiences prefigure mystical ones. For telepathic experiences to occur the I must find itself, says Gerda Walther, as an "isolated I," an I that has lost all of its ties with the outside world and its fundamental essence. Here the ego can be considered completely "free." She speaks of the foregoing state not as a possible experience, but as an actual experience that she underwent in 1918 when visiting her gravely ill father.[28] On her return visit home, she described herself as losing touch with her body, the embedment of her being, and with her own lived-experiences. She described herself as being isolated in an "abyss," which completely surrounded her.[29] She admits that such a situation was difficult to bear. When such abysmal states afflict human beings, they feel they need to seek something other, greater, and more stable (namely, the Divine).

Here two possibilities present themselves. First, one can turn inward and be in touch with oneself and others while linking oneself to human things and persons. Second, one can remain on the path of solitude and seek a definitive Something,[30] which one may not know fully but for which one may be nostalgic, as mystics do. But, in the case of the latter possibility, if one has nostalgia for this Something, does not one know that this being exists, and how does one access such a being? The only possibility, then, is that this Something is already present in our deepest being, in the seventh room, to borrow a metaphor of Saint Teresa of Avila.

Walther believes, however, that this Something must be external: the I calls it and waits for it. It does not live in the human being. The difference between Something that resides internally as opposed to dwelling externally is the precise difference between Edith Stein's position and Walther's view on the relation between the human and the Divine. Walther's position is justifiable, given that she does not wish to reduce the Divine to a human possession. Having "nostalgia" for Something Divine cannot be explained unless the I already had known that the Divine already existed, because it is present in us. Here we are dealing with a dynamic of presence–absence insofar as the Divine leaves a trace in us, which was not produced by us, otherwise we would not seek it. But, this trace does not capture the whole of the greatness of the Divine being. The Divine is greater than us and it transcends us. If it wishes to be known it must manifest itself.

The descriptors of the Divine trace or spark, to follow Meister's Eckhart's description, are not accepted by Walther because she holds that the relation between the essence of the human being and that of the Divine are incommensurable. For Walther, one must move beyond oneself to find God, and God can only be found if God chooses to manifest himself. Here, we are speaking about grace. She excludes religion as an originary, "natural" fact, ultimately affirming religion as something given by God and as being purely spiritual.[31] Walther is speaking here of Divine revelation, albeit

---

[28]Gerda Walther, *Phänomenologie der Mystik*, 139.

[29]Gerda Walther, *Phänomenologie der Mystik*, 138.

[30]Gerda Walther, *Phänomenologie der Mystik*, 143.

[31]Gerda Walther, *Phänomenologie der Mystik*, 183–184.

she never explicitly uses such terms. Further proof for her position on the primacy of Divine revelation can be found in her discussion of the two modes of relation: Either God manifests Himself directly to the human being or does so through a mediator to whom He has already shown Himself.

The case of the mediator presents two more possibilities for consideration: Either the mediator is Divine (that is, it is God Himself as is the case with the Incarnate Christ), or it is other human beings who refract the Divine light and speak of God. Human mediators (for example, the reformers of historical religions) always bring a limited message because it belongs to certain people. Walther's insight here is very interesting because it justifies the possibility of a plurality of religions in that many religions refract the Divine against a plurality of human beings, all of whom possess their own unique characteristics. Every expression of religion, then, captures aspects of the Divine, although such aspects never fully capture the Divine. Often, these Divine qualities are mixed with human ones. One can speak of a universal religion only if the mediator is God, which is the case for the incarnate Christ.

For Walther, religion is always linked to an *ab extra* revelation of the Divine; religion does not come from the presence of the Divine in us. Stein, however, reminds us that revelation can be both public and private. The former is given to the founders of various historical religions and it passes through various human filters. The message is directed to both individuals and the collectivity, as is the case in diverse religions. Hence, religion may be viewed as both a subjective and inter-subjective phenomenon. The latter consists of a direct revelation, which does not require a mediator. Communion with God is established, which is often referred to as a "mystical union." Communion can only happen between persons, and this is why, for Stein, communion is possible between human and Divine persons. The desire to bathe in the rays of Divine light and love, however, is not communion. In this sense, then, the Nirvana of Buddhism is not sufficient. One may also enjoy the desire to bathe in the light of nature, for example.

Let us pause to consider the qualities of mystical union, which Walther considers in her work by distinguishing communion with God from mystical union. She asks whether or not we can do something to achieve such union. Certainly, one cannot bring about a mystical experience by himself or herself. I am in agreement with Walther and Stein on this point. However, one can become inwardly disposed to be in contact with the Divine, one can desire and ask for the Divine presence. There is no guarantee that the presence will manifest itself. Saint Teresa of Avila used to tell her fellow sisters that entry into Carmel never guaranteed mystical union.

Responding to "rationalistic" skeptics[32] of mystical experience, Walther notes that often mystics will lapse into contradictions. On one hand, mystics may describe themselves as having entered into "nothingness," including the nothingness of the self. On the other hand, they recount what they have seen, as is the case in all historical religions. It is through such testimony that we know about mystical experience. Walther justifies the validity of such contradictions. First, the rigidity of the body, as mentioned earlier, may be viewed as stemming from the extraordinary concen-

[32]Gerda Walther, *Phänomenologie der Mystik*, 262.

tration on what is being lived or experienced in the moment. Second, entering into and describing nothingness is attributable to the I-center that feels itself isolated and immersed in a surrounding abyss, an experience that Gerda Walther herself experienced. Although Walther does not explicitly speak of herself as undergoing a mystical experience, albeit one may consider what she describes happening to her I-center as pre-mystical, she does understand that one can abandon oneself to the sea of lights without losing one's self, understood as a cognitive subject. Walther's insight can be confirmed by comments made in Teresa of Avila's *Interior Castle* and Edith Stein's *Finite and Eternal Being*.[33]

The subject (I) and the object (God) are never absolutely unified, even though a relation of unity is established between them: the creature can never identify or become God. Some mystics, however, view their experiences as being privileged and, therefore, they view themselves as being deserving of special honors, which ultimately should be directed to God who dwells in them. Such mystics do not suffer from excessive pride or self-entitlement; rather, they feel themselves humble before the greatness of God. They view themselves simply as the bearers of such greatness.[34]

In every religion—be it Hinduism, Buddhism, Christianity, or Islam—swami monks, bhikkhus, priests, and Sufis speak of themselves in the third person. They also take on a new name because they feel themselves "reborn," as they themselves have been completely decentered by God. Walther ends her *Phenomenology of Mysticism* with the foregoing claim, and this is important, for even in the 1920s and 1950s she anticipates more contemporary forms of interreligious dialogue and one of its more important themes: Dialogue between religions is necessary, and mystical experience provides a fertile ground for it. God directly manifests Himself to religious human beings without human "mediators," and this demonstrates His uniqueness. Beyond what religious doctrines are able to affirm, mystical experience shows that God is a Divine person. For example, in Sufism, Allah is considered to be so unreachable that He is unable to be defined. Hence, he can only be understood as a Divine "person". Though God can never be fully known Sufi mystics employ the pronoun You in reference to God, testifying to the fact that God is experienced as a person in their internal dialogues, when God responds to their invocations, and when he dwells in them. Undoubtedly, Sufis have suffered much persecution on account of such claims: other forms of Islam do not believe that such privileged encounters with God are possible.

The Trinity and Mysticism

Despite her openness to mystical experiences in other religions, Walther privileges Christianity in her analysis of the phenomenon of mysticism. She dedicates the last chapter of her book to the Trinity, which she views as personifying an important

---

[33]Edith Stein, *Finite and Eternal Being*, trans. by Kurt Reinhardt (Washington, DC: ICS Publications, 2002).

[34]Gerda Walther, *Phänomenologie der Mystik*, 272.

relationship between humans and the Divine. The "matter" out of which God is constituted is compared to a resplendent sun; she imagines this matter as divided into three parts bound together by a band of light. She invokes the image of a triple sun with each part having its own unique rays, although all parts belong to one and the same matter.

The relationship between the human being and the Triune God is different vis-à-vis mystical union. We can imagine the mystic as a small candle that is lit by one of the rays of the suns. Hence, it receives light, but it is not the source of light. The matter, the substance of the light, gathers together as one of the three suns. The Divine matter is never confused with the human one, which is created. This difference is most clear in the Christian Profession of Faith, in which Christ is not "created," but generated. The difference refers to the way Christ proceeds from the Father and the Son. Father, Son, and Holy Spirit exist in a dynamic relationship, which implies no creation of one by the other. Concerning the Holy Spirit, Walther posits that the love between the Father and the Son, a love that is endowed with an I-center, constitutes one of the principal aspects of the Holy Spirit.

In the human being who unites with God, however, there remains only the wick, the I-center immersed in a sea of light that does not liquefy like the candle (the body); rather, it remains the same in its singularity. This conservation of one's singularity allows one to recount what happens in the course of mystical experience. Walther does not appeal to philosophy and/or theology to explain her idea about the Trinity. She deploys images and metaphors to make her point understandable.[35]

It is important that Gerda Walther's thoughts receive more attention. She widens the horizon of our understanding of mystical experience by making reference to mystics in other religions. Moreover, she is not afraid to draw upon her own personal experiences to explain key aspects of her phenomenology of mysticism. Her analysis in the end remains concretely objective, and she succeeds in giving an account of mystical experience that is both rigorous and deeply enlivening.

Angela Ales Bello is Professor Emeritus of the History of Contemporary Philosophy at the Lateran University. Former Dean of the Faculty of Philosophy, she is now visiting professor at the Universities of Saint Paul and Campinas, Brazil. She is the President of the Italian Center of Phenomenological Research in Rome. She is also the President of the International Society of the Phenomenology of Religion and the Italian Edith Stein Association. At the Lateran University, she is the Director of the International Research Area Dedicated to Edith Stein and Contemporary Philosophy. Her recent publications include: *The Divine in Husserl and Other Explorations*, trans. by Antonio Calcagno, 2010; *The Sense of Things: Toward a Phenomenological Realism*, trans. by Antonio Calcagno, 2015; *Il senso del sacro. Dall'arcaicità alla desacralizzazione*, 2014; *Il senso dell'umano. Fenomenologia Psicologia, Psicopatologia*, 2016; *Tutta colpa di Eva. Antropologia e religione dal femminismo alla gender theory*, 2017.

[35]Gerda Walther, *Phänomenologie der Mystik*, 277.

Phenomenological Approaches to the Uncanny and the Divine: Adolf Reinach and Gerda Walther on Mystical Experience

Kimberly Baltzer-Jaray

Abstract Adolf Reinach (1883–1917) and Gerda Walther (1897–1977) were two figures of the early movement who gave phenomenological description to mystical and uncanny experiences; and, while the phenomenological approach each employs is slightly different, both commit to phenomenological description of the experiences of God and the uncanny, including the foreseeing of one's death, in a manner that is open-minded and unprejudiced. In this chapter I will discuss the experiences of foreseeing and of God for both Reinach and Walther. I will rely on their first-hand accounts of such experiences, utilizing the battlefield notes of Reinach from WWI found in his *Sämtliche Werke* and the mystical experience Walther describes having in 1918 in her book *Zum Anderen Ufer*. In the end it will become clear that phenomenology is an approach for all kinds of experiences, even those that are most unconventional, and thus the potential for further and fresh research is great.

Keywords Adolf reinach · Gerda walther · Phenomenology · Mysticism
The uncanny

While phenomenology is said to be a discipline that studies the structures of experience and/or consciousness, the types of experiences it often chooses to explore are of the everyday person: speech acts like promises or judgments. Willing, valuing, empathy, fantasy, and feelings like love or anxiety or disgust have all been discussed at great length. But, what of mystical or uncanny experiences? Are they not also worthy of description and exploration for the phenomenologist even though they are not everyday experiences or happen to everyone?

Adolf Reinach (1883–1917) and Gerda Walther (1897–1977) were two figures of the early movement who described mystical and uncanny experiences phenomenologically, and while the phenomenological approach each employs is slightly different, they both seek to avoid two things: first, this kind of phenomenological study cannot provide a causal explanation of mystical events, nor can or should it reduce

K. Baltzer-Jaray (✉)
King's University College (UWO), London, Ontario, Canada
e-mail: kbaltzer@uwo.ca

A. Calcagno (ed.), *Gerda Walther's Phenomenology of Sociality, Psychology, and Religion*, Women in the History of Philosophy and Sciences 2,
https://doi.org/10.1007/978-3-319-97592-4_11

them to something accepted by the principles of science or the laws of psychology; second, the purpose of such an endeavor is not to prove or disprove the experience, it is not an argument about validity or truth, but rather such a study must simply describe the experience so as to apprehend its essence. Reinach and Walther commit to describing the experiences of God and the uncanny phenomenologically, including foreseeing one's own death, in a manner that is open-minded and unprejudiced, and they both do so while utilizing personal experience as a springboard. It is interesting to add here that they both begin this descriptive phenomenological journey at the time of WWI: Reinach in 1916/1917 while fighting at the Western Front and Walther in 1918 around the time of the Armistice.

Both Reinach and Walther are overlooked figures in the history of philosophy; however, Walther's book *The Phenomenology of Mysticism* (1923, 1955, 1976) and her work in parapsychology are well known to scholars familiar with her. Whereas Reinach's notes on foreseeing and the experience of God are relatively unknown and go unmentioned in studies of his phenomenology. In this chapter I will discuss the experiences of foreseeing and of God for both Reinach and Walther. I will rely on their first-hand accounts of such experiences, utilizing the battlefield notes of Reinach from WWI found in his *Sämtliche Werke*[1] and the mystical experience Walther describes having in 1918 in her book *Zum Anderen Ufer*.[2] I will provide a translation for Reinach's textual fragments on the experience of God and Walther's mystical account in the Translation Appendix at the end of this chapter. When it comes to the phenomenological approach and analyzing the structures of these experiences I mainly turn to Reinach since his notes are lesser known. They precede Walther's, and the way he engages with these unusual phenomena is both accessible and highly probative; his analyses are the perfect example of his phenomenological realism. The goal of this chapter is to provide an understanding of the religious or uncanny experiences of both Reinach and Walther, how each uniquely approached describing such incredible phenomena, and then how Reinach sought to address the issues of knowledge and metaphysics surrounding such surreal experiences. In the end I argue that phenomenology is an approach for *all* kinds of experiences, even the most unconventional, and thus the potential for further and fresh research is great.

The Phenomenological Approach: Munich and Göttingen

As mentioned, Reinach and Walther approach uncanny phenomena differently, and the obvious reason for this has to do with their phenomenological teaching. Reinach was a member of the Munich Circle and a committed phenomenological realist. He was taught by both Theodor Lipps and Edmund Husserl, so his approach to phenomenology is a blend of the ideas of those two thinkers. Lipps, like Husserl's

---

[1]Adolf Reinach, *Sämtliche Werke*, ed. by Karl Schuhmann and Barry Smith (Munich: Philosophia Verlag, 1989).

[2]Gerda Walther, *Zum Anderen Ufer* (Bonn: Otto Reichl Verlag, 1960).

teacher Franz Brentano, actively researched and taught descriptive psychology (that is, the defining and classifying of various types of mental phenomena, including judgment, perception, emotion, etc.). Lipps, in fact, had his own conception of phenomenology and it predated Husserl's. The phenomenological themes he lectured on before the turn of the 20th century included: (1) objective contents of consciousness and spatial–temporal relations; (2) the ego; (3) the relations of objective consciousness to the psyche.[3] These themes were eventually modified and appeared in his paper "Psychische Vorgänge und psychische Causalität" ("Psychic Processes and Psychic Causality"), in which Lipps termed his methodological procedure "purely phenomenological" [*rein phänomenologisch*]. What was entailed by this method was the unprejudiced description of contents. For Lipps the phenomenological method is a tool to separate the psychical from the physical. Reinach took this idea and expanded it ontologically, saying that descriptive psychology, "… is not to explain and reduce to other things. Rather its aim is to illuminate and expose. It intends to bring to ultimate, intuitive givenness the 'whatness' of experience, from which, in itself, we are so remote."[4]

Husserl introduced ideation in *Logical Investigations*, and as a method it was understood as "the seeing of an essence" or "essential insight" [*Wesensschau*]. Ideation is an act whereby consciousness presents something itself (namely, essence). The essence originarily shows itself and this establishes an insight into the universal style of being of the individual entities that stand under the eidetic universality.[5] For Reinach this translated into an intuition of the essence, and the necessary laws that govern them, as well as states of affairs and apriority. That orange is similar to yellow is grounded in the being of the color orange; it is capable of irrefutable evidence and obtains regardless of whether anyone thinks it so, and I come to understand this truth by using ideation. His approach is often referred to as utilizing "pure intuition" into essences so that one can attain or apprehend the necessary laws that govern them and their instantiations, and states of affairs.

Reinach's phenomenological approach does not separate epistemology from metaphysics, they are done together, and this sets him apart from Husserl and firmly sets his phenomenology as ontological. The phenomenological realist holds that there exists a real world independent of human consciousness, and that some things in this world exist and others subsist. This necessarily leads to the understanding that different types of objects are given to us in different ways—sounds heard, sweetness tasted, ideal laws intuited, states of affairs apprehended, etc.— and the only way we can uncover the different modes of gaining knowledge is by engaging with beings

[3]Reinhold Smid, "An Early Interpretation of Husserl's Phenomenology: Johannes Daubert and the 'Logical Investigations'," in *Husserl Studies* 2: 267–290 (1985).

[4]Adolf Reinach, "Concerning Phenomenology." In J. Crosby (ed.), *The A Priori Foundations of Civil Law: Along with Lecture, "Concerning Phenomenology"*, trans. by Dallas Willard (Heusenstamm: Ontos Verlag, 2010), 147.

[5]Eugen Fink, "The Problem of the Phenomenology of Edmund Husserl," in *A priori and World: European Contributions to Husserlian Phenomenology* (Boston: Kluwer, 1981), 48.

that are known. Hence, he simultaneously does metaphysics and epistemology. We must regard all epistemological and logical terms, then, as primarily ontological.[6]

To be clear, for Reinach and other phenomenological realists, essences and states of affairs subsist in the world, and while some are timeless and others temporal, they subsist independently of my acknowledgment. When Reinach looks to describe phenomena like foreseeing one's own death or feeling dependent on God, he does not look inward at the structures of consciousness; rather, he looks outward at what the experience is and its ontological structure: What is the essence of foreseeing my death or dependence on God? What are the states of affairs obtaining that I am grasping about my impending death, etc.? When he speaks of the experience of God the investigation must address: (1) how we talk about such an experience both epistemically and metaphysically; (2) where we feel ourselves being sheltered by God; (3) what do we know about the existence of God (that is, immediate and mediate knowledge); (4) how we can have such knowledge while lacking empirical data or a standard object–perception relationship.

Turning to Walther, her teachers included Husserl and Alexander Pfänder. She began her studies at the University of Munich in 1915/1916 with Pfänder. Reinach was already at this time fighting at the Western Front. In 1917 she studied with Husserl, who now was established in Freiburg. Husserl was also committed to a more subjective, idealist type of phenomenology. In *Ideas I*, published in 1913, Husserl's phenomenology was said to be a descriptive analysis of the essence of pure consciousness, a science of pure consciousness. In this work we also see the introduction of eidetic reduction, bracketing, the pure ego, and the key moments of intentionality *noesis* and *noema*. The approach largely looks inwardly, and not at the real world outside, at the structures of consciousness to obtain their essence.

In 1919 Walther returned to Munich and in 1921 defended her dissertation under Pfänder. The training she received during this time is reflected in her style: While Walther is focused on essence, like Reinach, the way she goes about things is different because she starts from the standpoint of the subject and works outward to the world. Pfänder's phenomenology is referred to as a "subjective method" in that it is the subjective and descriptive study of psychological phenomena. He began his phenomenology with an investigation into the nature of willing, in which he explored the experience of willing with its conscious components from the inside, without referring to its accompanying physical or physiological elements. After exposure to Husserl, around 1916 this subjective method evolved with an emphasis now on the need to obtain explicit insight into the essential structure of the phenomena and their relations to psychological facts.[7]

---

[6]Lucinda Ann Vandervort Brettler, "The phenomenology of Adolf Reinach: chapters in the theory of knowledge and legal philosophy." Ph.D. dissertation, McGill University, 1973, 116.

[7]Herbert Spiegelberg, *The Phenomenological Movement: A Historical Introduction*, 3rd revised and enlarged edn. (Dordrecht: Kluwer Academic, 1994), 175.

Walther begins her *Phenomenology of Mysticism* with a discussion of the constitution of persons and human essence, since only persons can have mystical experience. The person, according to Walther, consists of three aspects: the I-center; the self, and the essence (which is composed of body, soul, and spirit). God is the ground of essence. When she seeks to answer how we can grasp God in a mystical way, Walther starts her approach at the I, the subject who is experiencing God in a way that is unreflective, direct, and non-rational. This experience is within oneself, as if the divine stream opened a hidden source inside oneself that allows the rays in from outside. The I then turns toward its own essence and sees itself through the light of this other (that is, the eyes and heart of God). It is in grasping God that one can purely and fully experience one's own essence; it is only in the full knowledge of God that this can happen.

Uncanny Experiences

Walther's mystical experience has two distinct elements: a moment of foreseeing into the future, and then feeling the presence of something Divine. Her story begins in the winter of 1918, on the train ride back from visiting her father and stepmother in Baden-Baden. She recalls that prior to the trip she had been in a strange state: she had episodes of weakness sweep over her to the point of losing control of her body and most likely her consciousness too, and she tells of a growing distance from and disinterest in her life and all she cared about. She had one of these episodes while eating dinner with her father and stepmother, and she had to use every ounce of her strength to stay on the chair and eat. When traveling to the train station to return to Freiburg, she describes her movements as mechanical, robotic, as if her body were an automaton that she was remotely controlling.

Shortly after boarding the train the first and shortest element of her mystical experience occurs; it is something foreseen: "Suddenly, I knew with uncanny clarity: 'When I arrive in Freiburg, I will either be dead or mentally ill—or I will have found something entirely new, unknown, which gives a different meaning to my entire life.'"[8] She describes the experience of this foreseeing as something she feels with "unrelenting objectivity" where her mental, physical, and spiritual powers are used up. Then she feels as if she is sinking inwardly into a dark and endless depth, an abyss without end, that lacks any support or light:

> I felt how my strength faded more and more, I let myself sink into that inner depth without resistance, sink and sink constantly further. Only one thing I could still think clearly: It was necessary to hold oneself together with the final residue of strength in oneself in order not to lose consciousness as well. This consciousness actually consisted, of course, only in feeling that I was sinking and sinking without knowing where to—as if I was plunging through the empty, infinite, starless universe. I did and knew only still that it was necessary not to dissolve myself unconsciously in this dark infinity. I felt, however, that it was only a question of a

[8]Gerda Walther, *Zum Anderen Ufer*, 223.

> few moments, and my strength would be entirely used up—and then? What would happen with me?[9]

When she finally arrived in Freiburg, her foreseeing experience had come true, since she found herself alive and not mentally ill. She also found (or it found her) that incomprehensible, unknown "something" that had already in its brief occurrence given her life an entirely different meaning.

The next phase of her mystical experience, feeling the presence of something Divine, begins on the train ride and lasts a long time. Walther is feeling as if she is sinking into an endless, starless universe, and just after the candle at the window blows out and all seems rather dark she feels a new source of energy.

As I was so sinking, however, suddenly, something was streaming towards me from a vast, infinite distance—something that permeated me with a feeling of deepest safety and security—but I could not recognize what it was. It increased in intensity; a sea of warm love and kindness surrounded me. It stayed with me a long time.[10]

She describes herself as being barely conscious on the walk home, and when she gets inside her apartment she goes straight to the side of her bed, kneels, and puts her face into the pillows. The experience of the Divine then waves over her again and much more intensely. She describes this experience saying:

> Now, a bright inner glow was streaming toward me from that immeasurable distance; it surrounded me completely. All the suffering I had ever experienced seemed to have been extinguished, as if it had never happened, as if I had heard only being told about it, like about something that had happened to a stranger. From my very depths, I felt born anew and transformed. I did not know anything anymore about myself and my surroundings; I only felt that warm flood of love which had taken me up, I saw only that spiritual light that had penetrated me. Then, entirely gradually, that sea of light and warmth began to retreat again, slowly and gently releasing me from itself, but in such a way that I was still held by it as if from a distance for a long time and such that I did not again plunge into the infinite dark space without support and without strength.[11]

When this feeling starts to subside and her mental and physical strength return she realizes that she has been kneeling at her bed for about 30–45 min. She then wonders what has just happened, and if this divine experience was God himself or another higher entity serving Him. Later, she arrives at the conclusion that this was a mystical experience, something absolutely remarkable, given that she was raised as an atheist, and this experience leads her to give up her political ambitions in the Social Democratic Party and pursue an academic career. It also opened her eyes to all the experiences possible for humans, ultimately resulting in her interest not only in mystical experiences but also parapsychology (for example, séances, clairvoyance, telepathy, etc.).

[9]Gerda Walther, *Zum Anderen Ufer*, 224.

[10]Gerda Walther, *Zum Anderen Ufer*, 225.

[11]Gerda Walther, *Zum Anderen Ufer*, 225.

But how does one even begin to talk about this kind of uncanny experience in a way that is dignified and rational? How do you overcome the skepticism that you would no doubt encounter when telling the average person about feeling the presence of God or having a foresight into the future? Reinach attempted phenomenologically to tackle these questions roughly two years before Walther's mystical experience. He also had a chance to investigate both the foreseen and the Divine.

During WWI, in 1916 while fighting at the Belgian front, Reinach overhears conversation at his camp about soldiers foreseeing their own deaths. The particular conversation he describes in detail in the notes occurs between a staff sergeant and an infantryman: the infantryman and others of his rank are growing very concerned about their fellow soldiers, who have a foreseen experience, put their affairs and papers in order, wrote farewell letters home, then strode out only to be killed. The infantryman is convinced these experiences are real and true, whereas the staff sergeant thinks they are pure superstition, the result of exhaustion, and furthermore death in war is a very likely occurrence that can be somewhat predictable. In listening to this conversation he realizes that the only way to overcome the skepticism of someone like the staff sergeant is to provide evidence for these experiences and proof that knowledge is obtainable from them.

First, we must distinguish what foresight is and is not. Foreseeing does not consist of feelings or volitions; it influences things (that is, we develop feelings after the experience and then will our actions based on them). Reinach describes a moment of foreseeing as, "the subject here appears to grasp by means of foreseeing, correctly or incorrectly remains to be seen, something from the river of future events, which was previously not accessible to him prior."[12] In the case of the soldiers from the story, "What clearly stands out from this foreboding is the *horror of future fortunes*, which as a feeling springs from this grasp of foresight, as do all aspirations and reluctance, willing and not willing …"[13] Foresight is very sudden and striking, it hits the subject all at once that *this will happen*. What one foresees adds something new to their store of knowledge, the subject grasps something previously unknown about the future. The knowledge gained by the subject carries with it a necessity that is absolutely binding; there is no room for doubt or hope of a different outcome. Furthermore, the experience leaves one feeling very helpless, as if one had no control over one's own life. Foresight is a purely individual experience, it is a glimpse at the causal chain of that subject's life—it cannot be shared, it cannot be seen by another. This also relates to the aspect of certainty the subject feels after experiencing it, since it is something so highly personal and specific to his or her life that it cannot be a dream or a mistake.

[12]Adolf Reinach, "A Phenomenology of Foreboding/Foreseeing" ["Zur Phänomenologie der Ahnungen"]. In Michael Kelly and Brian Harding (eds.), *Early Phenomenology:Metaphysics, Ethics, and the Philosophy of Religion* (London: Bloomsbury, 2016), 27.

[13]Adolf Reinach, "A Phenomenology of Foreboding/Foreseeing," 27 (italics added).

To answer what a foresight is ontologically, and hopefully address skeptics like the staff sergeant, Reinach's investigation turns to knowledge, evidence, and structure. First, foreseeing is intentional—it has content that refers to something. That simply means foresight has an object, even if that object is not tangible like chairs and tables that actually stand before us. Reinach writes:

> That every foreseeing as such necessarily requires a related content—the "foreseen" as such—so far stretched is the boundary of its possible contents here. Not only, for example, temporally but even future forebodings can refer to something. Within a scientific investigation a foreseeing of the result can rise up within me; here something forms apparently timeless (atemporal)—a more or less determinate proposition [*Satz*] or state of affairs [*Sachverhalt*]—the related content of a foreseeing. But not this foreseeing content, it being also identical with the content of a judgment or an apprehension, but rather the foreseeing as such—not the noematic, but the "noetic" side, to which Husserl speaks about, presents the real problem.[14]

The challenge to validating the foreseen is the fact that while they have content and are felt and influence actions, the object that the content refers to is not empirically present. However, for Reinach, a phenomenologist with a wealth of experience investigating entities that span all kinds of being—real, ideal, and intentional; temporal and timeless—this obstacle does not pose such a problem. For Reinach the one experiencing the foreseen is grasping a state of affairs (the *being-dead* and all the particulars surrounding that event), making judgments based on when they apprehend, and this means the content of the foreseen is in the world:

> Through foresight we grasp—or rather we believe that we grasp—something that was previously concealed. And a conviction can also be grounded in the foreboding, which in strength and inner certainty itself need be in no way inferior to the conviction based upon knowledge. From the foreboding of immanent death arises the certain conviction of having to die soon.[15]

This also entails that foresight has an essence and essential structures, and so the phenomenologist must go to the grounding structures it has. Reinach never finished this fragment, instead turning to the experience of God. However, what he says in relation to God actually addresses both mystical experience and foresight.

According to John Oesterreicher in his book *Walls Crumbling: Seven Jewish Philosophers Discover Christ*, in 1915 Reinach began to discover God and he told his wife, Anna, that the first few weeks at the front were terrible, but then God's peace came to him.[16] He also wrote to Dietrich von Hildebrand during that year and told him that a change had come over him, "a change to the very roots of my being."[17] In 1916, while on furlough, Reinach converted from Judaism to Protestantism, and the reason he gives , gathered from letters to his friends, is a direct result of witnessing

---

[14] Adolf Reinach, "A Phenomenology of Foreboding/Foreseeing," 26–27.

[15] Adolf Reinach, "A Phenomenology of Foreboding/Foreseeing," 28.

[16] John M. Oesterreicher, *Walls are Crumbling: Seven Jewish Philosophers Discover Christ* (New York: The Devin-Adair Company, 1952), 122.

[17] John M. Oesterreicher, *Walls are Crumbling*, 122.

the horrors of war. In the biography of Dietrich von Hildebrand, *Soul of a Lion*, Alice von Hildebrand writes that Reinach told Dietrich in a letter "that the terrible sufferings that the two warring sides were experiencing had clearly the meaning of calling men back to God."[18] While it is not clear or documented if he had a mystical experience like Walther, as we do not have a first-hand account, his descriptions are similar to Walther's, which leads me to think something Divine touched him while at the Front. Reinach tells his wife in 1916:

> My plan is clear before my eyes; naturally, it is very modest. I should like to start from the inner experience of God, the experience of being sheltered in Him, and shall be content to show that "objective science" cannot gainsay it. I should like to expound the full meaning of this experience, to show how far it can claim objectivity, to demonstrate why it is a genuine cognition, though of its own kind; and finally, to draw conclusions.[19]

Reinach refers to God as *Das Absolute*: God is the sum of all being that is actual and potential; He is beyond all space and time; His attributes are identical to His essence, and His essence necessitates His existence; and God is all that He can be, infinitely real and perfect. Had God not created the universe and everything in it, there would only be Him. Creating goes hand in hand with sustaining, so with the same intense and conscious (and loving) act that called us all into existence God, at every moment, is concerned with everyone and with a love that is intensely beyond comprehension. Regarding the relationship between God and humans, God, before our minds, is absolute highest and we are absolutely below Him. This position dictates our conduct towards God: "The experience of absolute shelteredness permeating the one who up to now has lacked faith leads him to God and simultaneously—in accordance with [God's] absoluteness—to a God enthroned in absolute highness."[20] In other words, even one who has a mystical experience and was previously unacquainted with God will know that He is absolutely above and beyond. Someone like Walther, an atheist, can grasp immediately, when engulfed by the Divine, her position in relation to God because of His Absoluteness. Reinach never met Walther and yet, uncannily, what he writes here captures her experience.

Furthermore, on our relation to and experience of God, he discusses our feelings of dependence, gratitude, and love:

> We humans, standing in time and space and the earthly world grasp what is beyond the earthly. This is the most precious gift with which God has blessed us. And not only do we grasp what is beyond the earthly; but in the acts in which it comes to be given to us, there mirrors itself in a certain manner the absolute fullness which we have predicated [*zusprechen*] to what is beyond the earthly. In experiencing God, we feel dependent on him, we feel gratitude to him, we love him; and all these—dependence, gratitude, and love—are not relative and able to be increased as it is with the relationships between human and human, but they are of an absolute nature . In this manner, the earthly experiencing also contains a content beyond

---

[18]Alice von Hildebrand, *The Soul of a Lion: Dietrich von Hildebrand* (San Francisco: Ignatius Press, 2000), 170. This book is based on a very long and detailed account Dietrich wrote to his wife, Alice, later in his life.

[19]John M. Oesterreicher, *Walls are Crumbling*, 122–123.

[20]Adolf Reinach, *Fragment on Philosophy of Religion*, §1, paragraph 2 (see Translation Appendix).

> what is earthly—and this is even how it must be. For when that which is beyond the earthly is grasped in acts which take a position, then, there must correspond to the absoluteness which is being grasped an absoluteness of the content of these acts.[21]

The experience of God is an intentional one; it has content, and that content, as with the foreseen, is not the typical empirical, tangible data, but rather something beyond and ontologically different. This also entails that the experience of God, for Reinach, is something that can be a type of knowledge: there is a state of affairs that I am apprehending and the ontological status of it is unique.

As with the foreseen, Reinach speaks out against those who would say that the experience of God is something that belongs in the sphere of feelings, which means that it is not knowledge. Here, he specifically refers to the "man of science," the one who would see religious experience as something that fails to be valid, rational, and, most importantly, to present empirical evidence. In many ways this point refers to those, like Immanuel Kant, who saw belief as a judgment that was sufficient subjectively (that is, conviction; true for me) but insufficient objectively (that is, not certain for everyone); hence, it could be considered neither knowledge nor truth since the latter depends on agreement with the object. In religious experience that object is not one we all can see, and so men of science will talk about religious matters as based in beliefs and feelings. Reinach writes:

> By what right, though, does one relegate the experience of God into a sphere of feelings outside of knowledge? There are feelings which, without referring to objects, suffuse a person's mood or disposition, a joyful mood, a feeling of deep depression, which have, to be sure, their real causes as do all experiences, but which relate experientially not at all to something to which they refer. In this case, we certainly are beyond anything having to do with knowledge, beyond all opposition of true and false …[22]

The first way that Reinach responds to the man of science is to say that there are many ways that we can be affected: for some the object or cause is clearly visible and sometimes it is not. Psychology describes numerous cases of moods affecting us or a gut feeling or even something we foresee. In the case of Walther her mystical experience during the train ride and at her apartment contain no physical object, but rather a sinking feeling, something streaming toward her, a feeling of a sea of love and safety, a bright inner light, etc., and all of this she felt with the utmost certainty and with her whole body. The experience is *as real* and *as certain* for her as eating a sandwich or stubbing her toe. Reinach's point is that to require that all experience have an empirical object to be valid is to have a bias for the physically or externally present as well as to neglect the vast array of experiences we humans can have, ones that can provide knowledge.[23] Reinach continues:

---

[21] Adolf Reinach, *Fragment on Philosophy of Religion*, §2, paragraph 4 (see Translation Appendix).

[22] Adolf Reinach, *Loose Notes*, paragraph 2 (see Translation Appendix).

[23] When speaking about his plan to investigate religious experience, referred to earlier, Reinach says, "Of course a presentation like this has nothing to offer him who lives in God's sight. But it can steady the one who waivers, who lets the objections of science confuse him, and it can lead onward him who these objections have stayed from walking with God." See John M. Oesterreicher, *Walls are Crumbling*, 123. AU: is "lead onward him who" correct?

> One may speak at this point—sufficiently prematurely—about merely "subjective experiences"; we are, however, here first of all interested only in the fact that these experiences come to be present with the claim to grasp being, thus, to be knowledge, contrary to the experiences which do not make such a claim. We may here leave entirely undiscussed the justification of this claim. Such a *claim* we find, however, also in the case of the religious experience from which we have taken our point of departure. Inasmuch as the ego feels itself in a relationship to God, inasmuch as it feels, with blissful certainty, its dependence on him and its security in him, something new discloses itself to it, it grasps a connection which is now firm for it and to which it adheres knowingly through all time. It is certainly not the case that the subject would have pursued this relationship in an attitude of "seeking knowledge"; but even theoretical states of affairs can light up for us without any seeking and, so to speak, against our will.[24]

What we grasp when we feel ourselves in a relationship with God is knowledge, although it is not the same type of knowledge sought after by the empirical sciences. The last line of the above fragment rings very true for Walther's experience: she did not travel seeking to know God or experience Him, God found her—God sought Walther, the atheist Marxist. When we seek to know something, we have some kind of idea or guess what we are looking for, but then what is it to experience something you had no idea existed? This must add something rather unique to the knowledge grasped since it is of a kind that was unbeknownst to you and unsought; the "object" came to you and gave you an experience against your will. While belief in God can be a choice or a tradition, for some it is not of their choosing at all.

In his notes to "Structure of the Experience" Reinach distinguishes between two types of knowledge involved in religious experience: explicit and experience-immanent. In mystical experience as well as the foreseen the knowledge gained is the latter kind. It is knowledge that comes about only in experience itself, rather than after the fact, when we cognize, make judgments, and carry out acts. Reinach adds:

> The taking-as-reality [*Wirklichkeitsnehmung*] of the feeling of oneself sheltered [*Geborgenfuehlen*] in God is quite different; logically speaking, the former would be the presupposition for the latter. However, no one would draw a logical conclusion [from this]. Rather, it is immanently contained in the sense of the experience itself. Two aspects we must separate here: On the one hand, the knowledge of being sheltered and, on the other, the knowledge of the existence of God, i.e., an immediate and a mediate immanent knowledge. The experiences of gratitude and love contain only a mediate knowledge; as position-takings [*Stellungnahmen*] they are in a certain sense derivative experiences.[25]

Walther's mystical experience possesses the immediate knowledge, but it seems to lack the mediate variety. The first thing she describes is the feeling of security and safety, and that a warm sea of love and kindness are surrounding her. The immediate knowledge of God is immanent experience. These are things she can only know while being held in the experience. In this case, being an atheist, she lacks any prior understanding of what a religious experience entails. Because she still is unsure about what happened to her or why—she speculates it could be God or an entity close to him—she does not have the mediate knowledge of something like God's

---

[24] Adolf Reinach, *Loose Notes*, paragraph 2 (see Translation Appendix).

[25] Adolf Reinach, *Fragment on Philosophy of Religion*, §2, paragraph 2 (see Translation Appendix).

existence or a feeling of love or gratitude toward God. She will get there later, of course, in her studies, but at this point the description indicates she is dwelling in the immediate knowledge the mystical experience provides. Regardless, there is still knowledge in the experience of God. Just as Reinach, in his phenomenological realist ontology, sought to describe kinds of being beyond real and idea, here he attempts to detail types of knowledge that fall outside the regular parameters, so that all kinds of uncanny experiences can have their rightful share.

Reinach's experience of God is one of feeling not only sheltered but also absolutely dependent. The state of affairs obtaining here is intimately contained in the experience and part of experience-immanent knowledge, and the "object" that he perceives is not before him, but absolutely above and beyond him. The knowledge gained here is not something on which he needs to reflect; rather, it is immediately known to him that he is loved, sheltered, and dependent on God. This knowledge is certain and as real as anything else cognition has granted him. He writes:

> I experience my absolute dependence on God. Insofar as I myself am concerned with this experienced relation, the state of affairs does not stand before me, but rather I myself experience myself in this relation, which then naturally cannot be objective for me. In this manner, also, if I perceive an object, the corresponding relation between perception and object is not objective to me. Then, however, a difference immediately appears: in perceiving there arises in me, through reflection on it, the knowledge that "I perceive". In the experience of dependence, I find myself dependent without a reflection being necessary, which indeed could also lead only to the knowledge that I feel myself dependent.[26]

Concluding Remarks

As mentioned earlier, there is no documentation or letter stating that Reinach had a mystical experience like Walther did; there exists only the words of von Hildebrand and Oesterreicher in addition to Reinach's descriptive notes. Regardless of whether he had a full-blown uncanny, disorienting mystical experience or simply had a moment of deep realization that he, surviving on a battlefield surrounded by immense amounts of death, destruction, and constant risk, felt sheltered and loved by God, both count as an experience of God. Both result in knowledge, and both have an "object," even if that object does not exist in the same way tables and chairs do. Reinach has clearly shown that phenomenological realism has the tools to describe and explore experiences like that of God or foresight, and in a way that is objective and valid. But, he has barely scratched the surface of what phenomenology can do with uncanny and surreal experiences. Walther extended this phenomenological work even further into parapsychology, but because her work has been understudied her efforts remain far too silent. It is time to change: we must take phenomenology into the dark and mysterious corners of experience, the places empirical science dares not go.

[26] Adolf Reinach, *Fragment on Philosophy of Religion*, §2, paragraph 3 (see Translation Appendix).

Translation Appendix (Translated by Kimberly Baltzer-Jaray and Fritz Wenisch)

Adolf Reinach
Fragment: Remarks on a Philosophy of Religion (1916/1917).

Das Absolute (Paragraphs 5–7, 12)

Obviously, we must distinguish between [the following two items:] On the one hand, [there are] the positions one person occupies with regard to another and which subsequently color [the first person's] acts—his questioning, responding, etc.—with regard to the [second person] in a sense identical to these positions, or which prescribe from the outset acts of a specific content, such as demanding instead of asking; on the other hand, there is the determination of direction of the acts mentioned last. What is foundational in general is certainly the difference obtaining from person to person. It might very well be [the case], however, that it is only [*überhaupt erst*] certain experiences with regard to a person suddenly imposing themselves on me which compels me to assume a position at a certain level, that, for example, compassion with a human results in a simultaneous "looking down" on this human.

All these relations become absolute in God. We look up to him; but we do it in a manner different from [looking up to] humans. In these latter cases [here], increases in any way are possible. The phenomenal relation to the humans ranking highest is not of such a kind that relations still directed higher could not still be thought of. God, however, [stands] before [our minds] as the absolute highest. This earth's powerful may stand on steep heights; God is enthroned in heaven. The position we occupy with regard to him—an absolute "below" relative to an absolute "above"—prescribes to us our experiential conduct: Trust, love, dependence, just as other experiences, be it benevolence or generosity, are immediately recognized as meaningless. The position with regard to God is the determinant for our experiential conduct toward him. Here also, however, reversals of the relation obtaining in itself are possible for us. The experience of absolute shelteredness permeating the one who up to now has lacked faith leads him to God and simultaneously—in accordance with [God's] absoluteness—to a God enthroned in absolute highness.

Thus, we can speak of absoluteness in three different, naturally, of course, closely related, senses: God is given to us in absolute highness; accordingly, our individual experiencing is characterized by the direction pointing to absolute highness; and next to this formal absoluteness, there is also the absoluteness of the material content, the complete "being fulfilled" of trust, gratitude, and love. An inner reasonableness obtains between these [instances of] absoluteness; not in the sense, however, that one could be deduced from the other through a logical inference; but in a way that internally motivated transitions take place: What is [being] given as highest, what our experiencing lifts itself up to, deserves an absolute fullness [*Fülle*] of love; just as inversely an absolute trust filling me must seek its intentional object in absolute highness.

We humans, standing in time and space and the earthly world, grasp what is beyond the earthly. This is the most precious gift with which God has blessed us. And not only do we grasp what is beyond the earthly; but in the acts in which it comes to be given to us, there mirrors itself in a certain manner the absolute fullness which we have assigned [*zusprechen*] to predicated of that which is beyond the earthly. In experiencing God, we feel dependent on him, we feel gratitude to him, we love him; and all these—dependence, gratitude, and love—are not relative and able to be increased as it is with the relationships between human and human, but they are of an absolute nature. In this manner, the earthly experiencing also contains a content beyond what is earthly—and this is even how it must be. For when that which is beyond the earthly is grasped in acts which take a position, then, there must correspond to the absoluteness which is being grasped an absoluteness of the content of these acts. These all are meager theoretical expositions. But what is hidden behind them is the most precious core of our life, that which alone can hold us upright in the storms of life. [We may be] thrown to and fro in hopes and disappointments, in fear and anguish and expectation, in love and hatred, in gratitude and vengefulness, being confined in the steps of the more and inferior of all social relationships; but here is the domain of what is inviolable and of eternal firmness.

Structure of Experience[27]

One might ask whether in our experience [*Erlebnis*], which indeed quite certainly includes knowledge [*Erkenntnis*][28], if the knowledge under consideration is a priori or of an empirical character, or whether knowledge of a third and perhaps quite unique type is present here. Let us take a priori states of affairs as such, for which the predication through the subject according to its essence is required, and which thereby becomes known, so that we immerse ourselves in the essence of the subject, then there is no a priori knowledge here. But, on the other hand, there is also no empirical knowledge, for it concerns no contingent and temporally variable matter of fact. Here, two different intersecting distinctions must be separated.

[27]The German word *Erlebnis* translated here into English as "experience," must be understood to carry with it the idea that experience is something a person lives through or has lived.

[28]The German word *Erkenntnis* translated here into English as "knowledge," must be understood to mean knowledge that is cognized (that is, it is acquired through cognition and/or perception). It is a *knowing about*.

We separate explicit and experience-immanent [*erlebnisimmanente*] [kinds of] knowledge [*Erkenntnisse*]. So, the enjoyment of a work of art is not knowledge, but forms the foundation for and releases from out of itself the knowledge that a picture is beautiful. However, here one might ask oneself: the knowledge "it is beautiful," does it not have its own intuitive foundation [*Anschauungsgrundlage*]? Otherwise, a perception in relation to any knowledge of actuality is to be judged quite differently [*Wirklichkeitserkenntnis*], insofar as the latter must always refer back to the perception for its verification. After all, there is even in the perception a taking-as-real [*Fuer-wirklich-Nehmen*], though not also actual knowledge. The taking-as-reality [*Wirklichkeitsnehmung*] of the feeling of oneself sheltered [*Geborgenfuehlen*] in God is quite different; logically speaking, the former would be the presupposition for the latter. However, no one would draw a logical conclusion [from this]. Rather, it is immanently contained in the sense of the experience itself. Two aspects we must separate here: On the one hand, the knowledge of being sheltered and on the other the knowledge of the existence of God, i.e., an immediate and a mediate immanent knowledge. The experiences of gratitude and love contain only a mediate knowledge; as position-takings [*Stellungnahmen*] they are in a certain sense derivative experiences.

I experience my absolute dependence on God. Insofar as I myself am concerned with this experienced relation, the state of affairs does not stand before me, but rather I myself experience myself in this relation, which then naturally cannot be objective for me. In this manner, also, if I perceive an object, the corresponding relation between perception and object is not objective to me. Then, however, a difference immediately appears: in perceiving there arises in me, through reflection on it, the knowledge that "I perceive." In the experience of dependence, I find myself dependent without a reflection being necessary, which indeed could also lead only to the knowledge that I feel myself dependent.

Skeptical Considerations

He who has been blessed with such an experience may be raised above all hardships and doubts of life; he may experience a reversal and transformation in himself that is comparable to no other occurrence in his life; he may have attained a firm direction that now makes all steps of his life firm and certain—but what has happened beyond this pure individual event in the existence of an individual? Especially, to what extent is true knowledge fostered? How can such a subjective experience lay claim to validity for the individual or for all humankind in general? So many doubts will make themselves felt in the positions [*erkenntnismäßigen*] of most people regarding knowledge, there will be so much rejection from the outset that one will scarcely take the trouble to formulate the deliberations precisely.

Loose Notes (1916).

Assessment of the Experience

It does not take an involved debate of how people face this experience [*Erlebnis*]. The pious person sees in it one of the many paths that lead to God. The man of science[29] [*Wissenschaft*] and the scientifically educated person relegate it to the sphere of mere feelings which—whether or not deceptive—in any case lack the objective dignity of knowledge. If he believes in God, he will assign to this experience its place in a province which lies not only beyond his own special science, but beyond all science altogether. And if he is a convinced atheist, he will counter it with all those objections which objective science can hold against it. In both cases, he will, as a follower of genuine science, see in it only an *object*, but not a *source* of knowledge; for him, there can only be the question in what way that experience comes about, how it is motivated in the total stream of psychical experiencing, and how its effects take place.

By what right, though, does one relegate the experience of God into a sphere of feelings outside of knowledge? There are feelings which, without referring to objects, suffuse a person's mood disposition, a joyful mood, a feeling of deep depression, which have, to be sure, their real causes as do all experiences, but which relate experientially not at all to something to which they refer. In this case, we certainly are beyond anything having to do with knowledge, beyond all opposition of true and false. We come already closer to it in all those cases in which there is an "about" of feelings. Certainly, one can speak of a justified and an unjustified sadness about an occurrence, no matter how far we are even here still removed from the function of knowledge. One can speak of real knowledge only in those cases in which a recognition of a state of affairs takes place, where something that obtains is "apprehended," where a "discovering" is possible and a knowing which finds its foundation in discovering and grasping. One is, in this case, not only to think about the seeing of theoretical connections, about the cases in which a mathematical state of affairs illuminates us, in which an event in the world of senses vividly confronts us: Even when moral values and disvalues, for example, are vividly grasped by us or when we most intimately sense the value of love or the disvalue of envy—even here exists "discovery," "grasping," and knowing based on it. One may speak at this point—sufficiently prematurely—about merely "subjective experiences"; we are, however, here first of all interested only in the fact that these experiences come to be present with the claim to grasp being, thus, to be knowledge, contrary to the experiences which do not make such a claim. We may here leave entirely undiscussed the justification of this claim. Such a *claim* we find, however, also in the case of the religious experience from which we have taken our point of departure. Inasmuch as the ego feels itself in

[29]"Science" here needs to be understood as an academic study that includes natural sciences, social sciences, and the humanities.

a relationship to God, inasmuch as it feels, with blissful certainty, its dependence on him and its security in him, something new discloses itself to it, it grasps a connection which is now firm for it and to which it adheres knowingly through all time. It is certainly not the case that the subject would have pursued this relationship in an attitude of "seeking knowledge"; but even theoretical states of affairs can light up for us without any seeking and, so to speak, against our will.

Gerda Walther

Selections from "Sturz in eine andere Welt," a chapter in Zum Anderen Ufer (pp. 222–225)

I was getting more and more into a strange state. Everything around me became for me inwardly strangely unusually distant and of no concern, as if basically, it had nothing to do with me. To be sure, I saw and heard everything that happened around me, but it was strangely shadow-like as if it was not really there at all, as if the actually real in which I would be able to be really fully immersed, with which I was entirely able to resonate internally, must lie somewhere else. The sun was shining as always, but everything was so oddly pale—just what was this? At times, I was filled with a strange inner tension, as if I had to hold myself together with all my strength so as not to fall apart, as if I could no longer hold on to my thoughts, and suddenly had to lose consciousness. In such moments, a sudden fear seized me that my strength might suddenly fail, and that I would no longer be able to hold myself upright. I succeeded, however, time and again to overcome, with the greatest exertion, these states of weakness so that no one, not even father, noticed anything about them.

During the Winter Semester of 1918, I had again, as usually, on a cold weekend, traveled home to Baden-Baden. I was sitting for dinner with father and with "Aunt Sigrun." Soon, it was time to travel back again. Once again, that strange weakness overcame me. I feared to fall off the chair; I was able to stay calmly seated and continue to eat only through the utmost exertion of all strength.

Father asked, "Why are you suddenly so quiet?" He almost had noticed something.

I responded calmly, "Oh, I just remembered a very difficult problem from a lecture."

Father stated, smiling: "Leave your tricky problems alone at least on a Sunday."

I had to hurry if I did not want to miss the streetcar to the train station. I asked myself, "What will possibly happen when I come here again—will I do it at all?"

I traveled mechanically to the train station, showed my ticket, and boarded the train. It was really as if I did not do all of this myself, but [rather] an automaton with which I was somehow connected to over a very far distance. With this, I was secretly surprised that everything went so smoothly, that I inserted the ticket correctly, changed trains in Oos, and that there, in the next train, I correctly took a seat in a compartment.

At that time, the trains ran without illumination. Besides myself, two vacationers sat by the window ahead. They had attached to the folding table a small candle stump that weakly illuminated the nearest surrounding. I squeezed myself in the opposite corner at the door.

Suddenly, I knew with uncanny clarity: "When I arrive in Freiburg, I will either be dead or mentally ill—or I will have found something entirely new, unknown, which gives a different meaning to my entire life."

I felt it with unrelenting objectivity: All my mental, spiritual, and physical powers were exhausted. I seemed to myself like an entirely burned down candle—even smaller than the stump over there by the window, like a wick that only flickers a bit now and then and threatens to become extinct at any moment. Then, it felt to me as if I was sinking, sinking inwardly in a dark, endless depth in which there was nowhere a support or a light. At the same time, it seemed to me as if I would become more and more distant from everything that up to now had been dear and valuable to me. I did not care, however; there was nothing that could hold me back. Father? He had Aunt Sigrun, and soon, he would himself die. Professor Pfänder? He had his wife and his work. Socialism? Many were fighting for it; so, one more or less did not make any difference. The unfolding of my foundational essence [*Grundwesen*], of the nucleus of my soul [*Seelenkern*]? What did it matter? Thousands fell victim to the war, why then should just I outlive it? I would have liked to continue living only if there would be something that would give all of it an even higher, ultimate meaning, something through which the entire world would suddenly look totally different—but what was that supposed to be?

I felt how my strength faded more and more, I let myself sink into that inner depth without resistance, sink and sink constantly further. Only one thing I could still think clearly: It was necessary to hold oneself together with the final residue of strength in oneself in order not to lose consciousness as well. This consciousness actually consisted, of course, only in feeling that I was sinking and sinking without knowing where to—as if I was plunging through the empty, infinite, starless universe. I did and knew only still that it was necessary not to dissolve myself unconsciously in this dark infinity. I felt, however, that it was only a question of a few moments, and my strength would be entirely used up—and then? What would happen with me? I myself had no reserves anymore; if some new strength would not stream to me from somewhere else, yes, then I would possibly be extinguished. The thought about this was, however, no longer uncomfortable or even dreadful.

Now, the candle stump by the window also went out—just as if the exterior darkness should correspond to the darkness within me.

As I was so sinking, however, suddenly, something was streaming toward me from a vast, infinite distance—something that permeated me with a feeling of deepest safety and security—but I could not recognize what it was. It increased in intensity; a sea of warm love and kindness surrounded me.

I stayed in this state for a long time. The train stopped: Freiburg! I had arrived at the destination of my journey. Thus, I had after all not become the victim of death or a mental illness! I had found, however, that entirely different, unknown, incomprehensible "something"; otherwise, I would have, on my trip, still been ruined mentally or physically—or both. As if sleepwalking, I left the train, crossed the barrier, and took the next streetcar to my apartment. I was still entirely engulfed by that distant sea that had taken me into itself. It was as if my consciousness was reaching out of it only to the extent that I could find home. I went, without turning on the light, straight to my room, I sank on my knees in front of my bed and pressed my face into the pillows—and there, it took hold of me even stronger: Now, a bright inner glow was streaming toward me from that immeasurable distance; it surrounded me completely. All the suffering I had ever experienced seemed to have been extinguished, as if it had never happened, as if I had heard only being told about it, like about something that had happened to a stranger. From my very depths, I felt born anew and transformed. I did not know anything anymore about myself and my surroundings; I only felt that warm flood of love which had taken me up, I saw only that spiritual light that had penetrated me. Then, entirely gradually, that sea of light and warmth began to retreat again, slowly and gently releasing me from itself, but in such a way that I was still held by it like from a distance for a long time and such that I did not again plunge into the infinite dark space without support and without strength.

I got up slowly. How long had I been kneeling in front of the bed in this way? I did not know; all sense of space and time had disappeared from me, but according to the clock, about half to three quarters of an hour might have passed. What was it that had taken me up? Was it God? A ray of His immeasurable love, His all-penetrating spirit? Or was it only a radiance of a higher being ministering to Him?

Kimberly Baltzer-Jaray is a sessional lecturer at King's University College (UWO) in the departments of Philosophy, and Social Justice and Peace Studies. She is the President of the North American Society for Early Phenomenology (NASEP) and author of the blog on Adolf Reinach, Hosted on the Open Commons of Phenomenology: http://reinach.ophen.org. She has spent nearly 20 years studying the body of work Reinach left behind after his death in WWI, and her recent publications include translations of his rough notes and letters from the battlefield, his contributions to the philosophy of justice, and the debates about the nature of essence he had with Jean Héring.

Bibliography

Selected Writings by Gerda Walther[1]

1922. *Ein Beitrag zur Ontologie der sozialen Gemeinschaften (mit einem Anhang zur Phänomenologie der sozialen Gemeinschaften).* Inaugural Dissertation. Halle: Max Niemeyer.
1923. *Ausführliches Sachregister zu Edmund Husserls "Ideen zu einer reinen Phänomenologie und phänomenologischen Philosophie"*, Vol. I. Halle: Max Niemeyer.
1923. *Zur Phänomenologie der Mystik.* Olten: Walter Verlag.
1923. Zur Ontologie der sozialen Gemeinschaften (mit einem Anhang zur Phänomenologie der sozialen Gemeinschaften). *Jahrbuch für Philosophie und Phänomenologische Forschung* 6, 1–158.
1925. Zur Psychologie der sogenannten "moral insanity". *Japanisch-deutsche Zeitschrift für Wissenschaft und Technik* 3 (May), 174–184.
1927. Zur innenpsychischen Struktur der Schizophrenie. *Zeitschrift für die gesamte Neurologie und Psychiatrie* 108, 56–85.
1928. Ludwig Klages und sein Kampf gegen den "Geist". *Philosophischer Anzeiger* 3(1), 48–90.
1928. Sören Kierkegaards Psychologie der Verzweiflung. *Zeitschrift für Menschenkunde, Blätter für Charakterologie und angewandte Psychologie* 4(4), 208–219.
1928. Betreffend Kierkegaards "Psychologie der Verzweiflung": Nachtrag zu dem in Heft IV/4 erschienenen Aufsatz "Kierkegaards Psychologie der Verzweiflung". *Zeitschrift für Menschenkunde, Blätter für Charakterologie und angewandte Psychologie* 4(6), 336.
1929. Parapsychologie und Mystik. *Zeitschrift für Parapsychologie* 4(6), 327–337.
1929. Ein Münchner Philosoph. *München-Augsburger Abendzeitung*, No. 124 (8.V.1929), 7.
1930. Ludwig Klages y su lucha contra el "espíritu". *Revista de Occidente* 87, 265–294.
1930. Ludwig Klages y su lucha contra el "espíritu" (Conclusión). *Revista de Occidente* 88, 117–136
1931. On the Psychology of Telepathy. *Journal of the American Society for Psychical Research* 25 (10), 438–446.
1938. *Ahnen und Schauen unserer germanischen Vorfahren, im Lichte der Parapsychologie.* Leipzig: Hummel.
1950. Der Okkultismus im Dritten Reich, I. *Neue Wissenschaft: Zeitschrift für kritischen Okkultismus* 1(2), 34–41.
1950. Der Okkultismus im Dritten Reich, II. *Neue Wissenschaft: Zeitschrift für kritischen Okkultismus* 1(3), 15–19.

[1]For a complete list of Gerda Walther's published writings, see the one compiled by Eberhard Avé-Lallemant in Resch 1983, pp. 50–78.

A. Calcagno (ed.), *Gerda Walther's Phenomenology of Sociality, Psychology, and Religion*, Women in the History of Philosophy and Sciences 2,
https://doi.org/10.1007/978-3-319-97592-4

1951. Der Okkultismus im Dritten Reich, III. *Neue Wissenschaft: Zeitschrift für kritischen Okkultismus* 1(4), 29–34.
1955. A Plea for the Introduction of Edmund Husserl's Phenomenological Methods into Parapsychology. In Eileen Garrett (ed.), *Proceedings of the First International Conference of Parapsychological Studies: Utrecht, The Netherlands, July 30 to August 5, 1953*. New York, Parapsychology Foundation, 114–115.
1955. Die Bedeutung der phänomenologischen Methode Edmund Husserls für die Parapsychologie, Parts I and II. *Psychophysikalische Zeitschrift* 1(2), 22–29.
1955. Die Bedeutung der phänomenologischen Methode Edmund Husserls für die Parapsychologie, Schluss. *Psychophysikalische Zeitschrift* 1(3), 37–40.
1955. *Phänomenologie der Mystik*, 2nd revised edn. Olten: Walter Verlag.
1956. Hitler's Black Magicians. *Tomorrow* 2, 7–23
1956. Die innerseelische Seite parapsychologischer Phänomene. *Neue Wissenschaft: Zeitschrift für Parapsychologie* 6(11/12), 364–373.
1957. Die innerseelische Seite parapsychologischer Phänomene, Part 2. *Neue Wissenschaft: Zeitschrift für Parapsychologie* 6(13), 408–422.
1958. Zum Problem der Visionen. *Philosophisches Jahrbuch der Görres-Gesellschaft* 66 (Festschrift für Hedwig Conrad-Martius), 347–354.
1960. *Zum anderen Ufer: Vom Marxismus und Atheismus zum Christentum*. Remagen: Otto Reichl.
1966. Die Bedeutung der phänomenologischen Methode Edmund Husserls für die Parapsychologie. In Hans Bender (ed.), *Parapsychologie. Entwicklung, Ergebnisse, Probleme* (Reprint). Darmstadt: Wissenschaftliche Buchgesellschaft, 683–697.
1975. Die Reichweite des menschlichen Erlebens. In Andreas Resch (ed.), *Mystik*. Innsbruck: Resch Verlag, 235–252.
1976. *Phänomenologie der Mystik*, 3rd edn. Olten: Walter Verlag.

Secondary Sources

Ales Bello, A. (1992). *Fenomenologia dell'essere umano: Lineamenti di una filosofia al femminile*. Rome: Città Nuova.
Ales Bello, A. (1996). Unterwegs zu einer weiblichen Philosophie. Hedwig Conrad-M*artius*, Edith Stein, Gerda Walther. *Edith Stein Jahrbuch*, *2*, 165–174.
Ales Bello, A., & Pellegrino, M.P. (eds.). (2014). *Incontri possibili: Empatia, telepatia, comunità, mistica*. Rome: Castelvecchi.
Bauer, E. (1991). Periods of historical development of parapsychology in Germany. An overview. In *The Parapsychological Association 34th Convention. Proceedings of Presented Papers* (pp. 18–34).
Baumann, G. (1995). *Dichtung als Lebensform. Wolfgang Frommel zwischen George-Kreis und Castrum Peregrini*. Würzburg: Königshausen & Neumann.
Beckmann, B. (2003). *Phänomenologie des religiösen Erlebnisses. Religionsphilosophische Überlegungen im Anschluß an Adolf Reinach und Edith Stein*. Würzburg: Königshausen & Neumann.
Benz, E. (1956). Gerda Walther, Phänomenologie der Mystik (1955). *Zeitschrift für Religions- und Geistesgeschichte*, *8*(3), 267–268 (Review).
Boehm, R. (1968). *Vom Gesichtspunkt der Phänomenologie*. The Hague: Nijhoff.
Calcagno, A. (2012). Gerda Walther. On the possibility of a passive sense of community and the inner time consciousness of community. *Symposium*, *16*(2), 89–105.
Caminada, E. (2014). Joining the background. Habitual sentiments behind we-intentionality. In A. K. Ziv & H.B. Schmid (Eds.), *Institutions, Emotions, and Group Agents: Contributions to Social Ontology* (pp. 195–212). Dordrecht: Springer.
Corbin, H. (1958). Gerda Walther, Phänomenologie der Mystik, zweite, umgearbeitete Auflage (1955). *Revue de l'histoire des religions*, *153*(1), 92–101 (Review).

Eppe, H. (2004). Gerda Walther (1897–1977)—ihr zweifacher Weg "aus dem Dunkel zum Licht". In Baumgartner, J. & Wedemeyer-Kolwe, B. (Eds.), *Aufbrüche, Seitenpfade, Abwege. Suchbewegungen und Subkulturen im 20. Jahrhundert. Festschrift für Ulrich Linse* (pp. 91–97). Würzburg: Königshausen & Neumann.

Fischer, M. (2013). *Religiöse Erfahrung in der Phänomenologie des frühen Heidegger*. Göttingen: Vandenhoeck & Ruprecht.

Hartshorne, C. (1957). Gerda Walther, Phänomenologie der Mystik (1955). *Philosophy and Phenomenological Research, 18*(1), 140–141 (Review).

Kelkel, L. (1957). Gerda Walther, Phänomenologie der Mystik (1955). *Les Études philosophiques*, Nouvelle Série, *12*(2), 270–271 (Review).

León, F., & Zahavi, D. (2016). Phenomenology of experiential sharing: The contribution of Schutz and Walther. In Salice, A., & Schmid, H.B. (Eds.), *The Phenomenological Approach to Social Reality. History, Concepts, Problems* (pp. 219–234). Dordrecht: Springer.

Lopez McAlister, L. (1995). Gerda Walther (1897–1977). In Waithe, M.E. (Ed.) *A History of Women Philosophers* (Vol. 4, pp. 189–206). Dordrecht: Kluwer.

Machnacz, J. (2005). Gerda Walther. Leben—Phanomenologie—Mystik. *Forum Philosophicum, 10*, 250–252.

Machnacz, J. (2014). Edith Stein und Gerda Walther. Vom Atheismus zum Christentum. In Haas, R. (Ed.) *Fiat voluntas tua. Theologe und Historiker—Priester und Professor. Festschrift zum 65. Geburtstag von Harm Klueting* (pp. 153–164). Münster: Aschendorff.

Mezei, B. (2013). *Religion and Revelation After Auschwitz*. New York: Bloomsbury.

Müller, A. (1926). Jahrbuch für Philosophie und phänomenologische Forschung. Bd. 6 (1923). In *Kant-Studien* (Vol. 31, pp. 370–371) (Review).

Mulligan, K. (2016). Persons and acts—collective and social. From ontology to politics. In Salice, A., & Schmid, H.B. (Eds.), *The phenomenological approach to social reality. History, concepts, problems* (pp. 17–45). Dordrecht: Springer.

Osborn, A. (1967). *The meaning of personal existence. In the light of paranormal phenomena, the doctrine of reincarnation and mystical states of consciousness*. Wheaton: Theosophical Publishing.

Parker, R. (2017). Gerda Walther and the phenomenological community. *Acta Mexicana de Fenomenología, 2*, 45–66.

Poortman, J.J. (1956). *Dr. Gerda Walther's beschouwingen over de mystiek*. Amsterdam: Theosophical Publishing.

Pouilly, C. (2006). *Dr. Gerda Walther's beschouwingen over de mystiek, 138*(3), 209–225.

Przywara, E. (1962). Gerda Walther, Zum anderen Ufer (1960). *Les Études philosophiques*, Nouvelle Série, *17*(2), 291 (Review).

Resch, A. (1983). *Gerda Walther*. Innsbruck: Resch.

Schmid, Hans Bernard. (2012). *Wir-Intentionalität. Kritik des ontologischen Individualismus und Rekonstruktion der Gemeinschaft* (2nd ed.). Freiburg: Alber.

Vendrell Ferran, I. (2008). *Die Emotionen. Gefühle in der realistischen Phänomenologie*. Berlin: Akademie Verlag.

Zahavi, D., & Salice, A. (2017). Phenomenology of the we: Stein, Walther, Gurwitsch. In Kiverstein, J. (Ed.), *The routledge handbook of philosophy of the social mind* (pp. 515–527). New York: Routledge.

Printed by Printforce, the Netherlands